# EMERGENCY KIT
# *for* FINDING
# COMMON GROUND

## Helping Americans Get Along

ANDREA MOLBERG, PhD

**EMERGENCY KIT for FINDING COMMON GROUND: Helping Americans Get Along**

❖ ❖ ❖

# Contents

Introduction: Survive and Thrive ........................................................ 1

## Part One: The Spot We're In

1. United We Stand ...........................................................................7

2. America's UNcivil War, a Nation Divided................................. 19

3. We are Biased, but Share Values ...............................................39

## Part Two: Changing the Situation

4. Starting with Empathy—for Both Sides.................................. 63

5. Managing our Differences ........................................................ 83

6. Building and Repairing Relationships.....................................101

7. Influencing Across the Divide ................................................ 123

8. Change Means Overcoming Resistance.................................. 141

9. Disagreeing Without Being Disagreeable .............................. 161

## Part Three: Changing Ourselves

10. Getting Off the Defensive......................................................193

11. Coping with the Stress of Now............................................. 209

12. Having Courage, Confidence, and Hope ..............................231

Conclusion: Putting It All Together ............................................. 247

## Appendices

1. Why all the Fuss About Competence and Fitness? ................249

2. Basic Differences Between Left and Right ............................. 260

3. Ten Core American Values ......................................................264

4. Improving Your People Presence ...........................................266

5. How Are People Influenced?....................................267

6. Methods for Dealing with Organizational Resistance ............269

7. Practice Coping through Positive Self-Talk..............................271

8. Using Appreciative Inquiry....................................272

9. Cultivate Confidence—What could you say instead?.............. 273

Notes....................................................................... 275

Recommended Readings................................................ 293

Acknowledgments ........................................................ 297

About the Author .........................................................299

**Survive and Thrive**

We need to heal from our politics. Polarized, scared, and exhausted, we're writing off family, avoiding neighbors, un-friending on social media, and tuning out within our hurting borders. Yet, if you love what this country should and could be, then engage and improve it, one conversation or citizen at a time.

Intense Trump era reactions have pitted us against each other, leaving us angry, intolerant, fearful, and depressed. As television's Dr. Phil might ask, "How well is that working for you, America?" Both empathy and action ought to replace finger pointing and complaining. Here you'll find solutions and salve—for individual Americans—to improve our current state of affairs and feel better too.

You can approach today's national divide from political, historical, economic, religious, racial, gender, and societal/cultural perspectives. *Emergency Kit for Finding Common Ground* takes a psychological one. This kit provides ways to manage our differences, talk to each other, and work together before and after the next election.

You have a right to know I'm an Independent who has voted for Democratic and Republican candidates, but never worked for and barely contributed to a single one of them. My life has been spent as an applied psychologist resolving conflicts, evaluating job candidates, developing leaders, teaching people skills, building teams, and helping people get along at work and at home. Never did I think about applying those tools to the political world or writing a book for American voters. Until now.

People living in these so-called United States need hope. We need to believe we can get along better. This collection of practical, evidence-based techniques from clinical, social, organizational, and positive psychology provides tools for how to help yourself, influence others, and get along. I hope it helps.

Chapters walk you through doable steps for gaining the confidence and motivation to actually implement sound advice for talking across the divide. Each chapter lists references, so if these doses aren't enough, you'll find recommendations for getting a full prescription elsewhere.

Admittedly, in study after study, the best outcomes from following advice were bolstered by support, feedback, and accountability. Violinists, chess players, memory experts, and athletes alike bear testimony to the value of training, coaching, and practice. Expect your collaboration and coping skills to improve with practice, and don't hesitate to have others help you.

## HOW TO USE THIS SURVIVAL KIT

Part One of this guide briefly describes the predicament we're in, while the second focuses on actions we Americans can take to change the *situation*, and the third on actions to change *ourselves*— something we have a lot more control over. You'll discover skills for handling conflict, decreasing polarization, and coping with the anxiety, depression, anger, and fear running rampant.

Because the chapters stand alone, you don't have to read them in sequence, yet they build on each other. Some techniques you'll recognize; some may be new to you. If necessary, skip to chapters that fit your urgent need. The "how to" ones begin with part two. Please use some well-researched alternatives to throwing in the towel with family, friends, or fellow citizens you haven't met.

## DUMP TRUMP?

Emergency kits are for dire moments—to sustain life until you're out of the woods or more help arrives. Stuffed with band aids, resuscitation equipment, water, food, flashlights, meds, and tools, they sometimes include maps with paths and marked dangers. Convinced that Trump is a danger to our survival, I've not only packed this book with communication and coping tools, I've put in why I believe America needs someone else leading our hike through Covid country. Included in the appendices are descriptions of the narcissistic personality disorder and criteria for selecting outstanding leaders. In Appendix 1 you'll see my duty to warn.

To heal and un-divide America which *wasn't* united before Trump took office, you can grab emergency equipment without taking my suggested route—a different president. On the other hand, I pray you'll consider the risks.

## HELP YOURSELF

Not written for politicians or political parties, this is a manual that I personally needed post the 2016 election. Finding myself becoming increasingly negative and irritable, I pulled books off my shelves, reviewed my client files, searched the internet, hit the library, went over the material in the almost one thousand corporate seminars I have taught, and asked myself what a good coach would tell me. After reflecting on what does work, I began consciously putting to use the constructive strategies that I employ when consulting and coaching.

Guessing you might need solutions too, I wrote them down. My favorites will be highlighted, but you may legitimately have different preferences. The approaches listed within these pages have been distilled from mounds of psychological thought, tons of research findings, and lessons learned from working with individual and corporate clients. What I have taught executives, MBA students, nurses, city officials, military personnel, engineers, balloon man-ufacturers, financial advisors, and the like I started to apply myself and *to* myself.

I helped myself to many items from this kit and subsequently helped myself *with* them. You can too. Applying the techniques re-energized this troubled American, so I hope you'll open-mind-edly start experimenting with the ones best suited to you and your situations. They all work—sometimes.

Which should be used? "It depends" is the competent consul-tant's answer. Situations and the people involved are extremely different. Approaches successful with a particular person or in a specific situation fail badly elsewhere, yet there are actionable strat-egies and techniques with good payoff probabilities. Commit to tak-ing away one suggestion from almost every chapter, but be choosy. If you want, you might simply ignore the other ideas or save them for later.

Let's protect the American dream. I'm grateful that my Norwegian ancestors left the old country and struggled to learn English, that I was born here, grew up with indoor plumbing (my mother didn't), received an excellent public education, and exited college debt-free thanks to my parents, scholarships, and multiple jobs. While I am blessed with more financial security than my par-ents ever had, plus well-educated daughters and good health care, many U.S. residents have received profoundly different treatment within these shores. Still, most of us realize it is a blessing to be American.

Let's live up to the old adage, "Blessed to *be* a blessing."

PART ONE

# The Spot We're In

# United We Stand

Americans aren't getting along too well in these so called United States. Some are sick, depressed, and anxious about the future. Some are so angry at the "stupidity" of fellow voters they won't try discussing political ideas, because they are certain it's impossible. Holding onto disgust has become awfully comfortable and even considered noble these days.

We are stunned by the vast differences between those who did and didn't put Trump in office and by those who would and would not re-elect him. There is talk of "civil war" on Americans' tongues, memories of a white supremacist rally on our minds, and fear of another massacre in our hearts.

In a tough spot, we have options: change the situation, adapt, or leave. We can do nothing, but I vote against that. Help yourself and this country. Though tired and disgusted, we the people need to listen, learn, and focus on commonalities to change what has been called this "culture of contempt."[1]

As an applied psychologist, I have two goals for us: (1) help bridge the nasty American divide and (2) feel better. Using tools for conflict management, relationship building, collaboration, change, influence, communication, negotiation, and performance, let's build.

Most Americans can change—if they want to. Ordinary people find ways to make a big impact, and positive psychology pioneer Charles Garfield studied 550 of them. He had been on the Apollo 11 team that put us on the moon, worked with cancer survivors, and experienced the thrill himself of hitting exceptional athletic targets, so he was intrigued by outstanding performance. His eighteen-year examination concluded: "The fact is the differences between peak performers and 'everyone else' are much smaller than 'everyone else' thinks."[2] Look and you can find success stories and strategies almost everywhere.

How do achievers overcome tough obstacles and perform so well? They persist. Why? Because they believe in their mission and their ability to accomplish it. We can shift how Americans treat each other. Nike is right—"Just do it." And do the math, if each of us just moves an inch, that's almost 330 million inches.

## WHY WORK ACROSS THE DIVIDE?

Preventing our circles of influence from being spheres of contempt will protect lives, our values, and our democracy. In 1861 at the brink of the Civil War, Abraham Lincoln told Americans in his first inaugural address, "We must not be enemies." This is certainly another time that every one of us should take up that call to encourage respect and peace within this nation of ours.

Let's make working on America's psychological climate a top priority. Years ago I started responding to anyone asking, "Is there anything else I can help you with?" with the answer, "World peace." My reply prompted quizzical looks, stopped a few, and got, "I'll work on that!" from many. Now my line is, "Americans getting along better." The frequent response is, "Wow, we need that."

Why even try? There is power in numbers. United we'll stand as long as enough of us do something constructive. Pulling as a team we'll meet more goals, thwart more enemies, and be happier and healthier in the process. Ever watched humans or horses working at crossed purposes? What a powerful waste. When Budweiser's horses work in tandem, they literally pull more weight and continue pulling longer.[3] However, even for horses, success depends on the attitude of each one in the team.[4]

If you tremble about America's future, remember individuals benefit from assisting each other.

## THE BENEFITS OF ENGAGING AND COLLABORATING

When people holding different perspectives work together, their collaboration produces high quality, creative, integrated solutions for complex situations. In business, marriage, science, sports, medicine, and the military, teamwork means success.

Like companies across the world, our nation itself faces the challenge to get and stay engaged. Fully absorbed, committed, enthusiastic people act in positive ways to further the interests and reputation of the people and institutions they care about. Business and industry repeatedly see engagement yielding increased innovation, productivity, and loyalty.[5] Americans have pulled together to face fires, tragedy, tornadoes, and Covid-19. Now we need to heal our political divide.

In his inaugural speech, JFK challenged individual citizens to "Ask what you can do for your country," and we got to the moon within a decade. Americans need to find out what engaging can do for a country in the 21st century. Plain and simple, we need to get more done and be proud of who we are.

When co-laboring well, we generate better solutions and end up liking each other at the same time. Accomplishment feels good. Members of winning sports and business teams describe their teammates more positively and stick with them. Joint effort toward common targets builds relationships, which in turn influences whether people cooperate or resist. To make coalitions stronger, successful teams recruit diverse talent and varied ideas rather than suppress or ridicule them.

However, differences also pull people apart, triggering stalemate in Washington and violence in our homes, places of worship, schools, malls, movie theaters, and streets. (See chapter 2.) If we could disagree without being disagreeable, think of the lives and time that would be saved. It literally takes more minutes, hours, days, and years to change an impression than the few seconds it does to form one.

Let's respectfully explore why we hold opposing views and find our common values (chapters 3–4, and Appendices 1–3). And, let's find better ways to manage political conflict (chapters 5–9).

As the Harvard Negotiation Project indicates, the chances of getting agreement rise when we attack problems not people.[6] Said Ronald Reagan, "Peace is not absence of conflict, it is the ability to handle conflict by peaceful means." Let's willingly put on our empathy caps, check our facts and feelings, realize our common humanity, and be open-minded.

Some were taught not to discuss politics and religion for fear of alienating others, yet failure to explore diverse viewpoints diminishes the chances of finding good compromises and ground-breaking solutions. Creative problem-solvers encourage first divergent, then convergent, thinking—in that order. They candidly explore a wide range of possibilities, some sensible and some a bit crazy, before narrowing to solutions which integrate a bit of one idea with a piece of another.

## THE POWER OF ONE

Don't underestimate the impact one person can have, because research on bystander apathy indicates we are actually more likely to intervene to help someone when we are alone.[7] Likewise, don't underestimate the impact of "social facilitation" and even public shaming. Being in a group and realizing others are watching is beneficial,[8] and the world is watching.

Some of us aren't ready to change the American landscape but do indeed need to cope. If that is you, head to chapters 11 and 12 to confidently manage the fear and demoralization in this Trump world with guidance from practitioners and researchers of resilience, stress, addiction and empowerment. Pick realistic alternatives to depression, obstruction, violence, and moving elsewhere.

Changing our divided world will require passion and perseverance—"grit."[9] We can toil, solve problems, and accomplish alone. The data on effective teams indicates we can often accomplish more with and through others. Let's do both—persistently pull hard individually and pull together.

## RECOGNIZE OUR INTERDEPENDENCE

Jointly tackling a tough project helps people realize how desperately they need and can help each other—like 9/11 fire fighters and Covid medical teams. Instead of using time and effort to defend our positions, we can apply those precious commodities to deciding which creative path America should take or how policies should be implemented to help as many as possible.

Pooling skills, knowledge, and resources enables us to get things done. Americans have had the mistaken belief that we must decide between standing on our two feet as individuals or sacrificing our uniqueness to accommodate to a larger whole, like a family, company, community, or country.[10] Interdependence doesn't preclude independence. Voters and politicians seem to forget how uniting to preserve democracy actually preserves our individual freedoms and how reaching national goals links to the achievement of their own.

As our fiercely independent and self-reliant ancestors discovered, there are benefits to working with others to raise barns, herd livestock, defend against predators, and protect water supplies. Twenty-first century farmers need loans from Wall Street, and those bankers need their produce. America needs allies and markets and global response to disasters.

We need scientists, grocery deliverers, manufacturers, nurses, construction workers, educators, child care providers, restaurant owners, pharmacists, and you.

## SURVIVE AND THRIVE

And, we need approaches for getting along and lowering stress. I'm starting there.

Besides overcoming the defensiveness of other Americans, learn to get off the defensive yourself (chapter 10). Why? Because amygdala activation draws metabolic energy away from the pre-frontal region that supports higher intellectual functioning.[11] Bottom line, when too upset, we and other Americans don't think straight.

The return on investment (ROI) for collaboration, improved American-to-American relationships, and stress reduction is that in the long term, we survive and thrive—both as individuals and collectively as a country. Constructive action not apathy or blind loyalty is needed in a Trump world. We need to say the addict's familiar prayer, "God grant me the serenity to accept the things I cannot change, the courage to change the things I can, and the wisdom to know the difference."

## MAKE A DIFFERENCE

And, as many have aptly put it, we also require the wisdom to *make* a difference. Each and every one of us can do something helpful. Working alone and/or together, we can change ourselves and fellow Americans, if we want to and know how. Social scientists have learned what encourages people to get involved and have seen bystander apathy cut in half. Now is the time to vigorously confront polarization.

Don't just stand around and watch. Show tolerance, put things into perspective, look for similarities, ignore some differences, and communicate with courage and compassion. Support those who tell the truth, lead, and heal. Begin now. Turning a big ship takes time, and another election is rapidly approaching.

Proven techniques are worth tweaking. Start short-circuiting bad habits by replacing them with new approaches that cause interference with the ones worth eliminating. For example, you can't be both depressed and highly energized at the same time, or voting while not voting, or effectively sharing solutions while refusing to talk. With effort we'll find common ground and reasons to celebrate. We can do this.

Skeptical? You may be thinking:

- Yes, but....
- How do we find the will to get along?
- Working with others takes skills I don't have.
- It's so easy to lose hope.

Keep reading. Hunt for useful approaches—techniques that are full of uses and applicable in multiple situations—and ones you're truly likely to use because you consider them appropriate and realistic. Choose and use a few tried and true techniques from this over-stuffed kit. If you select them yourself, you're more likely to try them, tweak them, and practice to perfect them. Neuroscientists have noted when people solve a problem, the brain releases a rush of neuro-transmitters like adrenaline.[12] This energy boost may be central to facilitating change and managing fear.

## FOCUS ON SOLUTIONS

Doing nothing is not usually a good choice, and our precious democratic republic can't afford it. We need to:

1. **Know what to do**
2. **Know how to do it**
3. **Believe it's possible**

Success relies on awareness of concrete actions under our control plus a belief in the probability of successfully implementing those badly needed action plans. Think what we can accomplish when we pull together to fight oppression, poverty, bias, and disease.

## LEARN FROM OTHERS

Follow the examples and utilize the techniques of those who get things done. There are vital differences between top and poor performers, spouses, leaders, patriots, and friends. They behave differently. Many research findings and remarkable stories illustrate success, and we can apply those strategies.

Kerry Patterson and his co-authors of *Influencer: The Power to Change Anything* provide memorable examples of individuals who have made a profound difference.[13] One of my favorites is Dr. Mimi Silbert, the founder of the non-profit Delancey Street Foundation, who hires the homeless, life-long drug addicts, and felons, typically those having four convictions. Over the course of 30 years she has changed the lives of 14,000. More than 90% of those who join Delancey never go back to drugs or crime.

## USE BEHAVIORAL CONTAGION

Not only is Covid-19 transmitted from person to person, so is behavior. Yawning, smiling, laughing, frowning, shivering, and risk taking are all contagious. Unfortunately, we also catch aggression and rudeness, harming how we perform and feel at the moment as well as how we perceive and respond in the future.[14] America, with our incivility we're harming ourselves.

Humans tend to do what others do, buy what others buy, espouse what others espouse. People keep up with the Joneses by purchasing bigger homes, abandoning sedans for SUVs, or going green. Instead of seeing behavioral contagion in criminality, drug use, and suicide, let's make treating fellow citizens with a curious, not contemptuous ear, catch on.

## POSITIVE CHANGE STARTS WITH COMMITMENT TO A MISSION

Unity is the issue—and Trump a huge obstacle. People unite against common enemies and toward common goals. We can collaborate—labor together—for equality, truth, justice, the planet, the economy, and the American way. Democracy and freedom are powerful reasons to work together.

Our way of government relies on checks and balances, sharing power, and wrestling with differences. Democracy has been called "messy" and the "worst form of government except all the others that have been tried" by Winston Churchill. We'll have this special republic only as long as we can keep it, and it's in danger.

A vision of freedom and hope sustained thousands venturing here, moving West in covered wagons, fighting under the flag, marching for civil rights, fleeing tyranny and poverty. By focusing on the American Dream we can reduce the rancor.

## ENEMIES, ALLIES, HEROES

Survival, liberty, and peace are compelling missions. At Pearl Harbor on December 27, 2016, in the presence of the Japanese president, Barack Obama eloquently spoke about shared interests and common values having turned the bitterest of enemies into strong allies. After the terrible losses of WWII, America successfully bridged the huge divide separating us from Germany and Japan. That kind of healing is what this country needs internally now.

BBC carried the entire presentations by the Japanese and American presidents, which I had listened to in the car on NPR.

NBC Nightly News' minimal coverage of the inspiring speeches struck me. That night the top evening newscast for the important demographic aged 25–54 devoted far more airtime to Carrie Fisher and George Michael than to the powerful stories of American heroism by Medal of Honor recipients. Americans revere celebrities not patriots, yet heroes are the reason we are alive and free.

On the first day of school in 2005 the kids discovered that there were no desks in Martha Cothren's history class at Robinson High School in Little Rock. With permission the teacher had all the desks removed, and when asked, "Ms. Cothren, where are our desks?" she answered, "You can't have a desk until you tell me how you earn the right to sit at a desk." [15]

The kids guessed—their grades and behavior—to which they were told, "No, it's not even your behavior." They called their parents to report what was happening, and by early afternoon television news crews were at the school to report about this crazy teacher who had taken all the desks out of her room. As the baffled students sat on the floor in the final period, Martha Cothren announced, "Throughout the day no one has been able to tell me just what he or she has done to earn the right to sit at the desks that are ordinarily found in this classroom. Now I am going to tell you."

This remarkable teacher opened her classroom door letting in twenty-seven U.S. Veterans, all in uniform, each carrying a school desk. Martha explained, "You didn't earn the right to sit at these desks. These heroes did it for you. They placed the desks here for you. They went halfway around the world, giving up their education and interrupting their careers and families so you could have the freedom you have. Now, it's up to you to sit in them. It is your responsibility to learn, to be good students, to be good citizens. They paid the price so that you could have the freedom to get an education. Don't ever forget it." Martha Cothren, daughter of a WWII POW, was awarded the Veterans of Foreign Wars Teacher of the Year for Arkansas in 2006.

## THE POWER OF PURPOSE

Many have experienced the power of purpose and been inspired by Holocaust survivor Viktor Frankl's powerful experiences described in *Man's Search for Meaning*.[16] A survivor of four concentration camps, he saw, "The prisoner who has lost faith in the future—his future—was doomed." Frankl's own survival mission involved helping fellow inmates find theirs.

Just as fighting Covid-19 has been a monumental cause, so is building the American bridge. Garfield, that student of the Apollo team, remarkable athletes, and outstanding employees, discovered peak performers believe deeply in both their mission and their ability to accomplish it.

Equipped with a clear target they expect to reach, high achievers persistently overcome obstacles in their path, and what was thought impossible happens.

> **"**
>
> **It has always seemed to me that the best symbol of common sense was a bridge.**
>
> Franklin D. Roosevelt

The old adage is the first step is the hardest. Why? Because we're all afraid to fail and all a little lazy.

> **"**
>
> **It seems to me that the most difficult part of building a bridge would be the first step.**[17]

## IT GETS EASIER

The good news is that we can learn to get off the defensive, listen, and defuse anger to deal with America's differences. We can apply lessons from good marriages, effective teams, and energized organizations—and with practice we'll get better.

We can develop resilience to keep from being overwhelmed and become more competent at regulating our own feelings and understanding the reactions of others. We can explore our differences, merge insights, cheer each other on, and take on the unprecedented. We can. And when we do succeed, even just a little, our desire to keep trying gets stronger. Having learned how to dodge some bumps, the path becomes easier.

## CHAPTER 2

# America's UNcivil War, a Nation Divided

With 58% of Republicans highly frustrated with Democrats, while 55% of Democrats return the favor, we the people are battling each other instead of our nation's problems.[1] Half of the country is not only angry but also afraid of the other half. Most of those polled (80%) think the country is out of control.[2]

On your way for emergency *interpersonal* assistance, pause here to quickly examine our wounds. We have an urgent need to improve how we view and treat each other, because big decisions—about economic recovery, health care protection, and leadership—loom over us. Many Americans have lost family, jobs, and medical coverage during the worst public health disaster in our lifetime.

Quickly take stock of how voters feel, the role of the media and authoritarians, and what happens if we remain uncivil and un-united. Some of us have amazing options while others feel left behind.

Everyday conversations around politics are now tense, difficult, and avoided. Overwhelmingly, Americans say the tone of our political debate has become more negative (85%), less respectful (85%), less fact-based (76%) and less substantive (60%).[3] Emotions are high. And as stressed as we are, almost anything sets people off.

Many in the U.S. are poor, poorly educated, and mistreated, while others are wealthy and privileged. With CEO pay 200–300 times that of the average worker,[4] our income inequality far exceeds anything in other advanced nations.[5] The pandemic has hit some Americans particularly hard. In addition, we can't ignore America's skyrocketing suicide and addiction rates.

To function, we need to understand and manage our differences.

## WHY VOTE?

Trump repeatedly mentions the last presidential election, because, though he won, more people cast their ballot for someone other than him. Hillary received nearly 2.9 million more votes. The 2016 election was the second in the past five where the winner of the popular vote lost in the Electoral College.

Americans have been questioning why they should bother to vote, since their ballot doesn't matter anyway and they disapprove of so many seeking office. Please exercise this important right—safely. More than 40% of eligible American voters stayed home instead of casting a ballot in the 2016 presidential election.[6]

Trump won with the support of barely 25% of the possible eligible voters[7] and took office as the most unpopular president in at least 40 years.[8] [9] The electorate profoundly disliked both 2016 candidates, giving them grades of C (Hillary) and C- (Trump).[10] Some voted against rather than for a candidate. More troubling, shortly after the election 52% of all Republicans polled, even 37% of the college educated ones, erroneously thought Trump won the popular vote.[11]

There are Russian hackers attempting to influence our elections, while our leader publicly denies CIA data and fails to make its prevention a high priority. Look out for trolls.[12] False news from local and foreign sources now rapidly flies across the internet, getting repeated, remembered, and believed. Facebook, from which 52% report they get their news,[13] uses algorithms to deliver more of the same, which we send on to our friends who agree.

However, the more we restrict ourselves to like-minded associates, the more extreme our positions become. How much accurate information do we get from and for all sides?

## WE DIFFER OVER FACTS AND
## DON'T TRUST THE MEDIA

Finding common ground begins with agreeing on something—maybe data. However, Americans are lacking facts and doubting them anyway. Only 13% of us trust the news media "a great deal" and 28% "a fair amount."[14] The majority don't. Compared to Republicans, trust of the media is much higher among Democrats and Independents.

Three-fourths of both Republicans and Democrats say news organizations should keep politicians in line—preventing them from straying from the truth and doing what they shouldn't.[15] Unfortunately, Republicans are about four times as likely as Democrats—59% to 14%—to say journalists are going too far as watchdogs.[16] Making matters worse, most Americans consider news organizations biased.[17] [18]

Some channels are clearly more persuasive. A vast amount of data has been integrated into an extensive model to estimate how effective Fox, CNN, and MSNBC are at persuading viewers. "Fox is substantially better at influencing Democrats than MSNBC is at influencing Republicans," the researchers concluded.[19]

Even though most Fox viewers are Republican, the sizable minority that isn't were particularly suggestible to the channel's influence. An estimated 58% of Fox viewers who were initially Democrats changed to supporting the Republican candidate by the end of the 2000 election cycle. (The persuasion shift in 2004 was 27% and 28% in 2008.) In comparison, MSNBC only persuaded 8% of Republicans to vote Democratic in the 2008 cycle.[20] Fox News is more influential than imagined.

If you were listening to prime-time Fox anchor Laura Ingraham advising only seniors to avoid congregating or prime-time host Sean Hannity praising Trump for managing the crisis well, despite the fact that we were still desperately short on tests and vital hospital equipment, you probably believed that we were going to be filling the pews Easter Sunday.[21] We certainly wanted that to be true. Hearing no need, many didn't take adequate precautions.

## FACTS AND OPINIONS DESERVE SCRUTINY

America should worry that Trump urges his followers not to trust scrutinized information. He labels media organizations "corrupt," any unflattering news about him "fake," and legitimate investigations "witch hunts." By repeating falsehoods and conspiracy theories—calling climate change a "hoax" invented by the Chinese and the coronavirus "the new hoax"—Trump validates and perpetuates false information. Be alert to propaganda from anyone and everywhere.

Loyal Trump supporter and conservative radio host Michael Savage, who is trained in epidemiology, said this about right-wing media's coverage of facts, especially those broadcast in the early weeks of the pandemic:

> "We're living in a terrible time in America where truth has died."[22]

His comments have cost him some of his 7.5 million weekly listeners. Though his show is still rated among talk radio's top ten, several major stations in markets like New York City and Washington took him off the air.

## GOOD INFORMATION MATTERS, BUT IT CAN BE HARD TO GET

At the same time that the world became more interconnected and information more essential, news programs became more like "Entertainment Tonight." Have we dumbed down? Financial pressure to attract the public encouraged an over-emphasis on the popular and trivial. Serious, dedicated reporting on complex issues suffered—putting America at risk.

As political scientists and historians warn, accurate information and a free press are crucial to preventing the rise of dictators. Autocrats actively suppress and discredit valid criticism to keep from losing popular support. Putin is reportedly a master at it, as was Hitler, which should trouble us all. "Since Auschwitz we know what man is capable of. And since Hiroshima we know what is at stake," wrote Holocaust survivor Viktor Frankl.[23]

Noting the striking similarities between Putin's and Trump's first post-election press conference behavior, Russian journalist Alexey Kovalev told the American media, "Welcome to the era of bullshit."[24] Kovalev warned that facts or reason don't work, you'll "always be outmaneuvered," and because of economic pressure

> "... you'll have to report on everything that man [Trump] says as soon as he says it, without any analysis or fact-checking, because 1) his fans will not care if he lies to their faces; 2) while you're busy picking his lies apart, he'll spit out another mountain of bullshit and you'll be buried under it."[25]

Competing stories erupt on the same day to divert attention, and Trump takes credit for what he hasn't done and denies what he has—paying off a porn star and encouraging us to consider cleaning our lungs with household disinfectants.

Making the situation worse, there is now a cottage industry of websites fabricating fake news to purposefully rile up one group or another. It's awfully easy to believe disinformation about someone you dislike. The lag of about 13 hours between the publication of a false report and the subsequent debunking is enough time for a story to be read by hundreds of thousands if not millions.[26] Fewer see the retraction.

## AMERICANS ARE NOT ONLY DISAGREEING, WE'RE HOSTILE AND UNCIVIL

Not only are we disagreeing and misinformed, bullying and violence are rising in the U.S. There were more mass shootings than days in 2019—a record number.[27] Americans suffer anti-social behavior in cyber-space, at school, and at work. "People are nervous that there's a certain amount of civil disorder that might come if huge numbers of people are sick and a huge number of institutions are not operating normally," said a gun industry expert explaining the recent spike in gun sales.[28]

Exacerbating the toxic environment is "hostile attribution bias"—our tendency to interpret others' ambiguous behavior as hostile rather than benign. It's far too easy to assume others are out to get us. Unfortunately there is a link between this bias and aggression. Well-known Christian author Os Guinness argues that rebuilding civility will affect whether western societies survive.[29]

We've had government shutdowns from both sides, and Americans voicing concern over the *erosion of civility*[30] in government, business, media, and social media:

- 65% say it's a major problem that worsened during the financial recession
- 70% say incivility has gotten worse since Trump was elected
- Students, especially those of color, are afraid[31]
- Since Trump won, hate crimes and racial/ethnic threats have jumped[32]

Trump supporters aren't the only culprits. A Chicago motorist was beaten while bystanders shouted, "You voted for Trump." People post, "What should I do when I'm bullied for supporting Trump?"

## SPEAK UP

As parents and dog trainers know, when aggressive, uncivil behavior has no adverse consequences, it's likely to continue. The depolarization organization Better Angels is renaming itself Braver Angels, highlighting that courageous pushback is needed when those who don't share our views are misunderstood and demeaned.

Everyone needs to hold everyone accountable for what they do. Political correctness and manners, which are scoffed at by some, helped Americans reign in their aggression. The Internet and Trump have helped unleash it.

## ROLE MODELS ARE POWERFUL

We should expect our leaders to be shining examples of tolerance instead of afraid to let our kids watch the news. Likewise, we should hold ourselves to that standard.

Albert Bandura, who is often described as the most influential psychologist alive today, demonstrated that observing others powerfully affects our behavior. In his most famous experiment, preschoolers watched a film of adults criticizing and beating a large inflatable "Bobo" doll. Later those children punched weighted dolls in the same and even more creative ways. As part of my training I watched Bandura's grainy films and never forgot them. They are still able to be viewed on youtube.com, if you want to see them.

Trump's name-calling is a model others may follow, and in 2017 our president retweeted an earlier video clip of himself punching World Wrestling Entertainment chairman Vince McMahon with CNN's logo superimposed over the wrestler's face.[33] He feeds division by encouraging Americans to "liberate" Michigan and Minnesota. Let's stop being red and blue states. Let's be America's united ones.

## UNPREDICTABILITY HARMS TRUST AT HOME AND ABROAD

Psychologically, we're also being threatened by the unpredictability of the man in the White House. If we don't know what to believe, trust, and expect, we have to be on guard ready to protect ourselves from our fellow Americans and our president. Our allies do too.

Unpredictability is useful for a sports contest or business (zero-sum) deal, when preserving the relationship isn't important. In those competitive and often one-time transactions, if you get something, then I won't. When winning is all that matters, power plays and tactics can be very effective. But, beware. People who get the short end of the stick often refuse future encounters. They even seek revenge down the road.

In true contrast, people in win-win situations want to win *and* simultaneously seek to ensure that others are satisfied.

> **Good long-term deals meet these criteria:**
> - **high quality solutions**
> - **mutual satisfaction**
> - **continued good will**

With family and allies, we want the process to be a positive experience, because then agreements are kept, trust is built, and the connection is maintained. Diplomacy and family decisions aren't just win/lose business transactions.

Of concern is that we're no longer viewed as a trusted ally—70% of the countries polled lack confidence in President Trump to do the right thing in world affairs.[34] We've been embarrassed on the global stage.

Collaboration relies on trust. Americans are wondering how to deal with a leader who violates the norms the rest of us live by, and someone who dismantled Obama's pandemic task force, told us the world-wide devasting illness was a hoax, said he had total authority, and answered, "I have no responsibility" for a slow response to it.[35]

## OUR COMMON ENEMY IS LACK OF RESPECT

The virus and other common enemies can unite us, just as common goals do. Some individual Americans have found common ground in stopping Trump. Like them, I'm asking you not to say the "new abnormal" or "that's just Trump being Trump." (See Appendix 1.)

His inappropriate behavior shouldn't be condoned—no matter if you're a registered Republican, Democrat, Independent, or infrequent voter. Lies, blaming, bullying, racism, misogyny, temper tantrums, etc. should not be the American way.

Americans attacking one other is no cause for American pride either. Our *true* common enemy is the lack of tolerance for each other. We need to be kinder, gentler, more civil, and more inclusive in this country that is supposed to be "of and for the people." What can be the magnet to bring us together? Respect—not anger.

Immediately, each of us can do something—we can treat each other better as we talk to and about one another—even six feet apart. We can assume the best. Disdain and name calling hasn't enabled us to collaboratively solve America's infrastructure, economic, climate, or pandemic woes. As Governor Cuomo said to a hurting country, "This isn't the time for politics."[36] Being divided will make things worse. It's time for a change.

## WITH OR WITHOUT TRUMP, AMERICA FACES AN INCLUSION PROBLEM

Trump isn't the only problem. Americans need to come together, but not in sub-groups attacking each other where polarization

27

intensifies. Our big, diverse country needs a unifying vision plus a focus on shared values and interests. We heal by putting country ahead of party and community ahead of self. Those health care teams stayed at work to help us. What an example. We owe them.

America used to take pride in being a "melting pot." The analogy switched to a "stew" where different cultural flavors (e.g., black and white, male and female) could still be tasted within a desirable concoction. Employee training sessions encouraging diversity started in the 1990s. Now most companies with an average of 10,000 employees provide diversity training for all levels of employees, but experiencing inclusion is far from complete.[37]

Many organizations promoting diversity were primarily motivated to avoid litigation with a focus on explaining discrimination and the law. Others like IBM stated that diversity was a moral imperative, and Xerox took on the social responsibility of hiring a more diverse workforce than the general population. Respecting differences was valued or at least encouraged.

Putting down minorities and women became inappropriate, and then, tragically, bashing white males became the thing for some to do. Women had been seen as lesser than, now males, especially white ones, were the brunt of jokes and last to be hired.

## RACIAL TENSIONS

Even where diversity training occurred, it wasn't enough to heal our racial divide. Social injustice lawyer Bryan Stevenson asserts that you are far better off in this country being white, privileged, and guilty than black, poor, and innocent. Part of his eloquent TED talk message is that many societies have enslaved other humans, but America has not sought redemption for doing so.[38]

To feel proud instead of guilty—to reduce the tension of "cognitive dissonance" described in the upcoming chapter "We are Biased, but Share Values"—American slave owners denigrated blacks to a position of being sub-human and have never reconciled this treatment. For healing, Stevenson believes we need to talk about our past as the South Africans, Germans, and Australians have talked about their atrocities.

Terrorism in American did not start with 9/11. Think of the lynchings, especially in the American South.[39] No wonder many reject the notion of making America great "again," because it was far from great for them.

America did elect a black president twice, but racial divide still remains. Even the millennial generation's racial tolerance may be overstated, because young people are not sharing similar school, policing, and housing experiences across racial lines. Our public schools are more segregated now than they were 40 years ago,[40] and the racial gap in household wealth has exploded since the 2007–2008 housing crisis.[41] Three-quarters of white people have entirely white friend circles.[42] On average, the lives of white people and those of color remain very dissimilar—hindering real understanding.

## GENDER, AGE, AND CULTURAL GAP

Years ago corporate training sessions also started teaching how to communicate across the gender divide and how to understand the four-generational workforce, which has now become five. The intent was to help people work together better. Managers were reminded that generational differences are real, so if it's right for you, it's probably wrong for your employees.

For the young who've been congregating rather than distancing during the pandemic, I wish I could remember the source of this wise admonition, "I've been 21 too. But, you've never been 78." I haven't been 78 either, but my point is that age gives people different perspectives.

In this land of opportunity for immigrants, companies also began to train to include individuals of different cultures, nationalities, and religions. One of my organizational clients was struggling to find ways to communicate emergency safety messages (e.g., "Stop!") to its workforce where 26 different languages were spoken on the manufacturing floor. Customers across the globe—such as many served by the Mayo Clinic and the hospitality industry—provided another reason for Americans to become attuned to cultural differences.

However, how much training for tolerance and globalization occurred outside of large organizations in the rural heartland, the South, or the ranching West? While Americans on the coasts and in corporate America were becoming accustomed to different co-workers and customers, those in small businesses and elsewhere were probably not being forced to appreciate those differences. My guess is that most Americans rarely think about and interact with the 77% of all 21st century workers on American crop farms who have been born abroad.[43]

Inclusion and similarities build strong relationships. Let's recognize how we are alike and how our communities, companies, and country need us. "We may have come on different ships, but we're all in the same boat now," said Martin Luther King Jr.[44]

## AREN'T AUTHORITARIAN PERSONALITIES THE PROBLEM?

Some have blamed Trump's popularity on authoritarianism which is on the rise across the globe. Shortly after the world fought Nazism in WWII, Theodor Adorno proposed that deep personality traits predisposed some people to prejudicial, totalitarian, and anti-democratic ideas. Looking at Nazi case studies, test scores, and clinical interview data, he concluded that individuals with authoritarian personalities tended to categorize people into "us" and "them" and saw their own group as superior.[45]

There is evidence that authoritarian personalities exist, but Adorno failed to explain why people are prejudiced against certain groups and not others. Not all prejudiced people conform to the authoritarian personality type and not all authoritarians have suffered harsh parenting, which Adorno considered a cause. Cultural and social norms and lower educational level seem to explain prejudice too.

Seeing a link to politics, "authoritarian-ism"—voters characterized by a desire for order and a fear of outsiders—started to be studied. Authoritarianism not only correlates with support for Trump, it seems to predict support for Trump more reliably than virtually any other indicator.[46]

## WHY IS AUTHORITARIANISM ON THE RISE?

When people scoring high in authoritarianism feel threatened, they look for strong leaders who promise to take action to protect them from outsiders and prevent the changes they fear. Years before Trump, political scientists concluded much of the polarization dividing American politics was fueled not just by gerrymandering or money in politics, but by an unnoticed yet large electoral group—authoritarians. Their theory was:

> "the extreme nature of authoritarians' fears, and of their desire to challenge threats with force, would lead them toward a candidate whose temperament was totally unlike anything we usually see in American politics — and whose policies went far beyond the acceptable norms."[47]

Early in the fall of 2015, as Trump's rise was baffling many, those researchers saw their predictions come true. They consider Trump a symptom of the rise of authoritarianism and right-wing populism that will have consequences beyond him.[48]

Authoritarians have been described as one of three groups who support the Republican Party *and* the most changeable.[49] The other two sub-groups? Anti-government-intervention types—Libertarians—and classic conservatives who are highly responsible, conscientious, and cautious about change.

When authoritarians perceive the moral order is falling apart, the country isn't cohesive, diversity is rising, and our leadership seems unable to manage the situation, it's as though a button is pushed. Their reaction is "in case of moral threat, lock down the borders, kick out those who are different, and punish those who are morally deviant."[50] About 30% of the U.S. population is authoritarian.[51] [52]

## AUTHORITARIAN-ISM IS A REASON TO ADDRESS FEARS

Chaos in Washington, massive global migration, and killings in Syria, London, and Las Vegas may be creating a more authoritarian electorate. What can we do? If certain personalities vote when they feel threatened, then making people feel safer should return that voting block to inactivity. How? With better economic conditions, more cohesion around a compelling vision, or functioning state and federal leadership. Reducing fear lowers many people's desire to vote.

When people are scared, they seek strength. However, authoritarian leaders aren't the right answer—they actually hinder constructive responses to crises by blocking information flow. Hiding the truth means the extent of trouble isn't known and responses are delayed. We saw it with Russia's slow reaction to Chernobyl, China's action toward the physician who discovered Covid-19, and Trump's claim we have the coronavirus under control. Someone said, "They lie and we die."

## DEMOCRACY DOESN'T LOOK SO HOT

The young are not that excited about Democracy.[53] [54] Finding special interest groups gaining privileged access to career politicians, believing elected officials don't care about them, and not having had experience with authoritarian rule, they are frustrated. The number of Americans who were alive during World War II who believe it is "essential" to live in a democracy stands at 72%, but among millennials, aged 20–36, that figure is only 30%.[55]

## CHAOS?

Worried more about chaos than fascism or authoritarianism, conservative NY Times columnist David Brooks saw Trump's administration as something to unite this country against. In January 2017 he wrote, "We've wondered if there is some opponent out there that could force us to unite and work together. Well, that opponent is being inaugurated, not in the form of Trump the man, but in the form of the chaos and incompetence that will likely radiate from him, month after month."[56] Many find Trump's incompetence evident with Sharpiegate—his redrawn hurricane weather map—and his mixed, inadequate Covid-19 messages.

## DON'T MAKE PEOPLE DEFEND, FIND A COMMON CAUSE

However, increased efforts to prove Trump wrong are likely to do the opposite—strengthen his base's determination to protect him. The same is true when far right Republicans attack the far left.

Loyal, those dedicated supporters perceive anyone who disagrees with their position is the enemy, and often they care more about who the policy is identified with than the policy itself. The more you attack their views or leader, the more they have to hunker down and defend them. Too many of us label ourselves Democrat or

Republican without examining the candidate's character and competence. See more about the halo effect in the next chapter.

Trump repeatedly uses the powerful tool of offering up an enemy to harness the power of anger. Notice his language. Disagreeing Americans—war hero John McCain and Republican Mitt Romney—are "traitors," and behavior the POTUS dislikes is "treasonous."[57] Trump has encouraged citizens to resist and protest when their governors ask them to stay home a little longer to prevent spreading the virus.

Neighbors and family are sick of this war. From a psychological perspective, lowering the need to defend our differing positions has the best likelihood of reducing rancor. Let's find shared concerns and common interests. We all worry about the virus causing both death and economic disaster.

Researchers have been seeking ways to promote peace. Tom Pyszczynski's terror management research team conducted a set of studies in the United States, Iran and Israel. First, they subtly reminded people of the threat of their own mortality. In all three countries, once people were "primed" by fear to cling strongly to their group identities, they were more likely to support violence against people out of their group. As expected, when afraid we stick with our own and attack outsiders.

The good news is that later research revealed that people's attitudes toward out-group violence *could* be changed, if they are reminded of a *common* human problem as well as their own potential death.[58]

## DISSATISFIED WITH CONGRESS

Gridlock, not just Trump, is a problem. Congressional Republicans refused to even consider a moderate Supreme Court nominee in 2016 when Justice Scalia died, leaving a vacancy for months. The Democrats pulled the same shenanigans for a shorter period in

2007, blocking George W. Bush's nominee. Couldn't Obama have reached out more to Congress? Sure. Could Congress work together better? Yes!

Congress' approval rating hasn't topped 30% in more than a decade.[59] Hundreds of bipartisan bills sit on Senate Majority Leader Mitch McConnell's desk, because he refuses to bring them to a vote. The country remembers that House Minority leader Nancy Pelosi told colleagues to quickly pass the lengthy Affordable Care Act so "you can find out what's in it," though she tried later to clarify what she meant. Members of Congress even get a pass from the health care system and other laws they craft. [60]

Those elected apparently forgot Americans put them in office to get our country's work done, until lately. In an historic moment, Congress passed the coronavirus relief bill with unanimous support from both sides in the Senate and only 40 House Republicans refusing. However, pettiness continues. No Democrat was invited to the signing. Plus, tax payer money going to millionaires has already been reported.[61]

Agreement among the populace hasn't translated to agreement or action in Washington. A bipartisan majority of Americans wanted Republican Senate Majority Leader Mitch McConnell to call witnesses during President Trump's impeachment trial.[62] Though about 90% of Americans favor background checks for all gun buyers, legislation hasn't been passed.[63] The Sandy Hook tragedy brought our country together without effecting change. Congress has failed us.

In the absence of Congressional action, presidents exert power through executive orders. In their first 3 years in office, Bill Clinton signed 89, George W. Bush 136, and Barak Obama 108. What about Trump? In his 3 years, from 2017 to early 2020, Trump's executive orders numbered 149. [64] Executive orders like Trump's travel ban started flying from the Oval Office immediately without involvement of appropriate departments or Congress. Lacking crucial support from the Senate, House, or courts, a president's executive orders get overturned and policies unfunded.

## ARE UNIFYING TRADITIONS DISAPPEARING?

As a psychologist, I look for factors that can unite us. Love of country and its symbols are some. One unifying action was pledging allegiance to the American flag. After the 9/11 terrorism attacks, bills making the oath mandatory in public schools were introduced in Colorado, Connecticut, Illinois, Indiana, Minnesota, Mississippi and Missouri, as many schools have stopped having children make the pledge, giving them the right to opt out. A fake news story even spread the rumor that Obama banned the pledge through executive order.[65] Encouraging love of country, brings people together.

Patriotism isn't childish; it protects our future. As anger at fellow Americans has translated for some into an aversive reaction to seeing the flag flown, we need reminding that America is beautiful. Individualism and patriotism aren't mutually exclusive.

## WHAT HAPPENS IF WE DON'T UNITE?

If we don't come together as a nation, we fail. Unity and respect are essential to foster peace within and abroad, so let's stop the demonizing, incivility, intolerance, and violence. Let's avoid falling like the Greek, Roman, and Persian empires.[66]

Slow decline may be the biggest threat.[67] Not referring to the 2016 election, Thomas Friedman and Michael Mandelbaum in *That Used to Be Us*[68] along with their critic Martin Sieff in *That Should Still be Us*[69] attempted to alert America to its downward slope. Many others have done the same.

In his 2013 *Forbes* article "How Dictators come to Power in a Democracy," Jim Powell, who covers economic and political history, wrote,

"...when people become angry enough or desperate enough, sometimes they'll support crazies who would never attract a crowd in normal circumstances."[70]

He went on to say:

"Those who dismiss the possibility of a dictatorial regime in America need to consider possible developments that could make our circumstances worse and politically more volatile than they are now—like runaway government spending, soaring taxes, more wars, inflation and economic collapse."[71]

We prevent our demise by fighting, but not each other. Let's unite by talking—by expressing different ideas and dissenting opinions in ways that will keep this messy, fragile, precious democracy alive. It's worth preserving.

We need to constructively bridge our differences, prevent our decency standards from slipping, protect Constitutional rights, uphold or change our laws, and remain economically viable. We need to heal our hurt. This book is designed to help.

In Appendix 2 you'll see a guide to understanding the other side with a bit of an "us v. them" view of how Americans on the left differ from those on the right. Most of us are more similar than what gets discussed by the media and have views more nuanced than this list suggests. Shared core American values are listed in Appendix 3.

Take a look in the next chapter at what we have in common—biases and values.

# CHAPTER 3
# We are Biased, but Share Values

S
tart recognizing Americans have some things in common—we are all biased. Regardless of political preference, humans systematically and unconsciously make judgment errors. None of us is the sound, rational decision maker, or voter, we'd like to think we are.

A biased American mind is a normal mind. For survival, we're wired to stick with our kind, embrace the familiar, and save energy. In the last chapter I mentioned our tendency—bias—to interpret people's behavior as hostile.

Frequently biases operate completely outside our awareness, so when you just can't understand how Democrats, Republicans, your kids, your parents, people across the country, people next door, Trump's base, and Never-Trumpers can ever think the way they do, remember we share these other well-documented cognitive patterns too:

- Halo effect = assume if people have one characteristic they have others
- Fundamental errors = attribute person's actions to their nature not situation
- Accessibility bias = rely too much on easily available information
- Conservatism bias = favor prior evidence over new

- Confirmation bias = listen only to information that confirms preconceived views
- Consensus bias = believing one's view is common and appropriate
- Cognitive dissonance = want to eliminate conflict between our beliefs or actions
- Negativity bias = pay more attention to negative information

## THE HALO EFFECT

People aren't truly objective. We see and hear what we expect. We can read words minus most of their letters and sentences without a word or two, since our minds look for patterns. We fill the gaps based on our assumptions and experience. If you possess one characteristic, we assume you have a bunch of others.

Hearing someone is a Democrat, for example, people attribute characteristics to that individual based on their mental picture of a Democrat. This so called "halo effect" can actually be positive *or* negative. To some, a Democrat holds certain views on health care, taxes, financial regulations, transgender bathrooms, and the environment.

Yet, of course, all men, women, blacks, whites, Asians, Latinos, Native Americans, gays, straights, or members of a party aren't the same. On a particular issue, some Democrats are more similar to someone in the Republican Party than to someone in their own. Certainly we've seen moderate Republicans wrestling with more conservative ones over health care, and the same is true for Democrats.

Generalizations aren't the same thing as stereotypes, and "generally true" isn't the same as what's true in a specific case. Plus, the differences between various groups' "average" positions—the average Democrat, Independent or Republican—are far smaller than the wide range within each group. For example, the average man is taller by about five or six inches than the average woman.[1] Compare a tiny female gymnast with an exceptionally tall female basketball player, and the wide variation *within* females is obvious.

Unfortunately, the tendency to categorize has us writing off other Americans and forgetting how different the individual members of the same group can be. We're dismissing people who aren't from our party, race, gender, or educational and cultural background, when we could be zeroing in on our commonalities.

## RECOGNIZE THE FUNDAMENTAL ERROR— BLAMING THE PERSON

Our "fundamental error" is attributing people's actions to their basic nature—their disposition—rather than circumstance. We conclude "that's the way they are" instead of considering situational factors affecting their behavior. So, a honking motorist is a jerk not someone desperate to get to the hospital. An American who supports late-term abortion is judged a baby killer rather than a grieving parent-to-be who terminated a pregnancy after learning the fetus wouldn't survive. A strong gun advocate gets labeled a redneck without us understanding he's terrified of being shot again by another home invader.

Recognizing how we ourselves are influenced by factors around us, we judge friends and self—"us"—kindly. We do the opposite for those outside our groups.[2] Playing a part in our especially unfavorable reactions to "them" is that "hostile attribution" tendency mentioned before. Be careful. Look for (hopefully positive) intentions, especially when situations are ambiguous.

## TRIPLE THREAT OF ACCESSIBILITY, CONSERVATISM, AND CONFIRMATION BIAS

Cognitive tendencies, especially several of them together, fuel polarization. Humans from all political persuasions suffer from "accessibility bias"—relying too much on easily available information. In addition, we're plagued by "conservatism bias"—favoring prior evidence over new. Both help us save energy yet keep us from being fully informed.

The point is we quickly reach conclusions and slowly revise them. Congratulate yourself for the times you were wrong and changed your mind. When might you need to repeat that feat?

People on both sides notice and remember what confirms already held positions, then fiercely defend their view. Once a judgment is formed, we *selectively* gather evidence to prove that point. For example, when shown the same presentation, people holding opposite views recall very different information from it, almost as if they had watched totally different videos. I was shocked the first time I saw that happen.

Evidence shows people also remember more positive than negative information about ingroups and believe their own groups are less prejudiced.[3] Identifying ourselves as belonging to groups we consider positive serves to help us feel better about ourselves.

"Confirmation bias"—this well researched psychological tendency to retain what fits the views we already had and tune out the rest—gets candidates elected and keeps us divided. It's awfully hard to change our minds when we so protectively insulate our brains from new or competing data.

Americans not only remember, they hunt for evidence to support their disdain for those who see the world, or cast their ballots, differently. Then, like-minded individuals tell us we're right, our reinforced pearls of wisdom get passed further, and the process repeats. Some people intentionally send out false news to get under others' skin.[4]

## IT IS EASY TO BELIEVE WRONG INFORMATION

It *is* easy to believe inaccurate information, especially if we want to. Mostly we get headlines, sound bites, and snippets of news from questionable sources rather than in-depth coverage. No, Trump did not call Republicans dumb back in 1998, but that story flew around the internet.[5]

Are we sufficiently analytical? Stanford researchers testing over 7,500 students from 12 states from middle school to college had serious difficulty distinguishing real news from "sponsored content" (advertisements).[6] More than 30% of students in their study thought a fake Fox News account was more trustworthy than the real one. The Stanford team concluded U.S. students are woefully unprepared for this new world and for their first-time voting responsibilities.[7]

Physicians think Americans ought to be getting more exercise. Psychologists and teachers think Americans ought to be getting more critical-thinking exercise. Even though adults, on average, tend to be good at identifying which social media sources are not credible,[8] emphasizing who published information made little difference to them.[9] A series of experiments involving nearly 7,000 Americans found emphasizing the source had virtually no effect on whether people believed news headlines or intended to share them. We're willing to pass on propaganda.

It looks like we're lazy. Susceptibility to partisan fake news is best explained by lack of reasoning.[10] First, our biases have us reaching faulty conclusions with accurate but insufficient info. Second, we're better at picking apart the logic of the *other* side.[11] Third, we absorb, retain, and spread disinformation which is easily attained and dangerously not scrutinized.

Making things worse, our emotions interfere with our reasoning—we trust our guts not data—when scared and vulnerable. Fear is our decision-making enemy. When the issues are highly threatening, health-related, or personally relevant issues, we discount cold, hard data and rely on poignant stories.[12] We tend to make more fact-based decisions when our emotional engagement is low.

Bad decisions, though, can have deadly consequences. Trump, a politician, dispensing medical advice to take hydroxychloroquine and chloroquine because, "What have you got to lose?" flies in the face of scientific evidence. Infectious disease doctors who've been studying other coronaviruses for decades explain what works for some people causes real damage for others.[13] Medical practice requires nuanced understanding of complicated situations. There is a reason cleaners are labeled for external use only.

Science takes a look at memorable anecdotes from a 35,000 foot view. Scientists study incidents over time looking for a pattern—and for exceptions. Does something occur only with certain types of people in certain types of situations?

## CONSENSUS BIAS AND CONSPIRACY THEORIES

Listening to conspiracy theorists discount Anthony Fauci's medical emergency guidance as "politically motivated to defeat Trump" terrifies me. The falsely informed will accidentally spread the virus. Getting around confirmation bias and its cousin "consensus bias"—the pervasive tendency to see one's own choices and judgments as appropriate and common—is difficult.

Dealing with conspiracy theorists? That's almost impossible, because they provide (wrong) explanations for the almost unexplainable, give structure to uncertainty, and false security to the anxious.[14] People are overwhelmed by the notion that Mother Nature could infect, kill, plus wreak economic damage so fast. Some would rather think the invisible enemy was concocted by the Chinese as a bioterrorism tool (for which they must have the antidote). Because conspiracy followers believe they know what others don't, they feel a bit safer, even when they aren't.[15]

Fear feeds conspiracy thinking, and so does society. Stories, like the Three Little Pigs and Hansel and Gretel, and TV shows, like *House of Cards* and *Ozark,* teach us the world is a dangerous place. Some of us are especially predisposed to react to fear, as you'll see in the next chapter.

## MYTHS AND ERRORS ARE HARD TO CORRECT

Correcting erroneous information—like the false belief that autism and vaccines are linked—is no easy task. Corrections of facts are less effective after a time lag between the delivery of the misinformation and the correction.[16] Corrections also work less well if the misinformation is attributed to a credible source and repeated multiple times first.[17] No wonder discreet Special Counsel Robert Mueller objected to Attorney General William Barr's short, misleading depiction of his lengthy investigation, which came out ahead of the release of Mueller's report. Barr created a narrative, the media repeated it, and the message became difficult to change.

To see how well media corrections and fact checking debunk myths, several researchers examined the erroneous notion that Obamacare included "death panels," a term coined by Sarah Palin.[18] In the experiment, people were given a news article with incorrect information about health care reform, and as expected, those who felt warmly toward Palin were more likely to believe in the untruth—death panels.

Interestingly, a correction of the facts affected people differently. Being informed that health care experts found NO evidence supporting Palin's death panel claims lowered belief in death panels for certain groups: 1) those who viewed Palin unfavorably and 2) those who viewed her favorably but had low political knowledge. Those results suggest corrections and fact checking improve policy understanding.

However, folks who liked Palin and knew more about politics actually came to more strongly believe in death panels after getting the evidence to the contrary. Attempting to correct backfired! As researcher Brendan Nyhan explained: "When evidence and beliefs collide, it is easier to change how we view evidence than it is to change our beliefs."[19]

## CONFORMITY CAN BE DANGEROUS

Failure to challenge our own thinking causes us to blindly or erroneously attack those who disagree with us. Even when wrong, we voters fiercely defend our positions often unaware of our biases, their payoffs, and their consequences. The trouble is, *prematurely* discarding competing ideas hinders creativity. Americans, we're threatening our chances to find innovative, workable solutions.

On the other hand, unless we *do* challenge others' faulty positions, we may blindly swallow and follow, especially if we don't have supportive people around. Stanley Milgram devised several experiments attempting to understand whether Nazi war crimes involved "just following orders." His frightening results, where participants believed they were delivering electric shocks, show remarkable obedience to authority. Instead of dissenting, we go along when we shouldn't.

Solomon Asch and others' conformity research also reveals individuals will do and say things they absolutely know to be wrong, when they are the only ones around espousing a certain view. When asked, for example, which line on the right matched the one on the left, if others unanimously say A or B which are obviously wrong, people go along with them.[20] The persuasive power of numbers works to interfere with productivity here. "How can they all see it that way?" we wonder. "Could I be wrong?" "What will happen if I voice a differing view?"

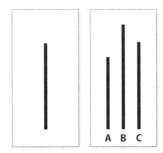

When another person holding our same view and giving our same answer is present, the strong tendency to conform diminishes. Having supportive buddies helps, so be one. Along with Senator McCain, two female Republican senators, Lisa Murkowski from Alaska and Susan Collins from Maine, are credited with defeating the health care bill proposed to scrap Obamacare. No doubt the presence of another female Republican senator enabled them both to refuse to vote with the Republican majority.

Yale's Cultural Cognition Project studies why so many people tend to make their beliefs about disputed facts (e.g., about whether global warming is a serious threat, vaccinations are safe, gun control makes us safer) conform to their cultural values.[21] Why do people stubbornly reject scientific data that doesn't fit with their worldview? Some people honestly believe the inaccurate information they have. In other words, they aren't bad people; they are misinformed and don't know better. However, conforming—following bad leadership—is deadly on the battlefield and in the pandemic fight.

Some people fiercely clutch beliefs, because they have a conscious or unconscious stake in their position being true. They are committed to a group, and the group's status or their standing within it depends on holding that belief. For example, gun advocates fear data that suggests gun availability is tied to violent crime,[22] because it's in their best interest to believe guns are not only fun but not harmful. Senators and supporters who've defended Trump for years face admitting they were wrong. It took courage for Senator

47

Mitt Romney to go against his party at the impeachment trial and vote to convict.

## COPING WITH COGNITIVE DISSONANCE

The psychological term "cognitive dissonance" refers to the human tendency to be stressed when there is a discrepancy between two of our beliefs or between what we believe and what we do. To make ourselves feel better, we attempt to reduce that tension by altering our perceptions and justifying our actions.

For example, when bystanders fail to help in an emergency, they choose to perceive no emergency exists, because it gets them off the hook. They are not, then, uncaring, apathetic or immoral people who failed to intervene. If the pandemic is a hoax, the Chinese's virus, or bioterrorism as conspiracy theorists suggest, maybe we are absolved if we spread or failed to prepare for it.

Citizens who voted for Trump do not want to believe his actions cost lives or that he threatens our Constitution, way of government, and position in the world. Americans say no person is above the law. To reduce cognitive discomfort, Republicans seek to believe Trump hasn't violated any emolument, campaign finance, or obstruction laws. Liberals, on the other hand, hate to perceive themselves as elitist, condescending, overspending, or insensitive to another's plight. It pains them to believe they left others behind.

Years of bystander apathy research found people are more likely to assist someone screaming for help when they are the only one around. They are less likely when others are present. Our justification is: If others aren't taking action, there can't be a crisis, so intervening to help isn't necessary. Those cognitive gymnastics get us off the guilt hook.

In a group, the sense of responsibility gets defused, and individuals don't step up to act. We tell ourselves some other American will do something. Not surprising, apathy is greater when situations are ambiguous.

What changes our minds? Many fathers of girls take up the cause of female rights, when their own daughter is affected. Many opponents of same sex marriage reverse positions when friends they care deeply about come out expressing love for another of the same gender. Personal experiences shape our thinking—moving us from apathy to empathy.

## WE PERCEIVE THE SAME SITUATIONS DIFFERENTLY

Our descriptions of identical situations vary greatly, so no wonder Americans hold different political positions. When coaching an executive identified as hostile by his peers, I captured a meeting exchange on video. Watching it together later, he described his behavior as appropriately strong, while others and I considered it unnecessarily aggressive. Hostile people typically describe the world as hostile and themselves as normal.

Conservative friends of mine perceived that when Obama said that Trayvon Martin, the young African American whose death sparked riots, could have been his son, he intensified racial tensions. From a psychological perspective, I had the opposite take on his message. One of the most effective ways to stop abuse is to help the abuser have empathy for the abused. To me, Obama was asking us to put ourselves in someone else's shoes and realize that skin color continues to affect and threaten Americans.

## SEE NEGATIVITY BIAS

In addition, humans carry a "negativity bias"—the cognitive tendency to pay more (and longer) attention to negatives. We dwell on criticism, quickly forget praise, and assume the worst, especially if we aren't actively challenging our own thinking.

Someone's negative traits carry more weight than an equal number of positive ones, and Jill Klein's research on presidential voting indicates character weaknesses typically influence more voters than strengths do.[23] Humans' focus on negative traits over positive ones is thought to be a result of behavioral expectations.

We assume people will generally behave positively because of social requirements and regulations. Therefore, negative behaviors/traits are more unexpected, salient, and influential in our judgments. Perhaps based on Trump's history, he wasn't *expected* to follow social norms, so his character flaws turned off fewer voters than normal. Some wrote off his behavior to campaigning, expecting he would become presidential when he assumed the office.

## CONTRAST EFFECTS

You've probably seen the example of a black dot being compared with others either larger or smaller. The same exact dot can appear to be bigger by placing it next to a small one. Some second spouses realize they look awfully good in contrast to the previous one. Like the conformity studies which revealed people's judgments are affected by what others say, studies have also shown "contrast effects"—what we see is affected by what we compare it with. So, Hillary looked more removed from regular people when compared with Trump. Trump looks less refined when contrasted with Obama than with Teddy Roosevelt or FDR.

Again, people try to cast themselves in the best light. Though we actually haven't changed a bit, we might try to make ourselves feel better by contrasting ourselves with folks living elsewhere, like those on the opposite side of the tracks. That is a change in perception *not* reality. Looking down on someone else, or assuming we're better, doesn't really make us better.

## SUPERIORITY ILLUSION

Our "superiority illusion"—the mistaken belief that each of us is better than average on almost any given metric including IQ, tennis, and driving skill—is well documented. Only half of us *can* be above average. Raised in Minnesota, I'm familiar with Garrison Keillor's Prairie Home Companion and its Lake Wobegon, where "all the women are strong, all the men are good-looking, and all the children are above average." We deceive ourselves. Is this what happens when kids get trophies for participation not achievement?

Thinking that you are better than you actually are is called the Dunning-Kruger effect after the researchers who showed that we are unaware of our own incompetence. Lowest performing students—those in the bottom quarter—estimated themselves around the 60th percentile, when in fact their performance put them down at the 12.5th percentile.[24] In contrast, those in the top quarter really did outscore others but underestimated themselves at about 75% instead of the achieved 87.5% or more. Studies of employees show the same tendency for underperformers to overrate themselves and outstanding performers to do the opposite.[25]

We have it backwards. The less we know about a particular field or set of skills—finance, medicine, gun safety, golf—the *more* we grossly overestimate our prowess and performance. We don't know we don't know. No doubt you've suffered through the singing of people who thought they would be the next Whitney Houston, Mariah Carey, Barbara Streisand, and Celine Dion. Mediocre athletes protect themselves from realizing they lack Michael Jordan and Wayne Gretzky's skill.

If people falsely believe they are basically about the same as those at the top of a particular field, they see no reason to strive to improve, learn, or clean up their act. Convinced they know as much as the industry experts, they deal with data that shows their perception is incorrect by simply ignoring or disparaging it. They are tough to influence. Unconsciously incompetent folks aren't comprehending, don't realize they aren't, can't recognize competence in others, and make up stuff.[26] Ignorance may be bliss, but it's dangerous.

Created by Joseph Luft and Harrington Ingham, the Johari window is a training tool used to help highlight that we have blind spots and areas of ignorance. All of us do. Some knowledge is open, free, public, and available to ourselves and others (top left quadrant).

## Johari Window

|  | Known to Self | Not Known to Self |
|---|---|---|
| Known to Others | Arena | Blind Spot |
| Not Known to Others | Façade | Unknown |

By w:User:Simon Shek  http://en.wikipedia.org/wiki/Image:Johari____ Window.PNG, Public Domain https://commons.wikimedia.org/w/index.php?curid=4565679

Some things about us are known to others but outside our awareness (top right quadrant), making input vital to our success. Think of the story about the emperor and his new clothes. Without honest feedback, the ruler made a fool of himself parading down the street naked. It's helpful to know when our slip is showing or fly is open. Feedback minimizes our blind spots—enabling us to correct a golf swing, improve our interactions, and excel.

Some information is known only to us and kept from others (bottom left), but we can become more transparent and make our facades shrink. Some information is known to no one (bottom right)—like our repressed feelings and unconscious motivations.

In theory, these window panes can grow or shrink. We can learn, be educated, get informed, take feedback, and become aware—thereby enlarging all the known-to-self window panes. To reduce the unknown, we can gain insight into ourselves and others.

## WE MAKE JUDGMENT ERRORS

Advanced education usually makes us realize how much we don't know. As we learn more about any field, appreciation for others' skills, knowledge, and expertise grows. Think of a teen who learns to enter accounts receivable data at her summer job and believes she understands the field of accounting. That was me. We can be clueless.

Interestingly, we are better at judging others than ourselves.[27] This gap between perceived and actual abilities is greater in the U.S. than, for example, in Asia where estimates match abilities more closely and individuals underestimate their abilities at all levels.[28] Asian cultures value modesty and self-improvement.[29]

So, in summary and in alphabetical order, research has documented these biases, errors, and cognitive patterns:

- Accessibility bias: relying too much on easily available information
- Cognitive dissonance: wanting to eliminate conflict between our beliefs or actions
- Confirmation bias: listening only to information that confirms preconceived views
- Consensus bias: believing one's view is common and appropriate
- Conservatism bias: favoring prior evidence over new
- Contrast effects: perceiving depends on comparison
- Fundamental error: attributing people's actions to their nature not situation

- Halo effect: assuming if people have one characteristic they have others
- Hostile attribution bias: interpreting ambiguous actions as hostile
- Negativity bias: paying more attention to negative information
- Superiority illusion: believing oneself above average on almost everything

## FOCUS ON SIMILARITIES

We share biases. Anything else? What is a common cause for this American population of over 325,000,000?

New census data is being collected to answer, "Who are we?" Data now indicates approximately 80% of us live in urban areas and suburbs.[30] The top tenth owns as much of our nation's wealth as the bottom 70% combined.[31] We are evenly split male/female. English is the language most often spoken at home, by 80% of us. More than half of the U.S. workforce consists of minorities, immigrants, and women.

The majority of our population is currently white, but American demographics continue to change with immigration and birth rates. African Americans are the largest *racial* minority (13.2% of the population). [32] Hispanic and Latino Americans (17% of the population) make up the largest *ethnic* minority living on our 3.8 million square miles. "How do we sew this coat of many colors?" asked correspondent Harry Smith.

In his intriguing book *American Nations*, Colin Woodard describes eleven rival regional cultures of North America and contends Americans have been deeply divided since the days of Jamestown and Plymouth.[33] Woodard believes many of these North American regional cultures still affect us today:

1. **Yankeedom,** in New England spread toward the upper Midwest, with a Puritan respect for intellectual achievement,

a focus on the "greater good," and an aggressive push toward assimilation

2. The short-lived **New Netherland,** NYC, modeled after Amsterdam with a strong tolerance of diversity

3. The **Midlands,** founded by the English Quakers and Germans, with government seen as an intrusion and no need for ethnic purity

4. **Tidewater,** the most powerful during the colonial period, with a high value on respect for aristocratic tradition and authority

5. **Great Appalachia,** founded by war-ravaged settlers from Ireland, England, and Scotland who have a deep commitment to individual liberty, personal sovereignty, and a warrior ethic

6. **The Deep South,** founded by Barbados slave lords, a bastion of white supremacy and aristocratic privilege

7. **New France,** the nationalistic Quebec area, which is egalitarian and multi-cultural

8. **El Norte,** in the southwest dating back to the Spanish empire, with Hispanic language and cultural norms and expected to be 29% of the 2050 population

9. **The Left Coast,** the strip from the Monterrey coast to Juneau, which combines Yankee faith in government and social reform with individual self-exploration

10. **The Far West,** inland from Arizona to Alaska, which depended on railroads and dams for its settlement, sees itself treated as an exploited internal colony by the coasts, and reviles federal government interference

11. **First Nation,** Native Americans in a vast area with a hostile climate who are reclaiming their sovereignty

Given the diversity of backgrounds in America, no wonder we see things differently.

## WHERE DO WE AGREE?

Similarities draw people together, so let's find some. Republicans and Democrats *alike* (over 80%) say the following are important concerns:[34]

- health care
- the economy
- jobs
- terrorism

Voters aren't hopelessly divided. In reality, polling shows most Americans agree that:

- protecting the environment should be a top priority[35]
- education warrants more attention[36]
- Roe v. Wade shouldn't be overturned[37]
- stricter gun laws deserve support[38]
- border security is important[39]
- DACA policy should be kept in place[40]
- corporations and the wealthy don't pay their fair share[41]
- Trump's tax returns should be seen[42]
- there should have been witnesses at the impeachment trial[43]
- Trump was too slow addressing the Covid threat[44]

These aren't just the Democrats' issues.[45] We are more alike than we may realize.

## WHAT COMMON VALUES DO AMERICANS SHARE?

Values unite us as well. Americans cite freedom of speech and freedom of religion as the top examples of America's superior values compared to other places in the world.[46] Eighty-seven percent

— almost nine of ten Americans — answered yes when asked: Do you believe in God? That percentage is down from the 96% who responded affirmatively in a 1944 Gallup Poll, but it was by far the strongest affirmation of any value in the 2012 Atlantic/Aspen Institute American Values Survey.[47]

Participants in the survey also said they are more tolerant and open-minded than their parents—and more than they were a decade ago. Half believe the economic system is unfair to middle- and working-class Americans, and more than 80% believe Wall Street executives don't share fundamental American values. Six in ten of us believe running a budget deficit undermines American values, since it means our children will have to pay for our spending.

In 2012, *before* Trump, two-thirds believed the country was heading in the wrong direction and 69% said the country's values have deteriorated since the 1970s.[48] Respondents cited political corruption, increased materialism, declining family values, and a celebrity-obsessed culture as culprits. Nearly half expected values to weaken further over the next decade.

## HOLD ON TO AMERICAN VALUES

I consider the U.S. still the best place to live on Earth, as does Muslim American filmmaker Kamran Pasha,[49] who blogs about our remarkable opportunities, freedom, kind hearts, and welcoming arms. Aren't you, like him, afraid of average Americans losing faith in what makes the United States so great?

What values are "American"? The Washington International Center staff has been introducing thousands of international visitors to life in the United States for more than a third of a century. They believe that if a foreign visitor really understood how deeply ingrained these 13 values are, the visitor would understand 95% of American actions—action that might otherwise appear strange or unbelievable from the perspective of the foreigner's own society's values.[50] We Americans need to understand ourselves.

The center advises, "When you encounter an action, or hear a statement in the United States that surprises you, try to see it as an expression of one or more of the values."[51] For example, America's impressive record of scientific and technological achievement can be seen as a natural result of 13 values, because:

> "First of all, it was necessary to believe (1) these things could be achieved, that Man does not have to simply sit and wait for Fate to bestow them or not to bestow them, and that Man does have control over his own environment, if he is willing to take it. Other values that have contributed to this record of achievement include (2) an expectation of positive results to come from change (and the acceptance of an ever-faster rate of change as "normal"); (3) the necessity to schedule and plan one's time; (6) the self-help concept; (7) competition; (8) future orientation; (9) action work orientation; (12) practicality; and (13) materialism."[52]

Examining the underlying values Americans hold in common can help us reduce division. Put yourself in others' shoes to comprehend what they care about, find common ground, and be more tolerant, because we are all flawed.

As the Washington International Center explains, the list of typically American values, which Americans consider positive, contrasts sharply with the values commonly held by the people of many other countries.

| U.S. VALUES | OTHER COUNTRIES' VALUES |
|---|---|
| 1. Personal Control | Fate |
| 2. Change | Tradition |
| 3. Time & Its Control | Human Interaction |
| 4. Equality | Hierarchy/Rank/Status |
| 5. Individualism/Privacy | Group's Welfare |
| 6. Self-Help | Birthright Inheritance |
| 7. Competition | Cooperation |
| 8. Future Orientation | Past Orientation |
| 9. Action/Work Orientation | "Being" Orientation |
| 10. Informality | Formality |
| 11. Directness/Openness/Honesty | Indirectness/Ritual/"Face" |
| 12. Practicality/Efficiency | Idealism |
| 13. Materialism/Acquisitiveness | Spiritualism/Detachment |

https://uucsj.org/wp-content/uploads/2015/12/L-Robert-Kohl-The-Values-Americans-Live-By.pdf

So, we Americans have different regional and cultural backgrounds, demographics, personalities, expectations, and experiences, yet espouse some core values.

Our precious democracy is built on them. Another similar list of Ten Core American Values is in Appendix 3.

We are part of the same tribe, though we frequently forget our identity. Some voters plugged their noses and voted for Trump to usher in a new administration they believed would protect their values. Most of those voters' intentions were good, even though we see things differently. My aunt voted for our 45th president because she believed, "Trump's going to take care of the poor." My hairdresser doesn't like Trump's behavior, but believes God put him there.

How do we find and build on common ground? Like Thomas Friedman I believe, "Most Americans are good-hearted people who are actually starved to feel united again."[53]

Let's build on our good-heartedness with the skills and strategies in part two.

# PART TWO

# Changing the Situation

**CHAPTER 4**

# Starting with Empathy—
# for Both Sides

Re-uniting America requires empathy, lots of it. Trump was elected for a reason, and Americans who put him in office have legitimate concerns that should be addressed by Congress, litigated in the courts, and discussed over dinner. At the same time, those who never wanted him in the White House have their concerns too.

Our intense emotional reactions—including the ones Trump sparks—make seeing another's perspective difficult. For each of us, our own point of view looks so obvious.

Sociologist Arlie Hochschild is trying to do something remarkable—overcome America's empathy wall. Her highly respected *Strangers in Their Own Land* brings the stories and fears she heard in hundreds of interviews in "Trump country" Louisiana to see if it's possible for liberals to empathize with Trump supporters.[1] What a wonderful place to start an American dialogue—with listening and understanding.

With her permission, here is her profound metaphor: Think of people waiting in a long line stretching up a hill, and at the top is the American dream. The people waiting in line felt like they've worked extremely hard, sacrificed a lot, tried their best, and were waiting for something they deserved. And more and more this line isn't moving or is moving more slowly as the economy stalls. Then they see people—immigrants, blacks, women, refugees, public employees, and even oil-drenched pelicans—unfairly cutting ahead of them in line and getting priority. To the side in this narrative is Barack Obama, the line supervisor who seems to be waving these people (and the pelican) ahead. Instead of hearing their distress call, the government seems to be on the side of those cutting in and pushing those in line back.

Hochschild took this story back to those she'd talked to and heard, "You read my mind!" She writes about real economic threat added to a cultural and demographic sense of loss and decline. About alarm coupled with a government that doesn't seem like it's heard your distress call. About ties to a community and an existential threat from outsiders who speak a different language, practice a different religion, or simply have a different sense about what matters in the world. She explains that big-picture stuff—emotional and financial self-interest—is what motivates our votes.

## WHY IS POPULISM SPREADING ACROSS THE GLOBE?

From the populists' perspective, if you aren't an economic or cultural victim, you're one of the perpetrators, which put journalists, scholars, bureaucrats, and technocrats into the enemy camp. Financial struggles played a role in Trump's rise, yet the bigger factors seem to be racial and cultural resentment—a backlash against modern values of globalism, multicultural tolerance, and openness to diversity.[2]

White working class voters with anxieties about the "American way of life" (79% of them) picked Trump.[3] Across the world, populist followers believe their leaders, even if they are billionaires, are straight talkers concerned about the average Joe or Jill. Making depolarization tough is that many think, "If you're not pro-Trump, you must be against me."

Trump's populism appeal is rooted in being an outsider. He claims to lead an insurgency on behalf of ordinary Americans disgusted with the corrupt establishment, incompetent politicians, dishonest Wall Street speculators, arrogant intellectuals, and politically correct liberals.[4][5] Unlike me, they think he's genuine.

## EDUCATED ELITES

To get along, encourage people to ponder why educated "elites" feel *they* are in grave peril. They worked hard in pursuit of that American Dream and may have been more fortunate in adapting to global changes. To them the world is now upside down—striving to improve no longer matters. Trump voters were scared of the direction the country was going. Trump stoppers are scared we're going backwards.

A progressive friend got my attention with this analogy: "I am trapped in a bus traveling fast in narrow, snow covered mountains. Driver is drunk, so are many passengers. There are also many sober terrified ones like me. We are pleading, begging for the drunk driver to stop or slow down or have someone else drive, but the other drunk passengers seem to be having a good time. I cannot get off the bus lurching around. Waiting to die."[6]

Those leaning left know Obama wasn't perfect, but they find Trump an offensive, narcissistic, incompetent huckster—out to take care of himself and his rich cronies. (In Appendix 1 you'll see "Why all the Fuss About Competence and Fitness?" plus my "Duty to Warn.")

## IS TRUMP SUPPORT ABOUT MONEY, EDUCATION, GENDER?

Empathy means genuinely trying to understand and feel *with* another. From caring instead of contempt, wrestle with, "HHHow could they believe that?" Look for common ground from the vantage point of both sides of the fence.

Trump was expected to help the economy and can claim credit for holding office during the longest bull market in history. Obama is credited for starting the 2009 recovery Trump built on. Remember—empathy for both sides.

Because close to half of America's households have nothing at all invested in the stock market, they didn't experience great benefits from the decade-long stock market growth.[7] The richest 10% control nearly 84% of the value of all stocks.[8] Among voters earning *less* than $50,000 a year, Hillary won 52% to 41%.[9] Economic victims flocked to Bernie Sanders.

Experience with Trump as our leader has the vast majority of Americans (83%) saying Trump cares about the wealthy.[10] "Indeed, 74% of Independents and even 23% of Republicans said Trump did not care about 'people like me.'"[11]

Who voted him in? According to political scientists, higher levels of Trump support came from those with[12]

- greater reliance on social security income
- *less* reliance on capital income
- living in racially isolated communities with worse health outcomes
- lower social mobility
- blue collar occupations earning relatively high household incomes that are not especially exposed to competition through trade or immigration

Among white voters who had not completed college, Trump won by more than two-to-one.[13] Approximately 1/3 of the U.S. population has a bachelor's degree.[14]

## CHOOSE YOUR WORDS CAREFULLY

More men than women put Trump in the White House,[15] and stereotypically male words—tough, practical, strict, and hierarchical—are used to describe Republicans, while female words—gentle, compassionate, nurturing, and egalitarian—get linked with Democrats.[16] However, flattering and unflattering terms are used for *both* genders—and *both* parties.[17]

At our core, humans long to be accepted and understood. Relationships are built with empathy, and that requires choosing words carefully—staying away from remarks that hurt and disparage. Because triggering the wrong emotion is like shooting yourself in the foot, notice how you talk about and across the partisan divide. Help prevent armed citizens standing off against each other or nurses and governors having to wear bullet proof vests.

Later chapters of this emergency kit offer specific phrases to use in tough spots, because everyday conversations will be affected by whether we refer to people as thrifty v. stingy, loyal v. obedient, and restrained v. inhibited. Minimize "us" and "them," so Americans can get along and make good decisions—together.

Be careful, because there are plusses and minuses to how we label ourselves. The more we identify as part of a group—conservative, liberal, moderate, alt-right, progressive—the more we like that group and its members, and subsequently exclude others.[18] Choosing to define ourselves in ways that bridge our divide is good medicine.

## FOR HAPPINESS AND MORALITY

America benefits if we can prevent opposites from turning to outrage. In pursuit of happiness, let's change our tone as we talk about fears, beliefs, and frustrations. The Dalai Lama teaches that *regardless of religion or position*, if we "have compassion for others and conduct ourselves with restraint out of a sense of responsibility, there is no doubt we will be happy."[19]

The tribes show contempt for one another, but neither party has the monopoly on morality. Jonathan Haidt, author of *The*

*Righteous Mind,* describes conservatives and liberals as voting for their moral—but different—preferences.[20] He contends liberals and conservatives alike believe in caring for people and place a value on fairness.

How are they different? People leaning right and those leaning left define fairness differently. Conservatives view fairness in proportional terms—that people should get what they deserve based on the amount of effort they put in. To liberals, fairness means sharing resources and parenting equally. Conservatives place an emphasis on values helpful for maintaining a stable society—loyalty, authority, and religion. Liberals prefer an egalitarian—not father/male-dominated—approach and strive to protect society's especially vulnerable.

Again, fairness and caring are common values, and many of us see softening our rhetoric as the moral—not immoral—thing to do. Dar al-Salam—literally, *"the house of peace"*—is the ideal society according to the Quran.[21] Pursuing peace is an imperative for those who follow Christ or study the Torah including Psalms 34:14.

## SPENDING TIME TOGETHER CAN MAKE A DIFFERENCE

See what spending time together can do. In September 2019, 526 voters—carefully selected to represent the diversity of Americans who are registered to vote—flew to Texas to spend a weekend together. The goal was to see if there might be a better way to disagree.

Political scientists James Fishkin and Larry Diamond launched this "America in One Room" event with about $3 million in funding raised by the nonpartisan group Helena. They argued that if you put a diverse group of folks face-to-face in a room, they're likely to mute their harshest views and struggle with how they refute others' positions, thereby becoming more informed and even more empathetic from being together.

That's exactly what happened. No indication of partisan preference was on their nametags as the chosen attendees debated health care, foreign policy, immigration, the economy, and the environment. Their political party often wasn't easy to discern. Trump was far from the only topic of conversation. After telling and hearing each other's personal stories of being helped or harmed by various policies, voters reported understanding each other better—and surprise at finding common ground.[22]

"Even though I imagined there would be significant changes in opinion, the results far exceeded my expectations. From both ends of the political spectrum, there was movement toward greater moderation and prudence," observed Diamond. "Our participants left with much more hope for American democracy—and so did I."[23]

In their carefully structured, road-tested Red/Blue workshops, the citizen-to-citizen initiative Braver Angels, aka Better Angels, has had similar results. Equal numbers of conservative and liberal participants across the country have arrived suspicious and somewhat hostile toward the other side and left hugging each other. About 79% of participants have reported being more able to understand and about 70% more understood by the other side.[24]

Red/Blue workshop exercises allow people leaning left and right to engage in a safe environment and learn from each other, even if they still disagree. Participants generate lists of misguided stereotypes and also wrestle with the kernel of truth in them. What they take away is more understanding and affection for the people of the other side.

A fellow participant told me, "I no longer can say, 'All PhD types think that!' because that would include you, and you don't." After a respectful exchange, one strongly "Red" attendee who came because his kids had stopped talking to him paid a Blue "opponent" what he considered a huge compliment, "You must be *light* blue." The immediate, positive reply was, "You must be pink." They both smiled.

Braver Angels' mission is to bring civility back to politics and have Americans see each other as friends, not enemies, no matter where they sit on the political spectrum. The organization was inspired by Lincoln's 1861 call to a divided nation to courageously "rise to the occasion" and be touched by the "better angels of our nature."

## A BETTER WAY TO TALK POLITICS

Changing deep seated views is a monumental task, yet a surprising field study shows a single, approximately 10-minute conversation when people are encouraged to actively take someone else's perspective can markedly reduce prejudice for at least 3 months.[25]

Canvassers trying to garner support for a transgender bill first asked individual voters to talk about a time when they personally had been judged negatively for being different. Then, they encouraged the voters to see how their own experience offered a glimpse into transgender people's experiences.

These brief personal conversations between canvassers and voters produced significant attitude changes that lasted over time. In contrast, the effects of attack ads and other political television advertising erode rapidly.[26] [27] Based on this model, Changing the Conversation Together has gone national.

There *is* a better way to talk politics—usually it's face-to-face, one-on-one, and begins with opening our hearts and minds to those who have differing perspectives. "Sometimes we get to change a broken world with our words," said Mister Rogers. While face-to-face is strongly preferred, other creative options—Zoom, Webex, FaceTime, Skype—can be used while we're social distancing or quarantining.

## HOW CAN WE BE SO FAR APART?

Start moving toward common ground with curiosity about how we can be so polarized. America was divided and government dysfunctional before Trump, and we should have been treating each other better. Now, our polarized country faces a monumental health crisis, millions out of work, and burning cities when we don't know who or what to trust.

Reds struggling to understand Blues may have forgotten many perceived "atrocities." Republicans vowed to make Obama a one-term president and for 18 months failed to even consider Obama's Supreme Court nominee. They wanted a Republican appointee. Trump denied intelligence on Russian interference, reneged on agreements with allies, lowered pollution standards, discounted climate change, and blanketly blocked information requested by the Mueller and impeachment investigations. More than 1,000 bipartisan former prosecutors signed a petition saying Trump deserved to be indicted on multiple charges for obstruction of justice.[28]

Then came unprecedented disaster. January through March 2020, President Trump misled the public about coronavirus facts and delayed responding. Examine the facts about when he was informed.[29]

On the other hand, angry left-leaning Americans may need reminding that many who voted Trump into office were appalled at Obama's failure to prosecute Wall Street's involvement in the housing recession, inaction at the crossing of a red line in Syria, inability to rally Congressional support, silence about Russia's cyber-attacks, and emphasis on bathrooms not jobs. A sizeable number of Americans were one-issue voters concerned about Supreme Court nominees or Second Amendment protection. Some leaning right support a Republican, but not Trump agenda. Some simply voted against Hillary.

Even though most of us learned that two wrongs don't make a right, more and more Americans show negative partisanship—voting against the opposing party more than for their own.[30] Having past presidential candidates from both parties brand Americans as despicable and deplorable hasn't helped. It looks like we love to hate.

## WE'RE PSYCHOLOGICALLY AND BIOLOGICALLY DIFFERENT

Not only do circumstances—zip codes, pocket books, and cultural heritage—affect us, there are psychological and biological differences between those leaning left and those leaning right. *Both* nature and nurture affect our politics. That's not good or bad, just real. Liberals and conservatives don't just see things differently, they *are* different—in personality, like openness to experience (liberals) and conscientiousness (conservatives), and even in their unconscious reactions to what's around them.[31]

Data shows parents' and their kids' political views are aligned more than those of people in general. Why? Studying twins helps answer the tricky nature vs. nurture question. Despite growing up separately, identical twins raised in different households share political views with each other more than with the siblings they grew up with. The same is especially true for sharing preferences and personalities. Genes play a role.

As the authors of *Prius or Pickup* highlight, our personality differences that appear in everything from politics to parenting to the workplace to TV preferences would be innocuous, if only we could decouple them from our noxious political debate.[32] We simply have to remember that being genetically different doesn't mean "lesser" or "better" than others.

## PEOPLE RESIST HEARING ABOUT HEREDITY

People do resist hearing about genetic factors, though a genetic influence both for party affiliation and strength of that affiliation have been found.[33]

Thomas Bouchard, one of my grad school professors, was one of the pioneers in the study of identical twins separated at birth. While Bouchard was collecting and examining Minnesota Twin Registry data, I stepped in one term to teach his University of Minnesota course on the psychology of individual differences. Preparing me for the assignment, Tom warned me that other students might stand outside the classroom protesting. They did. People don't want to think they're predetermined. We aren't. We simply inherit some tendencies.

Compare and contrast identical twins with fraternal twins. Identical twins being significantly more alike in their political views than fraternal twins provides added evidence for genes affecting political attitudes. Identical twins' views *are* more alike.

Twins were asked how much they agreed or disagreed with these and other statements: *"If wealth were more equal in this country we would have many fewer problems,"* and *"We have gone too far in pushing equality in this country."* More than half of the difference in self-identified political ideology (56%) and in authoritarianism (48%) looks like it can be explained by genetic factors.[34]

To measure authoritarianism, people were asked to react to 15 statements like, *"Our country needs a powerful leader, in order to destroy the radical and immoral currents prevailing in society today,"* and, *"Our country needs free thinkers, who will have the courage to stand up against traditional ways, even if this upsets many people."* Answers between Democrats and Republicans were significantly different, and identical twins' were more alike than fraternal ones.[35] Notice, though, that genes are only partly responsible.

## BASIC FEAR TENDENCIES

Our deep-seated tendencies to experience fear—tendencies that vary from person to person, partly for reasons that seem rooted in our genes—are related to political beliefs. Folks who have more fearful dispositions tend to be more politically conservative, plus less tolerant of immigrants and people of races different from their own.[36]

As researcher Rose McDermott carefully emphasizes, "It's not that conservative people are more fearful, it's that fearful people are more conservative."[37] Reeling from tragedy and terror, people of *all* political persuasions become more conservative, as they did immediately following September 11th.[38] Researchers found that simply asking Republicans to imagine that they possessed superpowers making them impervious to injury made them more liberal.[39] It looks like there is some range within which people can be moved.

Need some hope that we can get along? If political views lie on a continuum mediated somewhat by how much safety we need, everyone can shift a little depending on their current level of fear.[40] Make people feel more secure, and we might be able to move toward each other.

John Hibbing, who has spent years studying the psychological and neurological differences between liberals and conservatives, explains: "Conservatives who say liberals "just don't get" that the world is a dangerous place are right, "because they just don't respond [to world events] the same way."[41] For example, in tests of skin conductance—a measure of reaction—liberals show more response to images like sunsets, while conservatives to dangerous ones.[42]

To show that people don't experience the world identically, Hibbing uses smell as an example of inherited differences.[43] Because our olfactory systems are structured differently, people smell the substance androsterone very differently. To some it smells like cookies or incense, to others like sweat or even urine.

Despite the powerful illusion that the rest of the world experiences the world the way we see it, we don't. We have real differences influenced by genetics as well as by nurturing. Personality differences between my children were evident almost at birth—long before I had a chance to warp them.

From brain scans alone, political choice has been predicted with over 82% accuracy.[44] For example, Reds' and Blues' brains looked different when working on the same gambling task which had large successes and large risks. Republicans (according to their publicly recorded party affiliation) showed activity in the right amygdala, the brain's threat response center, while Democrats used the insula, which is involved in monitoring one's own feelings. Their bodies were acting *differently*.

## GENETIC AND ENVIRONMENT FACTORS INTERACT

We shouldn't forget that the environment interacts with our genetic nature. For example, novelty-seeking is another researched genetic difference. However, without certain experiences, having the novel variant gene doesn't lead to being more liberal. Ethnicity, culture, sex, or age alone isn't enough either. A crucial interaction is required.[45]

Only the people who have the gene *and* had a lot of friends during adolescence tend to be more liberal and open-minded. Because they had more friends, they were probably exposed to more views. While our genes give us a certain range of options, where we end up on that range depends on what life hands us.

Current research suggests not only that having a particular brain influences your political views, but also that having a particular political view influences and changes your brain. Reds and Blues have different brain structures—more volume in the amygdala (fear center) for Republicans[46]—and the causal arrow seems likely to run in both directions.

Our brains aren't fixed. Experiences change them. My favorite example of our brain's plasticity is that when people memorized London maps—because they were applicants for cab driving jobs and needed to pass a test measuring their knowledge of the city—the hippocampus or memory formation part of their brain grew.[47]

Here's more hope for getting along—if experiences change us, we have an even greater chance at bridge building.

## DON'T WAIT FOR MIRACLE CURES

Help repair our un-united states. Trump is not inspiring us all to have each other's backs, and Americans won't just miraculously get along. Don't get me wrong. Compelling data and numerous examples of individuals, teams, and companies who have altered their course and benefited accordingly exist. Medical treatments, cultural encounters, and religious experiences profoundly affect us.

People do change, but don't bet Trump will. Leaving him unchecked presents clear and present danger. Leaving Americans this hostile toward each other does too.

A strong body of evidence shows the best predictor of future behavior is past behavior. Situations (like a brush with death or job loss) and emotions (like romantic passion or fear for our children) can catapult someone down a totally new path, but typically one's patterns persist or return. Post impeachment as before, Trump has shown revenge and retaliation rather than remorse or reconciliation.

Be the empathy example he isn't. While more Americans died in a few months than they did in Vietnam, Americans sheltering at home learned about him in real time by watching his lengthy pandemic press conferences. Many were alarmed seeing Trump focus on his poll numbers, criticize New York Governor Cuomo's urgent requests, and order Vice President Pence not to take Michigan Governor Whitmer's calls for medical equipment because she challenged him. A rare prayer at Arlington or comment at the Space X launch hasn't dispelled the view that Trump is a spiritual black hole.[48]

## THE APPEAL OF UNDERDOGS

Empathy means trying to understand others' perspectives. For those with an authoritarian bent, Trump represents a strong champion. For some other conservative supporters, the president and his buddies are persecuted underdogs. To many liberals they are criminals.

Underdogs? Some Trump supporters may be rallying behind someone who repeatedly claims to have been a victim—especially if they themselves feel mistreated by societal and global changes. Plus, people love to cheer for underdogs. We feel sorry for them. Interestingly, underdog advertising is more effective with people who have stronger empathic concern.[49]

In addition, we react more strongly to unexpected successes (or failures) than expected ones.[50] And, we claim the successes of people who are in groups to which we belong.

In other words, just framing a team or candidate as a longshot makes people more likely to root for them, think they're likable, and find their win more gratifying.[51] That is the stuff of Disney movies. But, those opposing Trump see a totally different picture.

## HOW CAN AMERICA HEAL?

The nation is shifting. Governors are working together, and we recently witnessed unprecedented bipartisan support for a coronavirus relief package—in both the House and Senate. Trump's initial popularity bump for a leader-in-crisis dropped to his earlier levels. Former president George W. Bush called for unity. I thought this health and economic disaster would bring us together. It hasn't—yet.

The group of dedicated Republicans who launched the Lincoln Project contend, "Only defeating so polarizing a character as Trump will allow the country to heal its political and psychological wounds and allow for a new, better path forward for all Americans."[52] That's the cure—at least the start of one.

They ask all Americans of all places, creeds, and ways of life to join in restoring leadership and governance that respects the rule of law, recognizes the dignity of all people, upholds the Constitution, and defends American values here and abroad.[53] Vote Trump out of office.

## ENCOURAGE EMPATHY

Evidence from psychologists and neuroscientists feeds my dream that Americans will mend neighborhood fences, scale the empathy wall, and find common ground. Mirror neurons, or "smart cells" in our brain, allow us to read non-verbal cues, comprehend, and experience a portion of what others feel.[54]

When we see another person in pain, our brain activity is similar but not identical to what it is when we ourselves are in pain, and when we watch film stars kiss, some of the cells firing in our brains are those that fire when we actually kiss loved ones. Others' smiles activate ours. Mirror neurons enable us to imitate and understand others' intentions and put ourselves in their shoes, yet admittedly, brain scans show there are differences when Republicans and Democrats view the same images.

## PRACTICE HELPS

The good news is we can improve our ability to understand and relate to urban, suburban, and rural Americans—with practice. While some people are born with more interpersonal and emotional responsiveness, training in empathic listening helps therapists, leaders, spouses, and autistic children alike improve their relationships. For physicians, increased empathy yields more satisfaction, better health, and less depression in their patients.[55] Employees with empathic managers are less stressed.[56]

However, only the participants in Karina Schumann, Jamil Zaki, and Carol Dweck's study who considered empathy learnable showed enhanced empathy.[57] That means we're back to the importance of beliefs and expectations. We can become more compassionate, if we believe we can.

Empathy, which has an affective (feeling) and a cognitive (thinking) component, is part of what Daniel Goleman has labeled emotional intelligence.[58] Because of its role in interpersonal success, EQ—emotional quotient or competence—is often more important than IQ. Consequently, empathy is now a part of resilience training programs in schools, corporations, and the military.

Teaching compassion meditation, especially to pre-adolescents, may be a way to prevent bullying, violence, and aggression. If you examine brain scans in people with extensive experience practicing compassion meditation, you see that training dramatically changed their circuits used to detect feelings.[59] It works.

The problem is people avoid situations—especially when we expect empathy will cost us significant money or time. *Less* empathy is shown toward outgroups and also by people placed in power positions.[60] No surprise, we feel empathy for more victims when there is no financial cost.

Self-protection comes first. William Graziano and his colleagues suggest that by nature humans have two opposing motivational systems which act in sequence affecting prejudice and helping.[61] Difficult situations increase our distress (flight, fright, and fight) first, which hinders helping. Only later do the slower responses of sympathy and caring arrive on the scene. When people are reminded to act without inhibition, the balance shifts between approach and avoidance motivations, and bystanders then jump in to help faster and more often.

## SEVERAL CHALLENGES

If we want a nation united, we have several challenges—reduce fear, define ourselves differently, help Americans see the cost/benefit ratio favors empathy, encourage respect, and elect an empathetic leader—of either party—who will facilitate healing.

Spiritual giants Dalai Lama and Archbishop Desmond Tutu teach that compassion and generosity are sources of lasting joy.[62] Compassionate actions make people feel good—both those who perform them and those who receive them. Let's turn our backs on self-centeredness. Make empathy the norm, because as Barbara Fredrickson of the Making Caring Common Project argues, good feelings send "upwards spirals that transform communities."[63]

We habituate, hide, and become hardened to each other. We ignore and forget the dying and those seeking refuge. We vilify. But, people do learn, change, grow, and act when they see a big enough reason to.

## IT'S OKAY TO DISCUSS IN SAFETY AND WITH RESPECT

Americans—nearly two-thirds (65%) of us—say Trump was too slow in addressing the Covid threat, when cases of the disease were first reported outside the U.S.[64] Should we talk about it? Yes, I think we have to. We will soon face deciding if Trump deserves to remain in charge, and we learn and reach better decisions from listening to each other. But, how we talk matters.

Republicans are divided about whether it's acceptable for elected officials to fault the Trump administration's response to the outbreak. In early April 2020, 52% of the Republicans said it was unacceptable, while nearly half of Republicans (47%) agreed it is acceptable for officials to criticize the administration's response. Most Democrats (83%) consider criticism—hopefully construc-tive—the right thing to do[65].

As a psychologist and American, I am criticizing Trump's failure to show empathy to our badly wounded nation during this emergency. When asked by a PBS reporter about people getting sick and dying because he had downplayed the virus, Trump's *first* words were:

"A lot of people love me" and then, "I think we're going to win by a landslide."

This lack of sympathy is devastating for the families, friends, and colleagues of the more than hundred thousand who have died in this health emergency.

Devastating, too, is how Americans are treating each other.

## HOLD ON TO YOUR HUMANNESS

A worldwide health crisis has given us a window into others' circumstances. Newscasters have reported while fighting Covid themselves. Physicians have committed suicide. TV commercials have become more heart-warming. CEOs show tears.

As we've been hit with waves of grief, terrified, isolated, and shown the value of connection, there are signs of movement toward common ground. There are also signs of protest.

With the objective of understanding not fueling the fire, Appendix 2 has a guide to differences between Reds and Blues from two different sources. The previous chapter listed core American values which are also in Appendix 3 in a different format.

## UNDERSTAND WHERE OTHERS ARE COMING FROM

We're in a health, economic, and political emergency. So, start with empathy—some understanding of where others are coming from—and grab guide ropes for managing differences from the next chapter. Then, go on to later chapters to pick specific tools and helpful phrases out of the kit.

## CHAPTER 5

# Managing our Differences

E quipped with empathy and a sense of urgency from the last chapters, now tackle conflict. What causes conflict? Differences. Not really money, turf, power, status, or time. Our conflicts are about different **goals** related to those limited, precious resources. If I want power and you want me to have the power, we have the same goal. If I want it and you also want it, we don't. If you want Trump re-elected and I don't, our goals differ.

> **We differ over**
> - **Goals**
> - **Values**
> - **Approaches**
> - **Preferences**
> - **Facts**

Goals are related to **values**, and people are deeply divided when their values, morals, and ethics differ. Americans who value freedom of choice and who believe women have a right to control their bodies have trouble with the government telling a victim of incest or rape that she must carry a pregnancy to term. For others, abortions are never acceptable. Because the environment is a low priority for some, those fellow citizens don't place a high value on conserving water and reducing carbon.

Americans not only have different goals, we prefer different **approaches** to the same one. We may want to feel safe in America but not concur about which immigration or gun policies will achieve that result. And while a thriving economy or a good education for America's kids may be both your goal and mine, we can be at odds over which route takes us to that desired destination.

No two of us are alike. From the same events, fellow Americans reach opposite conclusions, and our conflicting views, expectations, opinions, beliefs, habits, and interpretations present serious challenges. What some call "telling it like it is" others find disgusting. What some deem horrific others consider "just fine."

Personality conflicts are essentially differences in style and **preference,** and remember there is a biological basis for preferences. Some of us like to be in charge; others hate the limelight. Some are compulsively neat; others are slobs. You may be comfortable with a large credit card balance and have a partner who feels insecure without a lot of money set aside for retirement. Differences like these trigger conflict.

Conflicts over **facts** are typically easier to resolve, because facts are less emotionally charged than goals, values, and preferences. Hold an eight-ounce, clear glass container with four ounces of water in it and ask for a description. "It's half full." "It's half empty." "It's glass." "It's filled with four ounces of clear liquid." All those answers are correct and verifiable. The point is people can be right and *still* differ, especially if they cherry pick. Unfortunately, these days Americans look willing to fight to the death to prove the correctness of their facts.

## BEING RIGHT DOES NOT AUTOMATICALLY MAKE SOMEONE ELSE WRONG

When irritated by a differing American, remember the story of three blind people touching different parts of an elephant. One accurately describes the trunk, but it sounds quite different from the second's description of the tusk and the third's of the tail. Rarely do we have the whole picture, and we don't know what we don't know.

It is common to differ over how facts should be interpreted. Two Americans may hear the same words from a politician and understand that message very differently. If I thought we were going to meet at 5:00, meaning anytime between 4:50 and 5:10, and you interpreted that as any time between 5pm and 6pm, you wouldn't see your 5:40 arrival as late or understand why I find you thoughtless.

We don't share the same assumptions or expectations. Perceiving motives, words, actions, and situations differently, we disagree on what is to be done (task), how to do it (process), and who should be in charge (authority). Though it's natural to differ, our differences, especially our intense political ones in the age of Trump, now threaten our relationships and union.

## DIFFERENCES TRIGGER FEAR

We know that people differ on almost every dimension, so how did differences become so negative? Differing should simply be normal. The problem occurs when you are thinking one way, I'm thinking another, and we realize at some level we have to choose.

Choosing carries with it the possibility of loss, and that triggers fear. I could lose by not getting what limited resources I want, by being made foolish, by being left out. At the perception of danger my body and yours automatically respond. Adrenaline and cortisol flood our system preparing us to flee or fight rather than to work together to find solutions. So, bringing Americans together hinges on minimizing loss and fear.

Called in when team members are at odds, direct reports hate a boss, or family members can barely stand each other, I watch people fight. My job is to help them work or live together better. What has this taught me?

1. Conflict is normal

2. How people handle differences matters

3. Wanting the hostility to end is essential

## CONFLICT IS NORMAL, HOW WE HANDLE IT MATTERS

Differences aren't inherently bad. *How* we handle conflict determines whether differences lead to hostility and relationship damage or to better understanding, innovative solutions, and stronger ties. Conflict can have positive or negative consequences depending on how our differences are managed. Global workplace evidence shows conflict negatively affects productivity and morale, yet 81% of workers have seen positive outcomes from conflict.[1]

## MINIMIZE FEAR

Managing American differences hinges on maximizing gains and minimizing fear for everyone involved. Fortunately with skill comes confidence—and more success—enabling us to more respectfully handle divergent views even about politics. Because no single way to handle conflict is always appropriate, we Americans should choose—not just use—a strategy.

Admittedly, you may endeavor to be collaborative with your different-minded neighbors or relatives, but they may be pushing for a win without regard for you. Consequently, besides selecting an effective style and being adept at using it, knowing how to handle others' reactions affects success. This chapter provides a map for matching style to circumstance. You'll find troubleshooting skills in upcoming chapters 6–9.

## CHOOSE A CONFLICT MANAGEMENT OPTION

Psychologists love 2x2 tables to simplify ideas, and below you'll see the model for Kenneth Thomas and Ralph Kilmann's Conflict Mode Instrument, the most widely used method of assessing conflict resolution styles. Thomas and Kilmann describe five styles for handling differences along two dimensions: cooperativeness (low to high concern for the relationship) and assertiveness (low to high concern for satisfying your own needs).

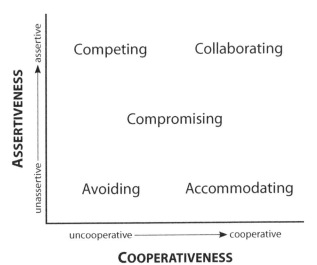

Thomas Kilmann Conflict Mode Instrument

Remember these conflict management basics:

- Each conflict mode is useful in certain situations
- Consciously matching style to situation yields better results
- Any one of us could be failing to consider others' needs
- We have choices
- Competing = forcing a win
- Avoiding = withdrawal and retreat
- Accommodating = smoothing and delay
- Compromising = splitting the difference
- Collaboration = problem solving and negotiation

## THIRD PARTY INTERVENTION

Two additional styles, mediation and arbitration, involve third parties intervening in a conflict. Mediators help parties voice their differences and reach an agreeable solution. Slightly different, arbitrators and judges listen to each side's arguments then dispense a decision. Occasionally arbitrators appear to be forcing a decision, which sparks anger, hurt, or resentment toward the third party.

Lacking neutral third party help, individual Americans and American sub-groups need more skill and will to get to agreement ourselves, when we find others willing to wrestle with differences. Take from this survival kit the reminder to choose, not just use, a style.

## WHEN *SHOULD* SOMEONE AVOID CONFLICT?

Avoiding, which I affectionately call the turtle approach, entails pulling back from a discussion of differences. Instead of addressing contrasting opinions and goals, we can withdraw from a threatening situation, sidestep temporarily, and postpone discussion until a better time. People using this conflict mode keep their mouths shut or dismissively say, "Forget about it..." or "I don't know" or "Let's not talk about it." Too often, however, ignored American differences simmer, heat up, and even explode.

Like each of the five conflict management approaches, avoiding has its uses. People ought to respond indirectly and uncooperatively (bottom left quadrant) when they don't believe there is a chance to change an outcome by speaking out. Please avoid if you know you are outmatched and sticking your head out could get it chopped off.

Because we spoke at some of the same conferences, I had the privilege of meeting motivational speaker Jackie Phlug, who in 1985 was shot in the head and thrown onto the tarmac off an EgyptAir hijacked flight. Her courageous, difficult, post-head injury recovery story is inspiring. My point here is that she stayed alive by avoiding—playing possum. After watching someone move and then be shot again on the Malta tarmac, Jackie played dead for five long hours. She quips that it wasn't all that difficult because she didn't feel that good anyway.

Though I am advocating that Americans learn to constructively discuss their differences, there are times when the costs of speaking out are so high that we have to keep quiet. Some elected Republicans probably feel that way—some friends and family do too. Speaking out could cost funding, White House support, and important relationships.

Avoiding is a good option when the issue is trivial or a tangent. Save your energy for matters deserving attention. Too often conversations get sidetracked by debating the unimportant or by bringing in old gripes. In marital conflicts, you can hear someone throwing in, "And your mother's the same way!" Leave that mother out. In political conflicts, "You people …" ignites a situation. Avoid a polarized debate about the merits of an entire group of people, because not everyone in that group is identical. Focus instead on the specific topics at hand, and better yet, one at a time.

Pick not only your battles, pick your battleground. Avoid confronting differences in the wrong place and at the wrong time. If the other person is coping with other high priority concerns, strutting for an audience, or overly tired, choose to bring up your political views some other time. Let people cool down.

Also wait to speak out if you need additional information, are getting the lay of the land, haven't yet reached a conclusion, and are still gathering facts and ideas. Voicing an opinion before you have your positions well researched could destroy your one opportunity to start the discussion well or make a good first impression.

If you've determined that others can handle the situation more effectively than you, let them. It may be their role, not yours, and they may be more eloquently prepared.

When the evidence is clear, try remaining quiet to give others a chance to follow that data and reach the conclusion on their own, because it is easier for them to convince themselves than for you to.

See the thought transfer technique and use of incomplete sentences in the chapter "Disagreeing Without Being Disagreeable."

## When should you avoid?
- **costs > benefits**
- **no chance**
- **trivial issues**
- **issue is a tangent**
- **cool off**
- **need information**
- **others can resolve**

## WHEN *SHOULD* SOMEONE CHOOSE TO ACCOMMODATE?

The accommodating style of dealing with differences involves preserving the relationship rather than focusing on our positions. High on cooperation and low on assertiveness, the smoothing and harmonizing American is essentially saying, "Whatever you want is okay with me." Think of the gentle lamb, but not the ostrich who hides its head in the sand. Sometimes accommodating is yielding, denying, and obeying; other times it is being generous and selfless.

Should we deny reality and just go along? No. Of course, on the other hand, if you discover that the other person's view is actually correct, you can get on board without even having to announce that you were initially misinformed. Accommodate when you realize you're wrong. Cooperation fits that situation.

If your relationship matters and the issue doesn't, go ahead and accommodate. For instance, if I was going to suggest that we eat Thai food for lunch and you mention Mexican first, if I don't have a strong preference, saying "Sure" is easy. I'll still be happily fed. If you want to tackle budget item number two before item number one, that approach may be highly satisfying to you without harming me. I can agree even though I had a different plan. Because getting along beats winning on trivial points, marriage counselors have more than once asked, "Do you want to be right or happy?"

Reaching an acceptable decision between warring parties can be more important than the issue itself. Use accommodation when concern over decision *acceptability*—agreement—eclipses decision *quality*. Imagine a nurse manager attempting to staff a 24/7 operation over the holidays. This client of mine considered staff members equally competent, so any combination of nurses would be an okay plan. Some staff, though, had strong feelings about which shifts they preferred, and tensions were high. While decision quality—the competence of who worked nights and who worked days—wasn't of concern, acceptability was.

When the head nurse realized she wasn't restricted to making assignments based on seniority, she turned over the schedule to the nurses to work out what seemed fair. I'm pleased to report they liked what they decided. The nurses more recently hired were able to spend Christmas morning watching their children open Santa's gifts, because the nurses who had seniority and grown kids kindly swapped shifts with them.

No doubt candidates Pete Buttigieg, Mike Bloomberg, Amy Klobuchar, and Bernie Sanders each believed they were a better pick to head the 2020 Democratic ticket, yet exited the race to endorse an acceptable moderate considered able to defeat Trump. For the greater good, choosing to back off means having your priorities straight.

Temporarily use the lamb approach, until the time for another conflict style is right. If a relationship between a Trump-loving daughter and her mother, a Warren-enthusiast, needs major repair, agreeing wherever possible preserves the connection. Later, when they tolerate each other better, they can gingerly revisit their opposite views on policy and politician. Go along to get along—for a while.

However, be careful of resentment. In the political world resentment leads to protests, name calling, and violence. In marriages it leads to divorce.

If I give in without you realizing I am, but then count my sacrifice and expect to be compensated later, I've actually created an unwritten psychological contract. If you thought I agreed and subsequently discover I didn't, you'll feel manipulated and see me as two-faced. Not aware of our unnegotiated agreement, you have a right to complain when I later think it's my turn and try to call in my markers. "I gave in on_____ and_____ and_____ ," gets met with, "I thought you were okay with that. I had no clue. Had I known you wanted something else, I would have saved my chips for a bigger deal."

People do accommodate to build credits for later, but doing so can backfire. There is less anger when people openly voice they are expecting something in return down the road instead of just postponing conflict without the other's knowledge. Make deals and expectations clear.

When outmatched, going along and yielding may be necessary for survival. If gang members shove a gun in your face demanding "Your money or your life," give them your wallet. Many politicians on both sides will toe a party line to stay in office, but sometimes an issue—like defending their oath to the Constitution—is so important they take a stand instead of being the lamb.

No doubt as parent, teacher, mentor, friend, supervisor, or leader, you have occasionally resolved differences by agreeing to something you considered less than best. You were not setting people up to fail; you were willing to try an alternative and permit them to learn from what you thought could be a mistake. In the process, you might have discovered their approach was equal or superior to your original game plan. Plus, because they were dedicated to having their idea succeed, they got it implemented. Sometimes when we believe we are right, getting out of the way to let others learn yields positive results for everybody.

## When should you accommodate?
- **when wrong**
- **issue much more important to other**
- **harmony is especially important**
- **build credits for later**
- **outmatched**
- **let others learn/develop**

## WHEN *SHOULD* SOMEONE BE DIRECT AND UNCOOPERATIVE?

The direct, uncooperative, competing conflict style (top left quadrant of the model) has also been referred to as forcing a win at others' expense. When people approach differences, such as nominating a Supreme Court justice, using an intransigent "my way or the highway" mode, their goal is to win. They care a lot about their agenda, but little, at least at that moment, about their relationship with others at the table. Often people assume that making others lose is the only way they can win what they want.

Competing operates on the notion that the issue is important while others' acceptability isn't, so use all the power you can muster to make what you want happen. Zero-sum negotiations and manipulation fall into this category.

In emergency situations when quick action is required, the direct competing mode for handling differences is appropriate. Instead of discussing, in operating rooms and hospital emergency departments, physicians bark out orders and others quickly comply to save the lives of patients needing them. Time is critical, and the common mission of patient care makes the direct, uncooperative style permissible. The same is true in military operations and when someone shouts to keep a loved one from being hit by an oncoming car.

For critical, split-second moments, there is no time to make the delivery palatable. However, unless there is sufficient trust and a clearly shared mission, repeated used of the direct, demanding, uncooperative approach damages the relationship.

According to an ancient African proverb, "If you want to go fast, go alone. If you want to go far, go together." American leaders, friends, and parents alike are at times so focused on an agenda—such as getting someone elected, implementing a necessary but unpopular policy, preventing sexual abuse, stopping discrimination, getting health care legislation passed—that they are unwaveringly direct. Passionate about their cause and convinced of their opinions—they treat others' reactions as insignificant and come across as aggressive and intimidating. Over time, our divide deepens and bridging our differences becomes more difficult. Instead of protecting Americans, they are destroying America.

In the short run, the strong use of power can intimidate others into backing down from their different positions. However, there are long-term consequences. My animal analogy is the shark. In his best-selling classic *Coping with Difficult People,* Robert Bramson distinguishes between two types of strong, dominant people—The Sherman Tank and The Bulldozer.[2] Most hostile, the frightening Sherman Tanks will be shooting at you, attacking with whatever they can. Refusing to be deterred, Know-it-all Bulldozers simply roll over anything in their way, don't bother attacking, or don't realize when they are. Both types destroy relationships.

When convinced of our political positions, we can become dogmatic and difficult about differences. Remember when I know the clear glass is filled with four ounces of liquid? I'm right! However, that accurate position still differs from the accurate description of the eight-ounce container as half-full. Being right does not automatically render someone else wrong or eliminate differences. And, if I have access to only part of the total picture, just the tail of the elephant instead of the whole beast, our views may be correct but not identical. How rare it is that someone has the whole picture.

What know-it-alls who discount others fail to comprehend is the extent to which people will avoid them. Research from marriage experts John Gottman and Joan DeClaire indicates that turning away responses, such as interrupting, ignoring, and disregarding a spouse ends a relationship sooner than combative, domineering, critical behavior does.[3] Know-it-alls can find themselves very isolated, unpopular, and unloved. Workplace exit interviews reveal people quit a boss or escape a difficult co-worker more than flee the company. People even move to get away from certain neighbors. Difficult relationships affect us.

What those who disrespect and bully others fail to realize is the extent to which people will retaliate. Don't underestimate the joy of revenge. While the attacked may cower and pull back, they regroup. Notice the size of the Women's March in response to Trump's misogynistic, demeaning, and dehumanizing behavior. Notice the amount of protest to Trump's order to separate asylum-seeking children from their parents.

Though working together to reach a common understanding is often preferable, being direct and uncooperative is sometimes required to protect yourself or others. Because a special friend of mine fought the man who knifed her on a cold winter day in a Minnesota park, she lived. Competing can be a good contingency plan when collaboration would fail. Keep it in your toolkit for certain situations.

## WHEN *SHOULD* SOMEONE CHOOSE TO COMPROMISE?

The person using the compromise conflict mode is saying, "Let's split the difference" or "Let's meet half way." When both the issue and the relationship are reasonably important, reaching a decent agreement where everyone gets something may be sufficient, and if full agreement is unlikely, tradeoffs might be necessary and acceptable. Cutting the pie in half, gives everyone at least something.

Compromise is used for division of labor, when neither collaborating nor competing works, and to expedite a decision when pressed for time. It's a fallback. Compromise may also be a temporary cease-fire allowing for full negotiation later.

However, some things cannot be easily divided to allow each a partial win. In the Biblical example, King Solomon faced two women each claiming to be the mother of the same child. Cutting the baby in half would have resulted in a lose/lose situation. Abortion bans, company policies, product quality, and legal judgments might not be up for compromise.

## WHEN *SHOULD* WE COLLABORATE?

When you have something important to resolve, relationships to preserve, and enough time, give collaboration a try. Issues, relationships, and time are factors to consider.

In the direct **and** cooperative mode of collaboration, those in conflict focus on both the important agenda items and their important relationship. A high quality decision that people consider acceptable is the goal. Maximizing gains and minimizing losses for all are the driving forces, so folks say:

*"My preference is this, please help me understand yours."*

*"Can we all live with_____ ?"*

*"What would be easier for all of us to accept?"*

When collaborating, there are two criteria for success—a high caliber decision *and* mutual satisfaction. If others trust you seek a solution that is in everyone's interest, you are inviting them to be an ally, not an adversary. Decisions made collaboratively get ratified and implemented.

Collaborative problem solvers want to learn from others' perspectives, because they are striving for solutions of both high quality and high acceptability. Co-laboring folks ask:

*"What else could be done?"*

*"What haven't we considered?"*

*"How can we make that easier for you to live with?"*

Working together they merge insights, integrate ideas, and creatively invent options to determine policy, draft legislation, suggest curriculum, tackle inequity, fight viruses, and improve the economy. They listen, explore, and build on each other's perspectives.

Because collaboration requires time, make the investment when you care about both the issues and the people involved. When done well, the process of attacking problems not people allows us to work through hard feelings and end up feeling closer, respected, and better understood. Although collaborators don't agree on everything or get all they wanted, they can be proud of their effort. Usually they get enough to be committed to implementing the decision and can explain it, so others come on board too.

Collaboration helps people maintain their connection, so in the future, new problems get met with a willingness to work together. Americans, let's do more of it. Hopefully we've learned something from the shared sacrifice of facing Covid-19. We're all in this together.

Being collaborative requires demonstrating that you are *BOTH* strong and reasonable. If you are not powerful, others will not need to listen or work with you. They will simply exert their power, forcing a win. On the other hand, if you aren't sufficiently cooperative, others withdraw or launch an attack to avoid losing.

## WANT THE CONFLICT TO END

Success with the various conflict management styles starts with a strong desire to have the conflict end. When avoiding and accommodating, people are fleeing from the tension of divergent views. In contrast, when forcing our positions, we want what we want and are fighting for it. When we collaborate, compromise, engage a mediator, or take a conflict to an arbitrator, we seek resolution.

Unfortunately, many people don't want a battle to end. An MBA student in one of my Pepperdine classes challenged, "Since you're a conflict expert, why aren't you in the Middle East solving that one?!" I sadly answered, "As long as one of the parties wants a conflict to continue, it will." Uniting won't happen if too many of us in this country take joy in keeping our conflict alive.

## COMMON GROUND?

Thomas and Kilmann's popular conflict mode instrument was developed 40 years ago using a few hundred managers who were quite similar to each other. Concerned about its continued relevance, results from a large diverse sample of 8,000 were recently examined. Scores from the two normative groups were remarkably similar, differing by only a point here and there. Kilmann made these comments about the findings:

> "In sum, although experience shows that there are strik-ing differences in behavior between male and female, black and white, young and old, non-supervisory per-sonnel and top-level executives, and southerners and mid-westerners—*conflict-handling norms are pretty much the same across these demographic distinctions and have remained largely the same for the past thirty years.* ... Perhaps the one behavior that helps define the essence of the U.S. culture is the way that its citizens—across the board—handle conflict situations."[4]

Good news—some common ground!

## MAKE IT A CHOICE

This survival kit's reminder? Adapt to the situation you're in and choose, not just use, a conflict management style. Because matching style to circumstance pays off, which style will you choose and when?

## CHAPTER 6 — Building and Repairing Relationships

G etting along is priceless. The scientific study of happiness reveals life's main sources of satisfaction are meaningful work—paid or unpaid—and close relationships.

Good interpersonal connections have a positive effect on quality of life, longevity, altruism, morale, loyalty, risk taking, and productivity. Getting along also helps us manage stress. Sadly, many American relationships are on life support—strained by ideological differences. My guess is this toxic, polarized interpersonal environment is not the kind of air you like breathing.

Though good people are divided by politics and religion, Jonathan Haidt pointed out, "If you can have at least one friendly interaction with a member of the 'other' group, you'll find it far easier to listen to what they're saying, and maybe even see a controversial issue in a new light."[1] Now the question is how can we have lots of friendly encounters in the Trump and coronavirus era?

## INTERPERSONAL ATTRACTION

For decades social psychologists have been accumulating evidence about who is drawn to whom and why. Four factors have consistently emerged that will help Americans get along better:

- **Reciprocal Liking**
- **Similarity**

- **Familiarity**
- **Proximity**

We like people who like us, are like us, are familiar to us, and are nearby.

## RECIPROCAL LIKING BUILDS RELATIONSHIPS

First and foremost, we like those who have the good sense to like us. Encounters with them are enjoyable and rewarding, because they care, agree, and help. They believe us and believe *in* us. It's hard to resist someone who makes us feel special, important, and appreciated.

If you want a good connection with an individual American or group of them, act like you like them, even if you don't quite yet. The good news is that if we act as if we feel a certain way, we actually begin to feel that way.[2] A wife, who felt so unappreciated that she decided to get a divorce, vowed to make her husband regret her leaving, so she began acting as wonderful as she had when they were first courting and in love. They ended up *both* falling in love again.

Because it is so vital, more about the "liking rule" and reciprocity is in the chapter "Influencing Across the Divide."

## SIMILARITY ATTRACTS

Improve your connections by pointing out what you have in common—limited toilet paper supplies, cabin fever, and Covid fear. We like, are influenced by, and defer to those who seem like us.

Finding common ground encourages people to link together and adopt each other's positions. Nations, organizations, and families alike have rituals and symbols highlighting shared identity, culture, and values—commonalities. Think how satisfying it is to discover someone who shares your hobbies, taste in food, and opinion (positive or negative) of Trump.

Still, don't forget opposites do attract. We like those who are different, *if* the difference benefits us. Broad-brush types appreciate having a detailed person on their team to complete the tasks they abhor. If you're quiet and shy, you may enjoy being with talkative, outgoing people who keep the conversation—political or otherwise—going. But, if you are quiet and prefer it that way, others' verbal tendencies will be irritating.

## FAMILIARITY ATTRACTS

We like what is familiar, yet you know familiarity also breeds contempt. Everything else being equal, people gravitate to places, food, music, and people they are used to, because the familiar requires less energy. It's safer. Don't get me wrong, we are stimulated by new situations and variety, but there is something special about home.

Think how we enjoy reminiscing about shared times with family and friends but hate having the same fight over and over. Repeated encounters and mere exposure builds familiarity and comfort, as long as those experiences are positive. Careful handling is required. With the right tools, spending time together is an evidence-based suggestion for strengthening ties, reducing relationship tension, and overcoming contempt. If we're unskilled, time together makes us want to pull our hair out.

## PROXIMITY MAKES BUILDING RELATIONSHIPS EASIER

We build relationships with people in close proximity—at work and school, in gyms, art classes, and apartment buildings—because we have more opportunities to do so. Close proximity allows increased familiarity, and, in turn, a chance to find similarities and demonstrate liking.

Once established, relationships can be maintained across great distances, but connecting with those nearby usually takes less effort. On the large, spread out campus of IBM's plant in Rochester,

MN, people routinely walk the same route from parking lot to work station. At first they pass each other in the halls without acknowledgement. Over time with repeated exposure, people begin to nod, then smile, then greet each other, and finally strike up conversations and friendships.

## DISTANCE MATTERS

De-segregation brings people of different races near one another, so they can grow accustomed to each other, discover similarities—we are all human and blow our noses—and begin to like each other. Foreign exchange programs for students do the same.

As both Michelle Obama[3] and Brené Brown[4] have emphasized, it's harder to hate up close, so the data cited in chapter 2 that America is becoming more segregated is worrisome. Coming together as a more perfect union takes getting out of our silos and getting to know Americans of different locales, ages, races, religions, preferences, and backgrounds.

Being up close and personal makes a difference. Though both have merit, in-person training differs from online or remote learning.[5] When we are with others, we instinctively pick up their emotions and even smoke and eat as much as they do.[6] Addicts, grieving widows, weight watchers, and exercise buddies meet in person for a reason—support. Failing to meet a commitment gets noticed and triggers a consequence, if others are near.

Electronics have facilitated communication and information sharing, but they haven't displaced face-to-face interaction. Not only does social media distract from relationships, a recent longitudinal study reveals Facebook use harms well-being instead of enhancing it.[7] [8] Connection quality isn't the same as many have experienced during the Covid-19 quarantining. Social animals like being together.

Most of what we consider social interaction with our close circle of friends happens in person. For good reason, business didn't abandon meeting in person when technology meant they could. Almost all (95% of the 2,211) *Harvard Business Review* survey respondents considered face-to-face meetings as central for negotiating important contracts, interviewing key staff, and understanding valued customers.[9]

Because distance matters, market researchers Ed Keller and Brad Fay emphasize:

> "All forms of communication work best when they lead to the sharing of ideas and recommendations ...But if we want to promote real change—as in our politics, public policies and cultural behavior—it's best we do it face to face."[10]

Unfortunately, in pandemics and when relationships are tense—as they are now between political groups—people avoid each other. A CEO I coached found himself irritated by a junior member of his executive team whose expertise he needed but whose mannerisms he disliked. Instead of increasing proximity and familiarity to develop a better connection, the CEO reduced it. When he made the simple commitment to say "Hi" every day they were both at headquarters, tolerance improved a lot. It doesn't take much to make relationships better.

Choose where you sit or stand to bridge the political divide, because interpersonal distance—proxemics—also affects how we relate. People sit closer to those they like and infer others like them if they have chosen to be near. Side-by-side seating and corner-to-corner seating typically seem more cooperative and intimate, while across the table more adversarial, so by not quite facing the camera squarely, you might improve your virtual meetings across the political divide.

Think about keeping your enemies close and defusing them by putting them on your right as your "right hand man." To get more discussion, be seated, choose a round table, and avoid the power positions at the end. The goal is to get along.

For good relationships, put the attraction principles into action—demonstrate liking, find similarity, foster familiarity, and use proximity.

## "FIVE FRIENDSHIP FACTORS"—STRATEGIES FOR ENHANCING RELATIONSHIPS

Years ago my father, who was an inspiring CEO of a non-profit, gave me a copy of Alan Loy McGinnis' book *The Friendship Factor: How to Get Closer to the People You Care For.*[11] McGinnis' work is now an award-winning, international best seller with more than a million copies in print.

Immediately, the strategies and inspiring examples from this pastor-and-family-therapist-turned-business-consultant seemed important to pass on. When I translated his relationship-building ideas into language for working professionals at places like IBM, First Bank, and the Mayo Clinic, I was delighted they valued his ideas too.

Here are McGinnis' rephrased suggestions for enhancing relationships. These friendship factors can bandage bonds strained by the political climate and forge new connections benefitting America. To build, maintain, and repair relationships:

1.  **Make relationships a priority**

    When you consider a relationship or group important, you give it what it needs—time, attention, and energy. Good relationships require a serious investment. Like beautiful flowers and tasty vegetables in a garden, relationships require planting, watering, fertilizing, and weed pulling. Time is a precious commodity, so spending some together is a way to signal how much you value the connection.

Care about strengthening our nation one relationship at a time. Start joking with neighbors of a different political bent, talking again to estranged relatives, and rebuilding associations across the aisle. Let's follow Stephen Covey's suggested habit of investing in relationships and take time to make deposits instead of withdrawals to our "emotional bank accounts."[12]

## 2. Be open

Openness leads to openness, so please don't hide behind a façade or wall. Allow others to get to know you and your political views, and be interested in knowing theirs. Authentic self-disclosure fosters good relationships.[13]

Selectively, courageously, and honestly telling people about ourselves and our perspectives yields others responding in kind. Bullying and poor conflict management does the opposite.[14] Regardless of the amount of similarity in our views, if people are friendly and receptive, we are more likely to continue disclosing—and that helps a trusting relationship grow.

Cultivating transparency does not mean letting it all hang out. We can reveal too much and appear too needy. For example, research suggests before revealing something quite personal to a new acquaintance, wait at least 8–10 minutes![15] If we turn every conversation back to "all about me," we are modeling narcissists not deepening our interactions. Both "un-disclosers" and over-disclosers are viewed negatively.

We need to be discriminate disclosers. Spouses who are happily married report they mention fewer negative feelings about their spouses than less satisfied spouses do. They usually report they've learned that uncensored frankness can be hurtful.

Blurting something out because you are angry is potentially harmful, while carefully phrasing something difficult to accept that you believe people should hear is commendable. Americans have been grateful for Governor Cuomo and medical advisors Anthony Fauci and Deborah Birx providing specific, truthful answers about the virus. When giving feedback or speaking your mind about politics, check if you are talking "truth from courage" or "truth from rage."

When the *only* things we disclose are negative, others will start to perceive *us* as being negative, so have fun candidly sharing positive thoughts and feelings too. Those who attack others' political views every time they talk are angry and anxious rather than frank and forthright.

In addition, remember that information is power. To be trustworthy what you do say should be honest, even when you must keep some things under wraps.

## 3. Spread compliments

Because McGinnis' third rule "Dare to Talk About Your Affection" might have sexual overtones and be misinterpreted in the workplace, my rephrase for the corporate world has been "spread compliments." Years earlier Dale Carnegie advised leaders, "Begin with praise and honest appreciation," which now has substantial empirical support.[16] Compliments facilitate teamwork, make us more influential, strengthen ties, and repair relationships.[17] Worth trying after there's been a Thanksgiving dinner debacle.

Because compliments pay off, be associated with them. Marital satisfaction and team performance are related to the proportion of positive comments to negative ones. John Gottman's research found five positives to each negative in marriages that flourish and less than one to one in marriages ending up in divorce.[18] Marcial Losada saw the same pattern with high v. low performance teams measured both by profitability and subjective evaluations.[19]

Though the exact ratio has been discredited, the idea of delivering more positives than negatives remains a good one. Instead of jumping in to criticize, consider Ben Franklin's advice: "Speak ill of no man, but all the good you know of everybody." Attack issues not people. Make it rewarding to be around you.

While visiting a friend, I experienced a noisy, crowded New York deli at lunchtime. We finally squeezed into a tiny spot after a long wait, and a waitress eventually appeared in a uniform stained with mustard, mayo, and who knows what. She threw the silverware and napkins on the table while brusquely asking for our order.

Deciding to see if compliments could work there, I told her, "You have striking eyes." She did. They were the same brilliant blue of her splattered uniform. She tossed me a disdainful, wary look but returned a few minutes later with our order and very gently placed it on the table with a subtle smile. Her delivery to our table was substantially less surly than what I'd witnessed to others. If it can work in NY, imagine what a compliment might do in your neck of the woods.

I've always liked Ken Blanchard's recommendation to "catch people doing something right."[20] Too many of us praise our pets' good behavior far more often than we do the same with fellow Americans. Let's speak favorably about others' helpful actions, ideas, and suggestions.

The more specific your praise, the more likely your comments will be believed and positively affect future actions. Employees report that when their boss only says "Good job," they doubt the leader has a clue about what's going on. In contrast, when told positive things about particular behavior or results, people know it was noticed and what to do again.

Frequently tell those in and outside your political tribe:

> *"Thanks for your input on_____ ."*
>
> *"Thanks for your kindness with_____ ."*
>
> *"I appreciate that you let me double check to get my facts straight."*

Also spread the positive news about them to others with:

> *"I really appreciated Taylor's help with_____ ."*
>
> *"Alex found those numbers for me, which really made a difference!"*

As you might expect, studies document that if the flatterer seems to have an ulterior motive or something to gain, people are skeptical.[21] Overdoing praise leads to denial and even tension.[22] To be a reward, praise has to feel like a reward.

## 4. Demonstrate caring

Compliments matter, yet actions toward fellow Americans speak even louder. Acts of caring don't need to be huge to help us get along. The husband of one of my clients brought her coffee every morning for 25 years, a kindness that got them through many rough patches. Too often we blame, shame, and erect barriers by thinking, "I'd be reasonable, if they were." Take the first step. Return anger with kindness and be out of sync with the hostility of other Americans.

There are *lots* of possibilities for demonstrating you care. Build relationships by passing on information, letting others talk, helping with a project and checking on progress.[23] You can buy lunch, honor a request, remember birthdays, swap recipes, and loan tools. Do something fun together. We get closer when we request someone's opinion or assistance. If we can't act on their advice, we show our appreciation when we explain why not.

As you know, observances like funerals and ceremonies like retirement parties signify caring. Regular Thanksgiving and holy day gatherings provide shared experience, add predictability, and strengthen our connections even in the midst of conflict. If virus mitigation allows, talk and break bread together with those you've been estranged from.

5. **Show respect and acceptance**

People don't want to be controlled, dominated, or judged, especially in this tense political climate. Because people want to be themselves, follow McGinnis' last rule—"create space in your relationships."

Hear views with an open mind that explores rather than criticizes differences. It's terrific to see birthdays through a child's eye and to learn how someone else reacts to a book or movie. Others' unique ideas and experiences make them interesting. America's diversity makes our nation strong. On purpose, successful organizations hire people with different skills and perspectives, because no one has it all.

Sometimes we forget that other Americans bring varied, valuable vantage points to the table. Imagine a three year-old at a table with toys on top and a teddy bear seated directly across. If you photograph the toys from each side of the table, lay out the four pictures, and ask young children to select the one that shows the way they are looking at the toys, kids choose the correct photo. But, if you ask them to point to the picture showing how Teddy is looking at the toys, they pick the same photo. Three year-olds don't realize it looks different from Teddy's chair. Respectful adults of all political persuasions do.

Remember that everything you need to know you learned in kindergarten, including "please" and "thank you." Try requesting and giving space with:

*"How about_____?"*

*"Next time would you_____ ?"*

*"Would you please give it more thought?"*

*"It would help me if_____ ."*

*"I'd suggest_____ ."*

McGinnis' friendship factors—invest time, open up, compliment, show you care, and respect others—are concrete ways to indicate liking and improve American interactions.

## WE NEED TRUST

Since high quality relationships help us feel good, live longer, and accomplish more, why don't we collaborate and get along regularly?

In win/lose situations when rewards go only to the winner, like sports contests and business transactions where a single firm gets awarded the contract, people compete instead of collaborate. Trump has been alienating our allies and aggravating the American divide with his frequent reference to "winners," "losers," and "America First." A leader should be inspiring us to get along and have each other's backs.

When people work on individual tasks or separately in silos, they're more likely to compete. Division of labor actually keeps family and team members apart. In contrast, joint projects requiring interdependency, exchange, and support encourage collaboration and respect for others' skills. For example, my husband and brother-in-law bonded over installing a ceiling fan.

To pull together, we need more opportunities to rely on each other, share, and unite on common ground. Historically, American communities came together to build schools and churches. We see bonding occurring now when communities deal with tornadoes, fires, floods, school shootings, and Covid-19.

## TRUST IS BASED ON PREDICTABILITY

Through experiences, Americans learn to count on one another. People trust those they predict have good intentions—who care and want good things for them. Trust is a positive expectation. Mistrust—its opposite—feeds competition. Because risk and vulnerability are involved, the trust components of (1) predictability and (2) positive intent don't carry equal weight.

Let me explain by describing two men I worked with in a consulting firm. One was jovial, outgoing, friendly, and extremely changeable. He was quick to sing my praises yet quick to storm out while slamming the door behind him. The other was stiff, abrupt, and cold 24/7. Which of the two did I trust the most? Colleague number two, though he had never treated me as well. His consistent behavior enabled me to predict what he would do, plan accordingly, and be less vulnerable.

Predictability carries more weight than good intent. What most of us mean by trustworthy is a predictable person with a positive purpose. What do you trust our 45th president to do?

$$\frac{\text{PREDICTABILITY} + \text{GOOD INTENTIONS}}{\textbf{TRUST}}$$

## TRUST PROPENSITY

Americans differ in their willingness to place trust in others. Based on our experiences, some of us have the propensity to be "until-ers" who start out trusting and continue to have faith *until* that belief is violated.[24] "If-ers" on the other hand withhold their trust to see *if* others are worthy of confidence.

Because the bulk of my encounters with people have been positive, I'm typically an "until-er," yet not always. When a book rep entered my University of St. Thomas office, I found myself immediately put off because the salesman had mannerisms reminiscent of someone I distrusted intensely. I was on guard to determine if this man was cut from the same cloth. Some Americans you encounter have been burned and left with reasons not to trust people like you. Some have a triggering effect on you.

Trust is "situation specific" and depends on others' ability, integrity, benevolence, and reliability. Trusting someone to have appropriate skill differs from trusting someone to follow through or speak truthfully. I'll trust certain individuals to fix my car and different people to replace my arthritic knee. Some neighbors and relatives may be trusted to tell me the truth as they know it—and be predictably ill-informed. Some politicians consistently mislead and misinform, while others promise and deliver—though not perfectly.

## HOW CAN WE FOSTER TRUST?

As you know, trust is built over time, bit by bit—in one-on-one encounters on the sidewalk or over the back fence, and in live group meetings or Zoom gatherings. When Americans from all over this country find common goals, occasions for interdependence, and rewards for joint effort, we'll collaborate.

### What helps develop trust?
- **Shared social norms**
- **Repeated interactions**
- **Shared experience**
- **Transparency**

Shared norms, repeated interactions, and shared experiences enable us to count on each other. With time we learn to forecast who will pitch in, perform competently, share power, and tell the truth.

Build trust through transparency. Smooth the way for people to guess what you will do and how you will treat them. I can relax if I expect your intent is positive, or at least be prepared if I predict you do not have my best interests at heart.

## EXPLAIN YOUR INTENTIONS

Increase trust by explaining your intentions. Clarify what you think, value, and support—and invite others to do the same. A phrase like this cuts down on interpersonal guesswork errors:

*"My goal is_____ ."*

*"I'm trying to_____ ."*

*"What I'm hoping is_____ ."*

*"I'm wondering how to find common ground."*

*"I don't want to_____ ."*

*"I didn't mean to_____ ."*

*"I hope you know that my intent was_____ ."*

*"I'd like to understand."*

Be aware if you attempt to improve interactions by changing your ways, at first you'll be *less* predictable—that means, less trusted for a while. Seeing you violate your norm, people who know you will wonder, "What is he or she doing (or pulling)?" Your sincerity might be doubted.

I recall a female exec in tears, because her team thought her reformed style was phony and manipulative. She slipped once after cleaning up her act, and that single mistake cost her months of relationship repair. How vividly she experienced that it takes only one action to destroy trust but countless, consistent attempts to regain it. Fortunately, restored trust and repaired relationships can be stronger than before. Hang in there.

Many people signal they are purposefully making an effort to improve a connection. They even explain why. One of my clients who had damaged many relationships told others I was his "charm school instructor." He asked me to walk the halls with him, so people could see he was getting coached. Sincere about wanting to change, he wanted others to observe he meant it.

Many leaders improve by letting direct reports, peers, and board members know what specific leadership and interpersonal skills they are attempting to perfect and by requesting input on their progress. Like lane assist in new cars, feedback speeds up learning—cuing us when we are on and off track. Learning agility predicts success.[25]

The tools of drawing attention to our attempts, asking for guidance, and getting estranged others invested in our development all work, because they increase the chances people will notice the change instead of seeing us as they always have.

## RELATIONSHIP REPAIR STRATEGIES

Relationship researcher John Gottman and his colleagues are able to predict with remarkable accuracy (80–90%) and speed (within five minutes) which married couples will end up divorced.[26] They've repeatedly witnessed the damage caused by contempt, criticism, defensiveness, and stonewalling. Be reassured, though, "Connecting is not magic. Like any other skill, it can be learned, practiced, and mastered."[27]

As Gottman explains, there are numerous ways to fix relationships. You can even announce, *"Repair attempt!"* What matters is not that you select a particular approach, but whether the repair attempt used is accepted or successful.

Keep relationships with fellow Americans from being irreparably broken by waving a white flag, sending "I belong in the dog house" cards, or wearing "I'm sorry" T-shirts. Develop expertise in sending, reading, and accepting repair attempts. When others soften their stance, make them glad they did.

## REPAIR WITH SELF-DISCLOSURE

When you sense the relationship needs repair or issues are right below the surface, proceed slowly. After watching lots of successfully married couples, Gottman recommends a "soft start" to discussions. Dentists first rub, then gently inject a little novocaine at a time to make fixing a tooth less painful.

To bring issues out in the open, try self-disclosure, because openness leads to both openness and liking. State you want to restore your relationship:

> *"We seem to be avoiding each other, and I want to change that."*
>
> *"Things haven't been the same between us since the election, and I'd like to fix that."*

Because disclosing your interest in relationship repair is taking a risk, it opens the door to others doing the same.

## GO FISHING TO INVITE DISCUSSION

Invite. To jumpstart the connection you could try, "We have to talk," delivered in person, via email, or by note, but sometimes such directness seems like a demand. Questions can seem accusatory too.

Here's my favorite example of a direct inquiry misfiring: Imagine a California mother searching desperately for her six year-old son after an earthquake has shaken the house. She yells "Matthew, Matthew, where are you?" His answer? "I didn't do it! I didn't do it!"

"Going fishing"—with a tentative, gentle, indirect statement followed by a long pause—is often a safer option for starting the conversation. Fish in a quiet spot when the repair can have your full attention. Because "What's wrong?" can trigger the fatal response "Nothing!" try one of these instead:

> *"Things haven't been the same between us lately"* ... *pause.*

*"Our conversation just shifted" … pause.*

*"This meeting suddenly changed" … pause.*

That silence is important. Carefully watch your voice, face, gestures, and posture as you quietly dangle the bait. If your indirect invitation fails to hook them into a discussion, add your best guess about the cause of the disconnection:

*"My guess is that I came on too strong about Trump's lying."*

Usually the other person will then respond strongly with something like, "Yeah! You went on and on, ranting and raving! You don't get it. The biased press just hates him. It's all a bogus!" Your guess hooked a fish, but a shark not a walleye. The tough part is stopping yourself from responding naturally.

Automatically defending or explaining everything away takes you farther away from your goal of restoring the relationship. Remember you wanted them to talk. Allow people to let off some steam, so you can eventually discuss what harmed your relationship, but don't get burned while they are venting. You might throw some cooling fog on the situation—which you'll find in chapter 10, "Getting Off the Defensive."

Return to talking about your intentions both (1) at the time the relationship was severed or strained and (2) your intentions now:

*"I was so upset by the latest news report, that I just spouted off. I wanted your take on it and didn't mean to attack you. How can I make things right?"*

*"I was ticked by what Steve said at the dinner party about the Mueller report. I shouldn't have gone off on you. I'd like to make things better between us."*

Your words, tailored for the person you know, will be more effective than those examples. Still, having some scripts ready is helpful. Practice saying:

*"I wish I'd said that differently."*

*"I didn't show it, but our relationship is important to me."*

Become an expert at
**sending and correctly reading**
repair attempts

## APOLOGIZE

No doubt you have witnessed your behavior fail to match your good intentions. Like me, you've irritated someone without meaning to plus insulted and angered people by accident. When that happens, rebuild. Communicate (1) what you had intended and (2) that you fell short, so they can predict you will struggle to keep from repeating that mistake.

You can apologize for the *result* while also reporting what you had planned:

*"I'm sorry! I had intended_____ ."*

*"That isn't what I had in mind. What I'd wanted was_____ ."*

*"I attempted_____ which didn't happen at all."*

Owning an error is a helpful form of openness. There is evidence that we like the person responsible to quickly tell us about a blunder.[28] Though people often prefer when others self-disclose late in a conversation, readily acknowledging "I goofed" can stop a mudslide.

Admitting a mistake shows we are human, humble, and concerned about preserving the relationship. Our trust in American institutions is a consequence of how much we perceive institutional leaders admit mistakes and take responsibility for them.[29]

## KEEP THE CONNECTION GOING

Forgiving, accepting others' efforts to make amends, and allowing the emotional tide to turn are all parts of repairing relationships in our families and across the aisle. Take the olive branch. Reach out to stay in touch until others calm down. All of us will at times speak out of turn, fail to show kindness, and reach erroneous conclusions. Let people save face when they do.

I like McGinnis' story of his friend who ripped into him because he was indignant about something McGinnis had done. Extremely hurt and angry, McGinnis cancelled their regular lunch date and was curt and icy when the friend called the following day to check on him. Though the buddy didn't apologize because he thought McGinnis had needed his feedback, the colleague continued to express his affection on the phone, in person the following evening, and consistently for several days until McGinnis stopped pouting. Time and effort heals.

## PRE-CALL TO AVOID FUTURE TROUBLE

Before relationship difficulties occur or recur, the pre-calling technique can be a beneficial tool. Make a deal about future consequences with something like:

> *"If that ever happens again, which I hope it won't, feel free to signal me."*
>
> *"Please give me the "time out" sign, if I cross the line again."*
>
> *"We have a deal that if I come on too strong, you can_____ ."*
>
> *"Would you be willing to give me a heads up, when I'm ticking you off?"*

Then, of course, follow through. Say what you mean and mean what you say.

Everybody makes relationship mistakes. Use these emergency kit devices to avoid missteps, keep transgressions small, quickly change direction, and start repairing.

## MAKE A PLAN

Good relationships don't just happen, so if you *don't* want to be an American who sees others as enemies, set aside time to build, maintain, and repair connections. Remember the CEO whose simple plan of greeting his direct report boosted their bond? Scheduling specific ways to strengthen important relationships pays off. American relationships are important.

Making a public announcement raises the likelihood of follow through, so you might tell someone else about your commitment.

**To increase the chances you'll execute, make your plan:**

- **small**—not too much time or effort required
- **specific**—definite and detailed
- **reasonable**—something you see value in doing
- **positive**—what you are going to start doing
- **repetitive**—done often enough that others begin to trust it
- **independent**—done regardless of their response (For example, you can invite but can't control whether they have lunch with you.)

Here's a **Do Plan** written by someone who recently joined a depolarizing effort and wanted to get to know people on the other side of the political divide:

1.  Once a week invite people, who have different views from mine, to a real or Zoom lunch
2.  Every Monday list two areas of agreement I can find with people of the opposite side
3.  Watch 15 minutes of news programming weekly with someone across the political divide
4.  Every month host or attend a gathering—real or virtual—of different-minded Americans

## FOCUS ON OTHERS

Known as the grandfather of all people-skills books, Dale Carnegie's extremely popular *How to Win Friends and Influence People* offers specific advice about how to make people like us and win them over, including:

- become genuinely interested in people
- encourage others to talk about themselves
- talk in terms of the other person's interests
- sincerely make people feel important

Because getting along matters, build good relationships with Carnegie's empirically verified tips, some trustworthy actions, and the friendship factors.

And, resuscitate damaged connections with some repair techniques from this kit. They are good medicine. More help is in the "Change Means Overcoming Resistance" and "Disagreeing Without Being Disagreeable" chapters.

## CHAPTER 7

# Influencing Across the Divide

**W**ant to influence how fellow Americans think or vote? As you can tell, I'm trying to influence you. If I could, I'd line us all up to get a shot of credibility. Without it, people dismiss or doubt us, making our attempts to influence them fail. To discuss differing perspectives, debate political policies, and influence outcomes, being credible matters—at least it used to.

## BOOST YOUR CREDIBILITY

Social scientists and communication researchers have been examining what it takes to be persuasive and believable. The basic ingredients in the credibility formula all start with the letter C, so I wish I could put several CCs in the syringe *in the right proportions* and inject us with charisma. To influence thoughts and actions, most of us, including those attempting to defeat Trump, need a credibility shot in the arm.

### Credibility

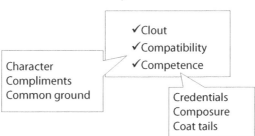

Character
Compliments
Common ground

✓Clout
✓Compatibility
✓Competence

Credentials
Composure
Coat tails

## CLOUT + COMPATIBILITY + COMPETENCE

People are influenced by those they respect and like. We admire others for their position, character, and expertise, but not all types of credibility are created equally. We may comply with a direct order made by someone with clout, because the person has sufficient power inherent in his/her role or position to force compliance, but that doesn't mean we do so willingly. In contrast, we gladly take the idea or suggestion of those we find compatible (likable) and those we find competent (know what they are doing).

In the right amount, the three ingredients of clout, compatibility, and competence yield charisma, which is almost magical. But, getting those proportions right is tricky and not the same for all people in all situations.

## DON'T OVERUSE CLOUT

Using your ability to punish, threaten, or coerce contaminates the credibility formula. Typically. But these are unprecedented times. Trump says, "You have no choice but to vote for me,"[1] which works with those who are afraid or can be bullied. Interestingly, clout appeals more to the authoritarian personality who when threatened seeks stability and an authoritarian leader to follow.[2] For others, his statement sparks backlash, defiance, and resentment.

Usually, too much use of position power, force, or intimidation spoils one's charisma. The moment someone demands we do something, we no longer want to. Known for our independent streak, Americans—red, blue, and purple—resist being controlled.

When pushed, many of us push back, but someone asking nicely is far easier to accept. "Ask questions instead of giving direct orders," advised Dale Carnegie.[3] Words like "You *have* to see it this way" or "You *must* agree" encourage others to say "No I don't," so suggest and request with:

*"How about_____?"*

*"Would you please give it more thought?"*

*"I'd suggest experimenting with_____ ."*

The indirect approach often—but of course not always—results in greater compliance, even though moods, convention, and amount of intimacy also have an impact.[4]

If necessary, you can fall back on any legitimate authority inherent in a role you have, such as a boss' assigned power to hire and fire, a senator's right to pass legislation, or a parent's ownership of a household car. However, once you use clout, attempting to influence through likability/compatibility becomes more difficult.

Be aware of gender differences. Linguist Deborah Tannen brought attention to the differences in male and female speech patterns,[5] and John Gray's best-selling relationship book of all time described how men and women seem to come from different planets.[6] Though not true of every male or every female, generalizable patterns exist.

Starting from a very early age females delight in finding similarities, emphasize closeness, and minimize status through rapport-talk. Males, on the other hand, use report-talk and typically communicate how they are different from or better than others. Consequently, males are less likely to be turned off by use of clout, though they may be challenged to fight it.

Again, the success of any influence approach depends on the situation and the people involved, so employ what works and keep refining your message. At times you'll need to appear stronger, at times more reasonable. Bernard Shaw wrote of the sensibility of his tailor who took new measurements every time he saw him.[7] What fits today may not tomorrow.

We have options—influence through compatibility, competence, or both. If needed, you can add a drop or two of clout in the syringe. Save big clout sledgehammers for when you can't find another way to break up others' views set in concrete. Usually, except with authoritarians, a better influence path is to de-emphasize status and instead rely heavily on a combination of compatibility and competence. When you can avoid resistance, you can leave the tools for overcoming it (see next chapter) holstered on your toolbelt.

## BUILD COMPATIBILITY THROUGH CHARACTER, COMPLIMENTS, AND COMMON GROUND

Because we are influenced by people we like, start with compatibility—likability. We listen to those who like us. Through character, compliments, and common ground we become more convincing and likable.

## DEMONSTRATE DESIRABLE CHARACTER

We like and trust individuals based on their character—and comply with requests from those we like, especially if we are female.[8] People value such character qualities as friendliness, humility, compassion, enthusiasm, commitment, honesty, and sense of humor. When you want to be credible, remember it isn't sufficient to simply *be* sincere; others must *perceive* you really are a likable person worth listening to.

How? Ensure that you are consistent in what you say and that your talk and walk are in sync. If not, explain why. Remember, people trust what they can predict and will be making assumptions about your motives and character. You know trust is broken easily but restored with difficulty, and you've seen trouble in the current administration. As Stephen M. R. Covey has written, trust "changes everything."[9]

## COMPLIMENT—SHOW GOOD WILL

Social psychologists like Elliot Aronson have clearly demonstrated another rule—reciprocal liking. We like people who have the good sense to like *us*. Charismatic people make us feel good both about being around them and about ourselves. What a difference if more of us complimented fellow Americans with:

*"I can tell you've given this a lot of thought."*

*"Thanks for mentioning that data."*

*"You're on top of the facts and know what you're talking about."*

*"I needed you to remind me of that."*

When people believe others respect and care about them, their receptivity to ideas—and their cooperation in general—goes up. Shaming drives people away.[10] Hillary, who had been plagued with poor likability throughout her campaign and career, no doubt cost herself a lot of votes by referring to Trump supporters as "deplorables." Mitt Romney made the same mistake four years earlier by saying his job was not to worry about the 47% of American voters financially dependent on government. To his credit, billionaire Trump convinced his followers he understood their economic pain and would do something about it.

A genuine interest in people is a powerful hook for their attention, so make people feel important like true friends, great partners, and loving grandparents do. Engage with others and learn about their views. Secretary Clinton established more rapport with her audiences in town hall situations, where she smiled, made eye contact, and showed a willingness to listen. Her husband was notorious for making everyone in the room feel he was focused on them alone. Infusing a situation with warmth and energy encourages others to listen and value what you say.

Market researchers have found we are highly influenced by friends, family, and those we like. Basically, if we like them, we like what they like, think as they think, and go where they go. Our "opinion leaders" sway our buying of products, services, and ideas. Despite the rise of social media and the attempts of advertisers, the social influence of our likable contacts remains strong. Marketers have tracked our on and off line talk, finding that 90% of our word-of-mouth conversations about brands occur in person, for all age groups, even teens and young adults.[11]

## MAKE OTHERS AWARE OF COMMON GROUND

Similarity pulls people together. When you want to influence by being perceived as likable and credible, highlight what you have in common. We not only like people who like us, we like people who *are* like us. People with similar beliefs, preferences, and approaches reinforce us by saying in essence, "Oh, you think that way too? We're so right!" Being around them is rewarding.

We even expect, see, and project commonality onto others. Suffering from the halo effect, we assume based on one characteristic that you have a certain set of perspectives. Our logic goes that if we share a characteristic, you must be like me, and if we're similar in ways I value, I'll think highly of you and follow your lead.

Noteworthy is that while a person's character is extremely important to whether we like that individual, our positive feelings for a *group* depend on the degree of similarity between the group and ourselves.[12] Do I belong? Is this my tribe? What will happen if I open my mouth here? Dissimilarity can lead to disdain.

If we see ourselves as a group member, we're likely to like the group.[13] The association between similarity and liking probably stems from the belief that if we have a lot in common, we can understand and predict what each other will do. Therefore, these relationships are safer and require less effort.

Admittedly, finding commonality has become more difficult as our nation has become more diverse. When talking across the divide, emphasize the similarities in your backgrounds, experiences, interests, and attitudes, while taking into consideration race, religion, sexual preference, age, education, economics, and geography. When interacting in a group, mentioning something for everybody is probably best. Using phrases like "we all" can tie us together, *if* they are true, but pull us apart when manipulative.

Showing your compatibility with references to local places, recent events, and familiar situations was easier when everyone in town went to the local high school's Friday night game or watched *Bonanza* and Walter Cronkite on one of three networks. We have vivid, shared memories of the Challenger disaster, 9/11, the coronavirus, and economic downturns, and we at least have heard of Harry Potter, *Star Wars*, *The Hunger Games*, *America's Got Talent*, *Shark Tank*, and *Survivor*. With gender lines blurring, referring to cooking and parenting along with computers and sports probably resonate with most. We do have things in common.

Because persuasion is both a cognitive and emotional task, find relevant examples, memorable stories, and good analogies that touch your audience's head *and* heart. Comedian Jimmy Kimmel's plea to protect those with pre-existing conditions like his newborn son resulted in Republican Senator Bill Cassidy saying that any bill must pass the "Jimmy Kimmel test" of not denying health care. Suddenly people saw those with pre-existing conditions differently—as someone's child, possibly theirs.

People need to see merit in your logical arguments and at the same time feel moved by what you say. Still, the backlash of negative emails Kimmel received calling him an elitist and telling him "go home and take care of your kid" signals the depth of our American schism. Even a powerful request will turn some off in this uncivil America.

In real and figurative ways, speak the language of others if you can, and if you can't, admit you don't but wish you could. Several of my IBM, Medtronic, and Mayo Clinic clients benefitted from learning to soften their style and "talk Minnesotan" when they moved from the East Coast. Be on alert for nonverbal and verbal missteps, and refrain from saying "I understand completely," because we never do.

Being influential with strangers usually involves helping them feel comfortable before getting down to talking politics or business. Virtual teams know the importance of pulling people together across distances and "take 5"—spend a few initial minutes—to discuss what is going on in everyone's lives and create rapport.

Politicians attempt to show connection with voters. Instead of appearing wealthy, highly polished, or out of touch with the less fortunate, Bernie Sanders inspired many as he spoke of economic disparity and his desire to address income inequality. Amy Klobuchar pointed out her practical Midwest roots, Mayor Pete mentioned his millennial age, and Elizabeth Warren referred to her humble beginnings in Oklahoma not her faculty spot at Harvard.

Trump, with his unabashed willingness to say almost anything, tapped the anger and frustration especially felt by working white males who hated political correctness. Linguists attribute some of Trump's appeal to his conversational I'll-let-you-fill-in-the-gaps-because-I-know-you-can style and his simple sentence structure, likened to grade-schoolers and standup comedians.[14] Anti-intellectuals applauded.

## BUILD COMPETENCE THROUGH CREDENTIALS

When expertise matters, modestly remind others of your special qualifications, training, and skills. We tend to believe those who are experienced and knowledgeable, unless they seem too condescending or too different from us.

Trump emphasized his business status, claiming to be "very, very rich" and good at making deals, to suggest that he would make money for all of us. Painting politicians as corrupt, he purposefully didn't want to be perceived to be one and sought the badge of the outside billionaire instead. The self-made and self-funding billionaires running for the presidency in 2020—environmentalist Tom

Steyer and financial guru Michael Bloomberg—highlighted their donations as well as their competently accumulated wealth.

If you want to be a credible influence, let others see that you grasp what's needed and know what you're talking about. Have your facts nailed down. In his first week as Trump's press secretary, Sean Spicer severely damaged his credibility with two obvious false-hoods—inauguration crowd size and degree of voter fraud. To quote Spicer, "I think there's been studies. There was one that came out of Pew [in] 2008 that showed 14 percent of people who have voted were not citizens."[15] Suggesting that Pew Research found 1 out of 7 voters were not U.S. citizens was of course untrue, and he should have known better.

Unfortunately, our society currently is becoming numb to mis-truth and placing less value on expertise. As our organizations have become "flatter," leadership styles more participative, and hierarchy less important, status has become less important.

People are of equal value, but what they know is *not* identical. Some have skills in construction; others are knowledgeable astrophysicists; others are talented artists, athletes, economists, teachers, surgeons, and mechanics. We have something to learn from each of them. We also have our own and others' superiority illusions (described in chapter 3) to overcome.

## COMPETENCE THROUGH COMPOSURE

Help people have confidence in you by staying cool under pressure and calm when attacked. (Specific tools to manage your defensiveness are in chapter ten.) Credible folks are perceived as poised, prepared, confident, and in control. If you were in a fire and a confident, composed person instructed you to escape via the side door and a rattled one directed you through the main door, wouldn't you follow the levelheaded one?

Preparation is the key that helps many communicate with assurance and remain on an even keel. Be ready for difficult conversations. You witnessed Lt. Colonel Vindman and Ambassador Yovanovitch testify with strength during the impeachment. Immunologist Anthony Fauci calmly, candidly, and competently informed America to take action to curb the spread of Covid-19, because the worst was yet to come.

Being composed differs, though, from being stiff, formal, cold, or mechanized. Elizabeth Warren purposely shifted her style by adding human stories to her "I have a plan for that." When popular candidates deliver parts of their stump speeches on autopilot, Americans are turned off. So, too, are your fellow citizens when your political conversations sound canned or insincere.

Don't be afraid to goof. People who suffer from being perceived as too competent are often liked better after they make a mistake, because they're now more human, real, and more similar to the rest of us.[16] However, research highlights that those who slip up when their competency *isn't* high are viewed less favorably after an error. Mistakes help compatibility but hurt competency.

## RIDE ON VALUED COAT TAILS

When appropriate, help others you want to influence see your association with organizations or people considered worthwhile, trustworthy, or prestigious. The credibility of others can boost ours, letting us ride a little way on their coat tails. Down-ballot candidates appropriately worry about the favorability of those higher on the ticket. Because our perceptions differ, selecting which affiliations to highlight depends on whom you seek to influence.

Consider having someone respected provide an introduction and mention your ties to the people you hope to influence. If someone likes Chris, and Chris speaks highly of you, you have a foot in the door. Mary Kay, Amway, and Angie's List all built strong businesses based on people's willingness to buy products and services used by neighbors.

Our behavior is guided by social proof—what others do and think. The rationale is, "You believe or like it, so I will." Researchers have demonstrated the power of testimonials, labeling something a best seller, and reporting that "countless others" have acted this way. When you want to influence, instead of mentioning those who didn't comply, which is "negative social proof," talk about all those who did.

## INFLUENCE PRINCIPLES

Robert Cialdini deserves the title the "influence guy." In his best seller *Influence,* which brought the social psychology research on persuasion from the lab to the public, he outlined universal influence principles you and I can use when trying to influence others. Ones not already in the credibility syringe are:

- **Reciprocation**

  Most people feel obligated to return a favor. So, if we thoroughly examine others' positions, they should do the same to ours. In addition, providing information, going the extra mile, or helping with a task makes a person more likable, so you can see why those actions would be persuasive when not deemed manipulative. Again, it is hard to resist someone who is so nice.

  Civilized societies rely on reciprocity, and knowing that, many charities send "gifts" to increase the likelihood we will contribute to their cause. Appealing to reciprocity and generosity outperforms the "if/then" approach. For example, when a hotel mentioned it had *already* donated on behalf of its guests and asked the guests to reciprocate by reusing towels to protect our planet, the guests were 45% more likely to reuse their towels than when the hotel offered to donate if they did.[17] Social obligation or reciprocity works better than incentives or bribes.

- **Commitment / Consistency**

People work to be consistent with a position they've taken, so if we can get a foot in the door with an easy "ask," it can be followed by larger requests. Because we want to reduce cognitive dissonance, we act in line with our values and with how we perceive ourselves. If we first comply because of reciprocity, we may *continue* to go along because of commitment and consistency. We've decided that's who we are. Consequently, asking for just an hour of someone's time or a little support can yield a lot more, and little by little over time people who once strongly opposed Trump start defending him.

Interestingly, when we observe ourselves doing something, we explain or "attribute" our actions to ourselves instead of concluding "the situation made me do it." Our actions change our attitudes and beliefs. Therefore, salespeople have shifted to having the customer, not them, complete a form to increase commitment to a deal or contract. Similarly, having people publicly announce they are dieting or giving up drugs helps them do so. Wearing campaign buttons or hats secures votes.

If you want someone to *change*, it's important to help the person see how the current situation is different and requires people to act differently. Times *have* changed. Facing the first pandemic in our lifetimes and weeks of racial protest, being united *is* more important than ever to our lives and our democracy.

- **Scarcity**

And finally, we try to secure something that is scarce, unique, or dwindling. If an opportunity or product is about to be discontinued or disappear, it suddenly becomes more highly valued, even if it hasn't been successfully popular up to this point. Think hand sanitizers and toilet paper.

While this seems counterintuitive, research data shows we want what others can't have.[18] Think freedom. Telling someone it's the "last chance" or "the deal is ending" often works, because we hate to lose even more than we love to win.

## LOOKING FOR MORE TIPS?

Intrigued and looking for more ideas to use in political discussions with fellow Americans? You'll find 50 tips for being persuasive based on these principles in *Yes!*[19] Authors Noah Goldstein, Steve Martin, and Robert Cialdini explain with excellent examples how too many choices are overwhelming and counterproductive (think of the number of 2016 Republican and 2020 Democratic presidential candidates), how we can make our position look like a good compromise (or better) in contrast with the right comparison, how too much fear causes people to tune us out, and why we should take the blame for our mistakes.

## INFLUENCE ROADMAP

Having a roadmap or blueprint helps get us where we want to go, so if you have only a few minutes to persuade people, follow these few steps:

1. Get their favorable attention with a **Grabber**, like a startling statistic
2. Establish your **Credibility** by tactfully mentioning expertise and common ground
3. Clearly and concisely make your persuasive point with a **Thesis** statement
4. Show your persuasive point has logical validity and **Thesis Credibility**
5. **Relate** to their needs, values, or interests to get them to care
6. Clarify and emphasize **Benefits/Rewards** to show "what's in it for them"
7. Call for **Action** and encourage them to respond appropriately

When conversing with people who already know you, you might start farther down the influence road, but when family and friends aren't coming along with you, the roadmap can be a guide to getting back on track. Where did you lose them? They may not find you credible on this topic or see any relevance to them. Do you need to change your tune, because they hate your song which they've heard too often?

## ADJUST TO YOUR LISTENER

Worth mentioning is that you'll be even more successful if you combine strategies and customize for those you're attempting to influence. Besides using basic credibility formulas and influence principles, refine your approach. Unfortunately, what works with one won't with everyone.

Speak their language. Understanding the personality types measured by the Myers-Briggs Type Indicator, which millions have taken, can help us skillfully adjust an influence attempt. Consider the style of those whom you would like to persuade and modify your message accordingly.

First, let me help you identify *your* preferred style:

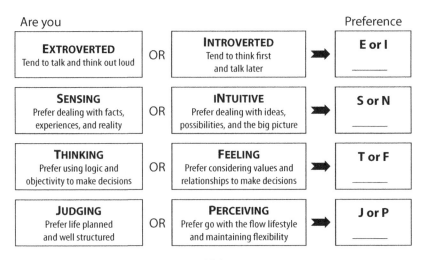

| Are you | | | Preference |
|---|---|---|---|
| **EXTROVERTED**<br>Tend to talk and think out loud | OR | **INTROVERTED**<br>Tend to think first<br>and talk later | **E or I**<br>_____ |
| **SENSING**<br>Prefer dealing with facts,<br>experiences, and reality | OR | **INTUITIVE**<br>Prefer dealing with ideas,<br>possibilities, and the big picture | **S or N**<br>_____ |
| **THINKING**<br>Prefer using logic and<br>objectivity to make decisions | OR | **FEELING**<br>Prefer considering values and<br>relationships to make decisions | **T or F**<br>_____ |
| **JUDGING**<br>Prefer life planned<br>and well structured | OR | **PERCEIVING**<br>Prefer go with the flow lifestyle<br>and maintaining flexibility | **J or P**<br>_____ |

People have different preferences along the MBTI's four major dimensions:

1. **E**xtroversion-**I**ntroversion—where we get our energy
2. **S**ensing-i**N**tuiting—what we pay attention to
3. **T**hinking-**F**eeling—how we make decisions
4. **J**udging-**P**erceiving—how we resolve issues

A large majority of Americans are considered extroverts, and if you want to influence or repair a relationship with one, it pays to try for a face-to-face encounter and let them speak and think out loud. Interacting energizes extroverts. In contrast, introverts think first and talk later, so they like digesting written memos and reports. Wait while they pause before answering you.

Sensors, about 65% of the U.S. population, pay attention to facts and details, specific real-life experiences, and information that would come through their five senses. They ask the practical "what" and "how" questions. Those with the intuitive preference like the big picture along with future possibilities, analogies, and hunches. Be ready to answer "why" when interacting with them.

The American population is split about 50/50 between thinkers and feelers. Thinkers will prefer you to quickly get down to business, use logic and cold, hard facts, and objectively weigh the pros and cons of each argument. More relationship than task-focused, feelers will need pleasantries first, resonate with personal and emotional examples, and expect you to value feelings and agreement.

Judgers, who are about 60% of the U.S. population, dislike uncertainty, prefer making decisions quickly, and jump in to take charge. In contrast, perceivers like to keep their options open, are flexible in their positions, and hold off making decisions as long as they can. They happily let others be in charge and can be okay with inconclusive meetings.

## CONSIDER THE SENSING/INTUITING AND THINKING/FEELING PERSONALITY DIMENSIONS

When attempting to influence your relative or neighbor, pay most attention to the important Sensing/Intuiting and Thinking/Feeling personality dimensions. If your message is, "To answer that, I need more information from Jack and Lauren," which of the following examples is best designed for a sensor, thinker, feeler, or intuitive?

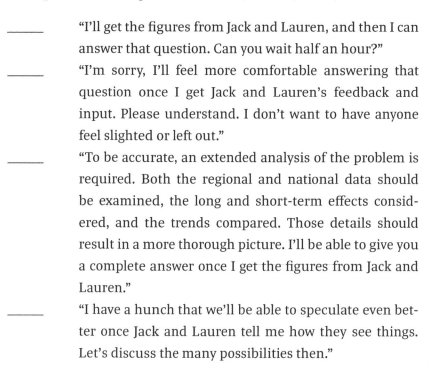

_____     "I'll get the figures from Jack and Lauren, and then I can answer that question. Can you wait half an hour?"

_____     "I'm sorry, I'll feel more comfortable answering that question once I get Jack and Lauren's feedback and input. Please understand. I don't want to have anyone feel slighted or left out."

_____     "To be accurate, an extended analysis of the problem is required. Both the regional and national data should be examined, the long and short-term effects considered, and the trends compared. Those details should result in a more thorough picture. I'll be able to give you a complete answer once I get the figures from Jack and Lauren."

_____     "I have a hunch that we'll be able to speculate even better once Jack and Lauren tell me how they see things. Let's discuss the many possibilities then."

Did you recognize the thinker, feeler, sensor, and intuitive, in that order?

When not careful, most of us send messages as we'd like to hear them, not as best received. While preferences fall along the MBTI dimensions in varying degrees, we can be predominantly an ST (Sensor Thinker) or SF (Sensor Feeler)—or, if we have a big picture orientation, either an NT (iNtuitive Thinker) or NF (iNtuitive Feeler). Give some thought about how to best interact with a differing American who is an ST, SF, NT, or NF combination.

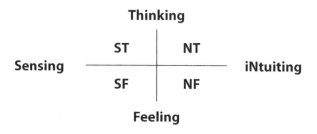

Here are some influence guidelines:

- To influence an ST, focus on the evidence and present it step-by-step, emphasizing logical analysis of the data and the tasks at hand.

- To influence an SF, show with details how people will be affected by what you propose. Relationships are important to these listeners.

- To influence an NT, start with an overview and then present a series of well-analyzed, practical options. Emphasize logical possibilities.

- To influence an NF, help the person see the big picture and how your proposal will positively affect people's lives, values, and feelings as well as achieve their vision.

Want to make an impact? Communicate unto others as *they* would have you communicate unto them. That *platinum*—which is rarer than gold—rule is precious.

## PERSUADING V. INSPIRING

Persuading someone to accept your view is different from *inspiring* someone to do what they've already decided is right. Structuring a persuasive argument involves acknowledging opposing sides and refuting the objections of those not yet convinced of your position. With those who already agree, simply point out how to get to your shared vision. Persuasive and inspirational approaches both urge action—like get out the vote or start treating Americans better.

| When your Purpose is to | |
| --- | --- |
| **PERSUADE** | **INSPIRE** |
| • Current condition | • Current condition |
| • Negative and positive futures | • Shared vision of improvement |
| • Key points | • Steps to take |
| • Undercut their objections | |
| • Desired future | • "You make the difference" |
| • Urge action | • Urge action |

## HOW ARE PEOPLE INFLUENCED??

Need a quick review or cheat sheet? Twenty research findings that summarize what is known about how to change someone's mind and heart are in Appendix 5.

For now, focus on that booster shot of credibility (**compatibility + competence**), think about tailoring for those around you, and keep the end—your destination—in mind.

## CHAPTER 8

# Change Means Overcoming Resistance

To bring Democrats, Independents, and Republicans together, most of us have to change—at least a little. The human default position is to simply confirm what we already believe and behave as we habitually do. What works to change that? The right tool used skillfully.

Trouble is, the right prybar for one person isn't the right one for another. And, because we aren't static, what fits today won't tomorrow. That's why I've packed a lot in this emergency kit. Just as patients with different kinds of cancer need specific chemo cocktails, successful change efforts for marriages, corporations, or voters require tweaking.

Change involves loss and sparks opposition. It also represents opportunity. What is tough to remember is Americans all along the political spectrum resist change.

People respond positively to different sets of events and react extremely differently to identical situations. A Republican National Committee leader tells the story of how he was crying with joy the night of the 2016 election while at the other end of the country his daughter-in-law was sobbing for the opposite reason.

Sometimes personal and political change brings losses that we're glad to be rid of, such as unpleasant responsibilities or elected officials we don't trust. Sometimes, though, we lose the sense of being competent, of having a handle on life, of feeling comfortable, of knowing what to expect. Some changes like the death of a child and severe injury are life shattering. Change requires adjustment and takes energy.

## HOW DO PEOPLE RESPOND TO CHANGE?
## DENY ➡ RESIST ➡ EXPLORE ➡ COMMIT

Denial is the initial reaction to a rumored or reported change, especially one we dislike. We tell ourselves the change simply can't or won't happen. No need to worry. The coronavirus won't get to my state and America won't go bankrupt. Trump won't separate asylum-seeking children from their parents. He won't get elected. Don't be too sure. As you know, millions of Jews tragically remained in Nazi Germany too long.

After hiding our heads in the sand for a while, when people realize change *is* occurring, denial shifts to resistance. We oppose the new position, policy, procedure, or politician because we are concerned about the potential impact.

With time, we become used to an altered state of affairs. We tire, long for normalcy, seek distraction, and tune out. Unless fear continues to be fueled, people stay on alert only so long—even those terrified of snakes.

Because our nervous systems habituate, repeated exposure works better than avoidance for dealing with anxiety. Confronting a picture of a snake again and again, and then repeatedly seeing a real one is a way we become more tolerant of them. Being with the snake first for a few seconds, then for half an hour, gets us accustomed to those critters. Bottom line, people get desensitized.

Finally, we begin to look for some positives in the new scenario, so we can scale back from our more extreme position of resisting. We rationalize our lack of arousal. People explore and subsequently find, for example, that automobiles have advantages over horses, that new computer systems outperform the old, and that people are paying attention to politics again. Payoffs.

## WE ACCOMMODATE

This human tendency to gradually accommodate both helps and harms us. Systematic desensitization and its companion—acceptance—are beneficial for children in newly blended families, people with phobias, and employees joining a team. Over time, many stop noticing what is upsetting them now. We get used to the new normal.

What's keeping public health officials up at night? We risk being like the frog in the pot with the water temperature rising so gradually that it doesn't realize it is facing death. Without adequate coronavirus testing, tracing, and treatment, we're shooting in the dark and spreading the outbreak. The anxiety that has us distancing in crowds will dissipate over time—maybe too soon.

We adjust, but sometimes we shouldn't. We get duped. If people hear something again and again, especially from sources they consider credible, they come to believe it. Disinformation is coming at us 24/7. False statements are being repeated *after* correct facts have been made known. According to my moral code, intentionally bearing false witness is out of line.

A cultural norm is something that is common, seen often, or done by many—but not necessarily right. With enough repetitions, people not only believe what is not true, their norms change, their morals decay, and we become less civilized. Witness lying, cruelty, and violence, or hear foul language often enough, and it no longer is jarring.

## SOMETIMES THERE IS A REAL THREAT

Sometimes resistance is warranted. Our bodies keep us alive by appropriately attacking foreign substances and struggling against infection. We *ought* to oppose inhumane immigration practices, interference with our Department of Justice, and waste being dumped in rivers. It's our job as citizens and friends to challenge unfounded allegations, investigate conflicts of interest, confront conspiracy theories, and speak truth to power.

Unifying our country depends on addressing the looming fears of those leaning left and those leaning right. Otherwise opposition will continue.

## REASONS TO EMBRACE CHANGE

When the status quo isn't working, people seek change. After the recession, many voters didn't see their economic condition rebound, and those Americans were eager to usher in a different administration. Trump's followers applaud that he fights with the press and world leaders, because they perceive his opposition as strength and believe someone powerful is fighting for them. But, Never-Trumpers see him as fighting on behalf of his ego not the country—costing America its allies and place as the world's leader.

Cultural changes, the erosion of the middle class's purchasing power, and the diminishing traditional role of the white male caused many to delight in Trump shaking things up. His supporters wanted things different from the way they had been. If our republic continues to be dysfunctional or chaotic, citizens will again welcome a new administration.

But, unless people see what is wrong with the current scenario, inertia takes over. For example, I won't readily jump onto a spacecraft to leave the planet, unless I understand that Earth is moments away from being destroyed by a huge meteor. Similarly, apathetic citizens don't vote.

We need reasons. A fruit distributorship asked me to convince its union employees, who loaded the fruit and drove its trucks, to put certain fruit in certain spots on the truck to avoid freezing and to routinely put oil in the rigs to prevent engine burn out. The leaders expected pushback. When I asked the management team whether employees knew the company was in financial trouble and drastically needed to cut costs, they admitted they had been withholding that news fearing workers might quit or tell their competitors.

I urged the leadership to reveal the financial situation and then leave the room after sharing this news. Acknowledging to the employees that I could only present their ideas as persuasively as possible—and could not promise management would listen—I listed on a flipchart the ideas they (slowly) offered. Not only did they suggest truck maintenance and careful placement of the fruit, their many recommendations included hiring part-time (cheaper) non-union help to do the tasks they didn't like doing. Keeping the company solvent gave them a reason for change.

## DESCRIBE THE VISION

Compelling visions rally people toward change, even when the present situation *is* satisfactory. Many a spouse has wondered why their partner wanted to redecorate or purchase a new vehicle, when the status quo was working just fine for them. The partner envisioned something better and desirable—something worth investing in. Astronauts, pioneers, and explorers leave the comfort of home and chase dreams. Inspiring leaders help us visualize exciting futures like getting to the moon, feeding the hungry, traveling in driverless cars, and harnessing the sun's power.

Encourage change by providing a better alternative and articulating a galvanizing future. To be influenced, we need to see a desirable outcome at the end of the road. Many folks did when Bernie outlined his vision of more income equality, national health insurance for all, and free college tuition. Voters left, right, and center are starting to coalesce around Biden to find America's soul. We want to heal our hurts and live by our values.

## GIVE PEOPLE CHOICES AND GET THEM INVOLVED

Need more tools for change besides status quo failure and a provocative vision? Use choice and involvement. Like you, I more readily embrace changes I choose rather than what's forced on me. We can avoid resistance by getting ideas, solutions, and participation from people who will be affected—and either take their suggestions or explain why we can't.

The ability to choose is often far more important than the actual choice itself. Ask others to experiment with new ways of doing things. Give fellow Americans choices. Though too many options can be overwhelming, too few are restrictive. Invite with:

> *"This might not be right for you, but which of these two do you think is best?"*

> *"Neither is perfect, but which option makes the most sense?"*

## REMOVING ROADBLOCKS

If you want someone to have a mindset, get rid of what's stopping them from thinking the way you hope they will. By definition, you're frustrated—your path is blocked. Admittedly, I'm trying to remove obstacles on the path to believing that Trump at the helm is dangerous.

## IF THE STATUS QUO IS OKAY

Remaining as we are is easiest, so folks comfortable with the status quo need to see a good cost/benefit ratio to think or behave differently. Think how difficult it is to break a habit or lose weight. Why should Americans back a different health care plan if they like their current one? To encourage a change find out:

> *"How well is the current situation working for you?"*

And point out:

*"Here's exactly why a change is needed."*

*"Trump's actions on trade are harming farmers and driving up
food costs."*

Too often the benefits of what people suggest are abstract rather
than concrete. Benefits have to be personal and understandable.
We are all wondering, "What's in it for me?" Highlight the payoffs
for supporting environmental protection, tax reform, limited campaign spending, gun safety, immigration reform, infrastructure
investment, diplomacy, etc. Explain how a truthful, inclusive leader
makes America collectively strong.

Shared interests bring us together, so tie what you are propos-
ing to what others already consider important. Instead of trying
to change their values—something both difficult and condescending—link to existing beliefs. Appeal to safety, morality, fairness, leg-
acy, kindness, and the greater good.

## IF PEOPLE ARE STRESSED

When people are already stretched too far, they balk. Your suggestions may simply be the final straw on a camel's back heavily bur-
dened with competing demands, health issues, or poor economic
conditions. Were they not overwhelmed, they might welcome your
view. Present ideas when people are ready for them. Ask:

*"When would be a good time for this?"*

*"What would make this easier?"*

*"Because you have so much going on, can you just do_____ ?"*

To make the change less demanding and acceptance easier, break
it into smaller, more manageable bites. Foster bipartisan efforts by
providing email addresses so that fellow Americans can easily contact their representatives. Supply facts and details, so folks don't
have to hunt for them.

## IF THEY MISUNDERSTAND

People resist when they are misinformed and disinformed, and when they don't understand. If we fail to recognize something is in our best interest, it is easy to wrongly object. Get into the details. Many Americans don't grasp that our national debt, which Trump promised to eliminate, passed the $22 trillion mark for the first time in history *prior* to the pandemic and its new relief bill. The 2019 tax cuts put us farther in the hole. Like most, I wish a college education could be free and student debt eliminated. I also honestly wish money grew on trees. Voters rightly ask, "Who's going to pay for it?"

Some clarification may enable your neighbors and relatives to accept or reject your idea based on its merits. Therefore, determine where you specifically disagree, go through the data, find out what is needed for their buy-in, and furnish that missing piece. If you know something they don't, you might offer:

> *"Let me explain."*
>
> *"Please let me clarify I'm talking about AR-15s not all guns."*
>
> *"I didn't point out_____ ."*
>
> *"Here's another way to look at those facts."*

Family therapists and consultants frequently ask clients to summarize others' positions before presenting their own. What the warring parties discover is they aren't as far apart as they thought. You might do the same to minimize misunderstanding:

> *"Would you please summarize what you heard me say, so that I can clear up any confusion I might have caused."*

Please avoid implying that others are stupid or closed-minded. Openly acknowledge that people see and hear things differently as you all determine where more data or explanation would be helpful. Be ready with additional information in bulleted lists and easy to digest charts. Go search Google together.

*"Here's what convinced me about assault weapons."*

*"Here's something that changed my neighbors' minds about health care."*

Explore their particular barriers, so you can remove what's in their way:

*"What would it take to change your mind?"*

*"What seems to be missing from Biden's proposal?"*

*"Who would you need to hear is in favor of this, before you support it too?"*

*"How well is the current approach working for you (or the poor, the LGBT...)?"*

*"If I could show you this much in savings, would you be on board?"*

## IF THERE IS TOO MUCH UNCERTAINTY

Just a little uncertainty lights up our brains, registering much like an error and sparking worry. People without information assume the worst. Think how awful it is to wait for test results about cancer. Not knowing is a type of purgatory.

Notice how a child clings when scared. We adults facing a pandemic, business closings, pre-existing health issues, and tax increases need reassurance and support, too. Once we know what we are dealing with, we can start coping, planning, and taking action, especially if we have help.

Our brains search for patterns. Neuroscientist David Rock explains that prediction is a primary function of our neocortex, and when our craving for certainty is met, there is a sensation of reward.[1] Many Americans admit to discounting and tuning out, especially when situations keep changing. We don't like ambiguity, uncertainty, and chaos, so offer phrases like:

*"Here's what to expect."*

*"What information do you need? I'd like to provide it."*

*"Here's what is known."*

*"Let me find out."*

Sometimes information must be held tight to the vest, leaving others anxious about their future. Because information reduces stress, if only so much is available for dispersal or too much is overwhelming, deliver frequent updates. Communicating a little at a time helps people feel more included, informed, and connected rather than left in the dark. Be frank and accurate.

## IF CAUGHT SURPRISED

Like humans who are uncertain, those caught surprised tend to drag their heels not knowing what is safe. Later, when hidden facts emerge, there is anger.

Get those you want to influence warmed up and ready just as a gardener loosens the soil, then plants and waters. Provide context and important background information so others become more comfortable changing their minds. Then, follow up with supporting data to grow those ideas. Fortunately experts and the legitimate press investigate for accuracy, supply information, and delve into back stories not clarified in brief sound bites.

Change initiators like executives and politicians often have been analyzing needs and planning action for a long time. They're much farther along in the change process. Unprepared constituents, employees, and friends feel stressed when they have to suddenly catch up, and their first reaction is usually "No."

Because insufficient support and too little guidance are roadblocks, minimize surprise. Get excellent ideas considered and implemented with:

*"Let me give you a little background."*

*"Step one would be_____ ."*

*"Support will come from_____ ."*

*"Here's what the process looks like."*

## IF CONCERNED ABOUT FAILURE

With concerns about their competence and fears about the future, some are reeling as they attempt to deal with a world they never imagined possible. A pandemic was thought to be science fiction. Just a few besides Bill Gates and George W. Bush saw it coming.[2][3]

Similarly, as technological advances and new energy sources permanently altered the American workplace, many didn't understand what was happening. Globalism shifted manufacturing to countries with lower labor costs. Mines were closed. Some had seen no reason to acquire skills for jobs outside those industries, while some made sure their kids did.

How could a sizable part of the American population not plan for our new global and technologically advanced economy? American ingenuity is our ticket for the future, but people fear it. Denial is normal. You might be tempted to shout, "Continuing to use bows and arrows after rifles and Colt 45s arrive on the scene means you'll be left behind—or wiped out!" However, you'll get further by asking:

*"What concerns do you have?"*

*"How can I help?"*

*"What training will you need?"*

If change asks for a different skill set, people question whether they can flourish in the new world. Respond to fears of failure with the medicine of empathy and support. People need skills, a realistic chance of success, and reassurance:

*"Here's what it takes. You really can do it."*

*"It will take work. Funding should help."*

*"Here's a way that can work."*

*"No denying, it's hard. You've handled some stuff like this before."*

*"We can do this—together."*

## IF THE RIPPLE EFFECT IS A DANGER

Fear of a specific change may actually be a general anxiety about what's next and what else may be ushered in along with it. For those worried about the ripple effect, hearing something like this may offer comfort:

*"Only for military style automatic weapons, not all guns."*

*"This is all that is proposed."*

*"Anything else requires your approval."*

## IF LOSING CONTROL IS THE PROBLEM

Though change is normal, Americans are dealing with change at warp speed. We resist both losing control and being out of control, which partially explains why people started stockpiling toilet paper. Purchasing a product is at least controlling something.

When our actions are voluntary instead of dictated, reasons to resist disappear. Our brains even release dopamine.[4] To help others handle something new, get them involved, help them see choices, and allow them to select their own route to a common goal. Getting to the destination is often far more important than which trail to take. Whenever possible, put the spotlight on what they *can* decide or implement. Seek their input, give them part of the project to manage, and place them in a driver's seat.

Parents are taught to handle situations with difficult toddlers and defiant teenagers by presenting options. Choices also help defensive Americans. Ask a toddler "Would you rather have daddy put you to bed or mommy tuck you in?"—choices you can live with— instead of "Do you want to go to bed?" Ask a teen "Would you rather clear the table or mow the lawn?" Ask an adult American:

*"Would you rather reduce spending or raise taxes?"*

*"Would you rather call or send an email to your senator?"*

*"Which is better—increasing the debt or decreasing spending on that?"*

*"Neither choice is great, but would you rather imprison drug users or fund treatment programs?"*

Ideally offer two acceptable actions instead of presenting a choice between action and no action. Because the first or last option mentioned is frequently chosen, you may increase the chance others will choose an idea you like by placing it last or emphasizing it with your voice tone.

Encouraging change involves preparing for resistance while proceeding as if you anticipate agreement. The psychological recommendation is "act as if." When your voice and behavior suggests that you expect agreement, you are more likely to get it. And, if you act as though you expect resistance, opposition is likely. Instead of inquiring "Can we make this happen?" you'll probably get farther by asking:

*"How can we make this work?"*

## IF THEY DON'T WANT TO LOSE FACE

Give people big enough reasons to counter resistance, because how much do you like owning that your past decisions and actions missed the mark? Democratic supporters loathe admitting that Hillary failed to provide the rust belt Americans with hope. Trump's base has trouble acknowledging how unpresidential he is—how he is abandoning decency, science, and truth. Agreeing with you may essentially mean, "I had it wrong," so work hard to minimize others' need to justify or protect their image.

If the new way of doing things involves admitting the old way they did things failed, face-saving could be causing resistance.

Honor the past before pointing out the present is different and requires a new approach:

> "_____ worked well when the situation was_____ . Now that we are facing_____ , we need_____ ."
>
> "We needed change in 2016, now we need stability."

Organizations that are merging or closing often have rituals, like funerals or retirement parties, where people gather to tell stories about how important the past was at the time, say good-bye, and usher in the new. After honoring the past, they paint a bright new future and symbolize the change with a slogan or new logo. America may need to follow suit.

## IF FIGHTING PAST FAILURES

If past change efforts were unsuccessful, people need extra convincing that your proposals will pay off. Attempts to prevent terrorism, improve healthcare, and stop illegal immigration have repeatedly had difficulty. Because people need to believe you are realistic rather than overconfident, investigate why previous approaches failed and, instead of defending, acknowledge:

> "That didn't work."
>
> "That taught us not to do that again."
>
> "That failed. What should have been done differently?"
>
> "Yes. We learned that didn't work. Let me show you what's different this time."

## IF FIGHTING RESENTMENTS

It's possible the Americans in the conversation may not reject the idea as much as reject the people advocating for it. You might be up against lack of trust and past resentments. Acknowledge that with:

*"Despite the fact that Trump suggested it, I think it's worth a try."*

*"Even though the idea comes from the other party, it has merit."*

## IF THERE IS PEER PRESSURE

Someone opposing you may be caving in to peer pressure—resisting because friends, family, and party members expect them to. Provide talking points to help fellow Americans explain the change to those who are actively rewarding them for resistance:

*"Would your friends see the merit in_____ ?"*

*"Earning their support is important. What do they need to hear?"*

*"I realize you're caught between supporting this as your conscience dictates and opposing it as your neighbors do. How can we get their support?"*

Because different strokes work for different folks, your challenge is to select the information best suited to their needs.

## WIN PEOPLE TO YOUR WAY OF THINKING

After studying human relations successes and critiquing more than 150,000 speeches, Dale Carnegie took 15 years to consolidate his recommendations. His sound advice for sales people, public speakers, leaders, and the rest of us includes these excellent ideas about how to win people over:

1. The only way to get the best of an argument is to avoid it.
2. Show respect for the other person's opinions. Never say, "You're wrong."
3. If you are wrong, admit it quickly and emphatically.
4. Begin in a friendly way.
5. Get the other person saying, "Yes, yes" immediately.
6. Let the other person do a great deal of the talking.
7. Let the other person feel that the idea is his or hers.

8. Try honestly to see things from the other person's point of view.

9. Be sympathetic with the other person's ideas and desires.

10. Appeal to nobler motives [like truth, justice, and the American way].

11. Dramatize your ideas [with compelling examples, metaphors, and stories].

12. Throw down a challenge [try it for a week, change ten neighbors' minds, find three areas of agreement].

## A STEP AT A TIME DEPENDING ON THE PERSON

Want change? Get others going in the right direction, one a step at a time. Start where they are—alongside them—rather than shouting at them to come to you.

With a *hostile* audience, set your sights on a little less hostility, not full support. Admitting to a minor weakness in your position can make the hostile audience a little less convinced an attack is necessary. Before advocating for your position, stress areas of agreement, build rapport, and show respect as much as possible. Acknowledge that your viewpoint isn't the only one possible, and use data from sources they consider credible. Ask them which sources they trust. To inch toward common ground—a more positive view of you and your ideas—plan to connect more than once.

With an *unfriendly* group, show you are fair and prove your supporting evidence is accurate. Listen, demonstrate you truly comprehend other sides of the issue, and point out any place you concur. State their position to their satisfaction. Only then carefully walk through your reasoning, describing where and why you differ. Ask them to consider or commit to something small. Easy does it.

To move *neutral* and *undecided* Americans, stress the link between your position and their needs and wants, steering clear of differing views when you can. No need to raise doubt that isn't there. Scrounge for common interests and common enemies to unite you, plus help them visualize improvements using great examples. Touch this group's heart even more than their head, and dare to draw stronger conclusions in your favor than you would with unfriendly folks. Undecideds are already a little closer. When you can, make small requests that they can agree to, so you have a foot in the door. Follow up, because when they hear arguments from others, they may reverse their allegiance.

The *uninformed* require that you point out your credibility and the facts supporting your side, but don't bury them in data. Clearly organize your thoughts, invite questions, and be ready to clarify. One-sided messages—mentioning your positives without mentioning the competing views—fit this occasion. It's time to stack the cards in your favor. Of course, offer evidence bolstering your view from sources they respect.

When blessed with a *supportive* listener, strengthen their commitment with vivid examples and testimonials, remind them they belong to your cause, and ask them to act as soon as possible. Because they are ambassadors, prepare them to counter those they will encounter who hold opposite views. The most important goal with actively supportive Americans is to keep them active and enlist their aid in encouraging others. Inspire them to be disciplined rather than militant by challenging them to keep their cool in this depolarizing effort.

## NEED EXTRA RESOURCES?

In the previous chapter about influence, there was guidance for inspiring others—for presenting only one-sided arguments supporting your view. Two-sided argumentation—debate by adding refutation of the "other side"—was outlined there too, along with how to modify your message to fit different personalities. Appendix 5 summarizes 20 research findings to answer, How are People

Influenced? Because we can also learn from how organizations implement change, check out Appendix 6.

## FIND EFFECTIVE TOOLS AND HEALING SALVE BY ASKING YOURSELF:

- What will show the status quo needs changing?
- What compelling vision will inspire change?
- How could you explain what's in it for them?
- Where do you agree?
- What might they misunderstand?
- What information do they need?
- How can you make what you want easier for them?
- What can they do to be involved?
- Which phrases and discussion starters are worth memorizing and using?

**Make change and transitions a little easier with:**
- **Reward for effort**
- **Information and clarification**
- **Guidance and training**
- **Involvement and choice**
- **Support and reassurance**
- **Respect for values and dignity**
- **Hope and confidence**

## IN SUMMARY

Understand why others are resisting, and then work to close the distance between their views and yours. Instead of threatening others' values, self-esteem, or power, give differing Americans a chance to

158

start experimenting with new ideas. Stop making them defend the status quo—or the past.

Let's minimize misunderstanding, fear, and uncertainty, so our differences get discussed on their merits over coffee or in committee. And, to overcome resistance, let's work to help Americans perceive that positive change is both possible and likely to be successful.

## CHAPTER 9

# Disagreeing Without Being Disagreeable

After a careful dinner discussion of widely different political perspectives, my dear neighbor emailed me what Thomas Jefferson had written to his political rival William Hamilton: "I never considered a difference of opinion in politics, in religion, in philosophy, as cause for withdrawing from a friend."[1] How wise. Even though sometimes we simply have to take issue with one another, Americans should be friends not enemies. Disagreeing is normal.

Finding common ground means moving from "I'm not talking to you!" to "I'm trying to understand." If we're skillful, our exchanges will up the chances others will switch from "Fine, I'm not listening!" to "I'm trying to understand, too."

I'm not talking to you!

Fine by me. I'm not listening!

I'm trying to understand.

Me too!

to

In the midst of contentious discussions, disagreeing without being disagreeable hinges on conspicuously displaying positive feelings as well as skillfully stitching and suturing. Affirm that the relationship is important. It is. Happiness relies on strong relationships and so does our democracy.

You want to preserve this tie, get this vote, and have Thanksgiving dinner with this relative. Besides, work teams, marriages, and communities prosper when different views get effectively combined into a greater whole, so dust off and perfect the use of advanced communication techniques to make a difference. Again, like other skills, they can be learned, practiced, and perfected.

Previous chapters offered ways to manage differences, strengthen relationships, be influential, and overcome resistance. You'll find 20 avoid-being-disagreeable emergency techniques in this one—hopefully you can adapt some to your own style and situation.

To successfully manage disagreement, technique, timing, and tone all matter. My daughters grew up out in the country next to real farmers and learned early that trying to catch feral kittens made them flee. If cornered, the critters would strike, and their claws were sharp. When the kids and I sat down, especially with something tasty in front of us, gradually the barn cats dared to approach, if we waited long enough. Success depended on making them feel safe, curious, and hungry.

Americans are already hungry for less division, so let's work on safety and curiosity—but we can't wait too long because this country is being led by the wrong person. Urgent action is required. Even grieving hasn't pulled us together.

## START SOFTLY

Trying to talk people out of their views only strengthens their resolve, so instead of forcing people to defend their position, begin by making discussion safe. You can disagree later if you choose.

Defensiveness is a huge roadblock to finding common ground. If I'm too busy protecting myself, I won't consider another point of view. Neither will you. Respectfully allowing others to voice their concerns, let off steam, and explain their perspective starts moving people toward each other.

Recall that relationship expert Gottman found "soft starts" reap great interpersonal results. We can discover what others think (and why) with gentle, open-ended questions that are either indirect or direct. Direct questions have a question mark at the end. *Indirect questions,* usually considered a little softer, end with a period:

> *"I'm interested in what you think about Trump."*
>
> *"Help me understand your views on Biden."*
>
> *"Tell me your take on how we're going to recover from the virus."*

Some open-ended *direct questions* are:

> *"What do you think about_____ ?"*
>
> *"How do you think that should be handled?"*

Open-ended prompts that get political conversations going are: what, how, tell me about, help me understand, and I'm interested in. The goal is to honestly learn and understand, not play gotcha. I'll bet you'd hold back, if you suspected an ambush, and so will they. Make it safe to talk.

Because the question "Why?" can seem accusatory, you're better off with:

*"Walk me through your thinking, so I can understand."*

*"Because I respect you, I'd like to understand your take on that."*

*"Valuing your opinion, I'm wondering what led you to that conclusion."*

Still, watch your tone. If you accidentally asked "Why?" and got a negative reaction, quickly add:

*"I'm just trying to understand."*

*"I'm not disagreeing, just trying to follow you."*

*"Only trying to figure out how you got there."*

## ACKNOWLEDGE

Once you've gotten the conversation started, the job is to listen, learn, and prove you're curious rather than prove you're right. These days most Americans aren't listening, they are reloading. Run the risk of being persuaded by another point of view, because as Ken Blanchard reminded us, "None of us is as smart as all of us."

Instead of "That's wrong," say and mean:

*"I'll give that some serious thought."*

*"That's worth considering."*

*"Oh, I hadn't seen it that way."*

*"Thanks for mentioning that."*

*"Let me think about that."*

*"I needed to hear that."*

Hopefully you've experienced others honestly trying to see your perspective on government size, candidates, health care, environmental regulations, guns, government debt, and the wall. You probably then, having been heard, found yourself more willing to examine their point of view.

Nod, smile, and grunt appropriately. Pause and give serious thought to why—either emotionally or logically—those Americans hold those opinions, so you can answer their concerns and head for an inch of common ground. They have a reason.

Agreeing with their opinions is certainly not required, but please show you are trying to understand them. Why should they listen to you, if you haven't listened to them? More than a simple summary, the tool *paraphrasing with empathy* proves you were listening to their views and to the emotions connected to them. Skillfully, slowly, and gently reflect thoughts and feelings with slightly less emotion than they were expressed:

> *"You're concerned about losing second amendment rights."*
>
> *"Bloomberg's stop-and-frisk policy really turned you off."*
>
> *"If I understood correctly, funding abortion is tough for you."*
>
> *"You were fired up about Buttigieg. Help me understand why."*

Proceed cautiously. An attempt to appropriately convey respect for both their feelings and thoughts can quickly seem condescending, if our non-verbals either fall short *or* exceed the intensity of theirs. Voice, face, and body alter the message. Too matter-of-fact comes across as disinterest, while too much emotion seems ridiculous—or like ridicule.

Because summarizing and reflecting feelings frequently misses the mark, when others are emotional, even trained therapists often fall back on a safe and simple:

> *"Ouch" or "Oh" or "Hmmm" or "Wow."*

Social psychology evidence suggests that repeating the exact words used by the other person generates good results, even though it fails to reveal how you interpreted what they said. Echoing or mirroring has been shown to increase trust and help people reach win/win solutions (67% v. 12.5% of the time).[2] Food servers who repeated an order word for word got much bigger tips than those who answered "okay!" or "coming up."[3] People want us to listen carefully.

Exact repetition removes the dangers of understating, overstating, and selecting the wrong word. When paraphrasing you may intend to signal understanding when saying, "That upset you," the person may in frustration react, "No, I'm ANGRY not upset!!" The successful echo falls somewhere along the tightrope between mere parroting and falling off the cliff.

## CLARIFY

Gently asking other Americans to clarify increases the chances of greater understanding between you. Plus, if you demonstrate and model curiosity, they hopefully will reciprocate. When others say, "Trump is doing what he promised," or "All Republicans are plain ignorant," inquire further:

> *"Help me understand what you mean."*
>
> *"Please give me an example."*
>
> *"I'm confused about your conclusion that Trump handled Covid-19 well."*

Don't confront right away. Wait 'til safety ropes are in place. Again, the implied tone or direct phrase "I'm not disagreeing, just trying to understand" is crucial at a point of friction. Back up when they seem to feel cornered, so they don't have to defend. And, if you start to lose it, pull out the tools from the upcoming "Getting Off the Defensive" chapter. Once everyone is back on track, you can compare ideas.

If they haven't shown interest in your perspectives, ask if they'd like you to clarify:

> *"Can I give you an example of what I mean?"*

## AGREE AND SIDESTEP WHEREVER YOU CAN

With the goal of getting closer, point out where you concur. Similarities pull people together, so when possible and accurate, mention:

*"We both want protection for the Dreamers."*

*"Like you, I care about safety."*

*"We agree there should be less campaign spending."*

*"Sounds like we all think bipartisanship is important."*

*"We agree on_____ and_____ . The only place we differ is how to get there."*

Hearing "yes" is almost magic to our ears, so hunt for opportunities to say:

*"Yes."*

*"Of course."*

*"Sure."*

*"Makes sense to me."*

*"You have a point."*

Even surface agreement can keep discussions from turning ugly. I frequently rely on the fogging phrase "It might look that way" described in more detail in the next chapter "Getting off the Defensive."

Though we could dodge a bullet, time and again partners, political rivals, and others would rather be right than get along. Instead of devoting emotional capital to proving the "other side" wrong, sidestep. Letting them save face instead of eat crow may make the difference in getting a bill passed, a desirable candidate selected, or a budget item approved.

If you elect to avoid a side issue, some ways to return to the main point are:

*"I'm still thinking about_____ ."*

*"Let's spend more time on_____ ."*

*"Can we go back to_____ ?"*

To let go and focus on priorities, you might ask yourself: How important will this be in 10 minutes, days, months, or years?[4] Sometimes we just need to tolerate something for 10 minutes.

## SHIFT WITH "FEEL, FELT, FOUND"

Traffic lights go from the cautionary yellow to red to green. With caution set a good tone, then stop—red light—and show you've heard, and *only* after that proceed to express yourself well—green light. The sequence "Feel, felt, found" starts with nodding and acknowledgement, then adds social proof and agreement, then finally introduces a different perspective. Here's what it looks like:

*"You feel_____ , right?"*

*"Many people felt that way until they found_____ ."*

OR

*"I felt that way. [nodding] When I found_____ , I changed my mind."*

## USE "I" STATEMENTS

When you want to collaboratively assert yourself, "I" can have a positive effect. Working with angry couples and families, therapists often witness the word "you" sparking a defensive response, so they encourage "I" statements. Consultants do the same in workplace interactions. So, for a better result, the recommendation is replace "You're wrong" with:

*"Wow, I see it differently."*

When your goal is showing you recognize others may have a different perspective, putting the word "I," "me," or "my" in a sentence serves to personalize the message, take responsibility, and soften the blow.

Even *"I* think you're wrong"—with the "I" emphasized—gets someone farther than "You're wrong," since it suggests more than one view is possible. Punch the "I," so "I" rather than "you" gets heard. Or, make a quick shift from "you said" to "I believe you said" to de-escalate a situation. Some more options are:

*"Oh, it looks different to me."*

*"From my perspective, that's not accurate, but maybe I've missed something."*

*"My understanding is_____ ."*

"You statements" take us down the rabbit hole of attacking people who state differing views. Instead, at home, at work, and in your community, offer your perspective while demonstrating a willingness to examine theirs.

Waiters and waitresses must have learned the dangers of "you," because I hear them ask, "What are we having for dessert?" Nurses notoriously announce, "It's time for our bath," even though they aren't partaking. They seem hesitant to say "you," just as we collaborative Americans need to be—unless it's time to grab attention as the World War II poster "America Needs YOU" did.

If we slip up when discussing controversial issues, adding "I," "me," or "my" at the end of a sentence can fortunately reduce the sting. Calm things down with an emphasis on "me" or "my" plus an accompanying voice tone shift to sound more open-minded. Tools for back pedaling from "You're wrong!" include:

*"... at least that's the way it looks to me."*

*"... from my perspective."*

*"... as I see it."*

Using "but" can also decrease some heartburn:

*"You're wrong, BUT that's just one view."*

## REMEMBER "BUT" IS AN ERASER

"But" has been called the giant eraser, eliminating what was previously said. The word is useful when you want a delete button and dangerous when you don't. Think of when you heard someone start with a compliment and suspected a "but" coming. The compliment seemed manipulative, so you probably didn't tune in until you heard that "but."

Too many of us have the "yes, but" habit—negating "yes" with "but." For example, "Yes, Trump changed the tax code, but that mostly gave tax benefits to the rich" fails to feel good to those who are on the fence or want him reelected. When you want *both* pieces of your sentence to hit home, delete "but." "Yes, Trump changed the tax code. (pause) What I'm having trouble with is that the change mostly gave tax benefits to the rich."

"Yes, I should have said that differently, BUT what I said is true!" nullifies your apology, so here's another example of avoiding "yes, but":

*"I should have said that differently. (pause) I'll work on saying it better, so people can hear those facts. I think they're important."*

Commas serve as a short pause, so a comma followed by "but" hurries the listener to the second idea. To avoid invalidating your first thought, use a period—which is a full stop and pause—and let that first comment settle in before moving on.

Once people have absorbed idea number one, some skilled senders start a whole new sentence; others insert "and"—avoiding "but"—before continuing. Both work. The other option looks like:

> *"I should have said that differently, and I'll work on saying it better, so people can hear those facts. I think they're important."*

Like the add-on phrase, "just a thought," when you urgently *wish* you had a delete button, "but" is a handy tool:

> *"I think you're way off base ... but I may not have all the facts."*

## SAY WHAT YOU REALLY WANT TO SAY— ABOUT THE *ISSUE,* NOT THEM

Describe your goals, views, values, desires, and approaches rather than voicing judgments about the Americans who hold differing ones. Talking about what you are trying to accomplish is more likely to spark a good response than an attack on your opponent will. It's possible to be tough on issues and nice on people.

So, replace outrage or an impulsive "Where on earth did you come up with that?! You (Republicans, Democrats, bigots, feminists, chauvinists, etc.) are all____ !" with an even-tempered disclosure or description of your political leanings:

> *"I'm hoping to reduce health costs."*
>
> *"I'm trying to find a way to be sure everyone has health care coverage."*
>
> *"The coalition is striving to give people health care options."*

People love explanations, so even though you can't imagine why they don't understand, explain. Your fellow Americans may have been tuning out. Grab their attention with:

*"My goal is_____ ."*

*"My intentions are_____ ."*

*"Having had success with something similar, I think it's worth a try."*

*"From_____ I've learned_____ ."*

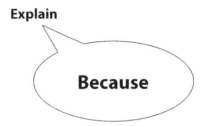

**Explain**

**Because**

## ADD "BECAUSE"

Because people will be inferring your motives—sometimes incorrectly—frequently pull from your interpersonal survival kit the word "because," because it works a bit like magic. We adults repeatedly wonder "Why?" though not out loud as often as children do, and we respond better when we understand the context and backstory for a request. Knowing why, it's much easier to comply.

Because analyzed responses differ from automatic ones, encourage people to think before deciding, acting, talking, and voting. Unless aware, our cognitive biases—our mental habits—have us deny, resist, and reach faulty conclusions. Emotions cause the same kind of trouble.

Most of us run away from rather than toward danger and don't help, until empathy kicks in. Our first responders, military, and amazing health care workers run toward—partly because of their nature, partly because they were trained, and partly because they've decided to. Help people reach good decisions by shining the light on good reasons.

To inch toward agreement with differing Americans, try some softly spoken expressions that include the word "because":

*"I'm surprised to hear you say that, because we both want _____ ."*

*"Because we both value _____ , your comment caught me off guard."*

*"Because we care about_____ , I thought we'd agree on_____ ."*

## REPEAT A CONCISE POINT

Despite good intentions, the longer we talk the more likely we are to lose our cool or lose our nerve. We may begin well with a reasonable statement like, "I think this might work" and within seconds we're saying, "And there's *NO* other option, it *has* to be this way! Only an idiot would fail to see that!"

Or, a calm "I'd suggest that we handle it this way," becomes "Well, it's, um, just an idea," "It probably won't work," and "Oh, never mind." Without being blunt or curt, remain focused on your main point and keep it simple. Fortunately, a concise message makes maintaining self-control easier.

Here's a time to emulate children. Kids are amazingly persistent and successful in getting what they want. They ask, we say no. They ask again, we refuse again. They continue, continue, and continue, and we give in. However, collaborative adult Americans need to repeat without whining, pleading, or yelling.

Simply state your well-phrased point. If they haven't agreed, in a relaxed, friendly yet firm fashion say it again. If you can remember that far back, act like a broken record that repeats without getting louder, attacking, or name calling. So, if the first message doesn't get the desired result, say it again and even again:

*"Here's what I think might work."* → *"I believe this could be done."*
   → *"I'm convinced it's worth considering."*

The words become slightly stronger, so the vocal tones need not. Masterful folks using this approach sound just as reasonable and nice each time they present the idea.

Or, if you have difficulty keeping the intensity out of your voice, repeat the same *exact* words as pleasantly as you said them the first time. Having an exact script helps those of us who aren't great off the cuff—allowing us to work exclusively on delivery.

Children have proven that persistence works, so just stay on point and hang in there. Depending on what's needed, you can repeat the same words or have some variation (slight word or voice change). An exact repetition typically sounds stronger, while a varied one seems more reasonable and less close-minded.

## HARNESS THE POWER OF POSITIVE WORDS

You've noticed that the way a picture is framed affects how it looks, and the same is true with messages. When genuine, "we" is a powerful hook signaling belonging. Use the pronoun "we" to link to others in and out of your immediate tribe—and to avoid too much "I," which claims undue credit and fails to include. Yes, "I" is frequently safer than "you," but a real "we" is great medicine.

Church leaders, military officers, committee chairs, and business managers are taught to use "we" to emphasize team involvement. However, many on their staff feel manipulated when the boss uses that word too broadly. "How are we going to fix this?" too often is heard as "How are YOU going to fix this?" If in doubt, try:

*"How are we, meaning both you **AND** I, going to fix this?"*

Be certain those across the divide perceive that you are including yourself, if you are. At the end of a tough business travel day, the hotel clerk checking me in inquired, "And, how are we going to pay for this room tonight?" My quick retort was, "Let's use *your* credit card." That night I'd lost patience with the manipulative "we." Many Americans have, so tread cautiously.

Besides the correct pronoun, select other positive words from customer service professionals' toolboxes. "I *get* to" sounds quite different from "I have to," *"My pleasure"* outperforms "No problem." If there is only one option, it's the *"best option."*

Be positive as you announce the limits you face. "I *can* do it Wednesday" sounds more agreeable than "I can't until Wednesday." With energy in your voice coupled with a smile or nod, turn "can't" into "can" and "won't" into "will":

> *"I can agree here."*
>
> *"I will go this far."*
>
> *"I'd suggest_____ ."*
>
> *"The best option is_____ ."*

## GIVE IN FANTASY

Authors Adele Faber and Elaine Mazlish taught me to give in fantasy what you can't give in reality.[5] Too often we lack the power to deliver what other people want. When you indicate you wish you could give them their heart's desire, they realize at least you understand and care. What does that sound like?

> *"I wish there was enough in the budget to do both."*

*"I wish we had votes for that."*

*"I wish I were at liberty to disclose that information now."*

*"I wish I could tell you that would work."*

*"I wish we had enough personal protection equipment."*

*"I wish there were enough accurate tests."*

When not said flippantly, *"If I had a magic wand, I'd make that happen"* is a handy variation.

That wise dentist of mine saw me wince while in his chair and asked if I was okay. When I explained that I was conditioned—I automatically responded like one of Pavlov's dogs—to be afraid at the sound of a dental drill, he kindly and gently applied salve with his words, "I wish that weren't the case." Often we wish it weren't that way. Go ahead and say it.

## WATCH YOUR NONVERBAL BEHAVIOR

As you know, much of what we communicate in difficult conversations is nonverbal. Our voice tone, pitch, volume, inflection, speed, and pauses alter the word message, making us sound more or less disagreeable. How much better the message is received when voice tones are respectful and informative rather than arrogant or condescending. With your relative and neighbor, sound as if you anticipate some common ground rather than suggesting with your voice that you expect a fight. Otherwise you'll likely get one.

One of my clients was leading a team in the middle of a difficult transition, and almost every message she brought the group was something they didn't want to hear. Afraid of their reaction, her delivery became worse and worse. Looking for something that might help, I asked if she had a friend or sibling who didn't always agree with her yet would give her a fair hearing. She said her sister Margaret would. When asked to pretend she was giving the information to Margaret instead of the team, her voice and demeanor dramatically changed. With her team she then switched to imagining she was speaking with her sis, and receptivity improved a lot. Because it works, I've often coached clients and myself to "Sound like you like them."

We can also appear more approachable by making ourselves look less poised to attack. Drop your shoulders, sit down, lean back, and decrease the observed tension in your face and arm muscles. Try backing up or turning slightly away. Basically, think of how a posturing gorilla would act and do the opposite, unless you desperately need to be seen as stronger at that moment.

Your attire can shift the tone, too, and that's an easy way to change an interpersonal climate. One of my clients who grew up fighting in the streets of her NY neighborhood came on too strong for her Midwest coworkers. While practicing hard to appear more collaborative, she found it easy to start wearing softer colors and flowing fabrics. Controlling her tendency to move as if she were ready to punch someone was admittedly more difficult. She rehearsed flopping her wrists and lowering her shoulder to avoid looking like she had a chip on it. All those efforts did help others work with her more willingly.

When wanting to be taken more seriously, people usually dial up the eye contact and make it more direct. However, too direct can appear disagreeable. Experimenting with this power strategy with a tame monkey in the Caribbean got me immediately bitten. My perceived aggression triggered his. Be careful with alpha-type dogs and humans, too. Depending on the circumstances, "dim the lights."

When you don't have to protectively social distance to avoid the virus, remember proxemics—interpersonal distance—affects relationships. Less space between you and others on the street or in a conversation can signal either intimacy or aggression. Turning our faces away and staying at least six feet apart might be taken as shunning the Americans we encounter on the street or in the grocery line. We're being challenged to find ways to show warmth while connecting safely.

Of course, be alert to regional and cultural preferences, so you send the agreeable message you intend. In a classic experiment, E. T. Hall put a north American and a south American in a 40 foot hallway. The South American moved in and the North American backed up, all the way down the hall. When asked their perceptions, the South American said the North American was "cold," and the North American perceived his South American counterpart to be "pushy." Reducing the physical space between you and others might signal liking, yet it can be inappropriate and uncomfortable, so be safe by monitoring how others react.

If things are tense, changing your behavior can change your mood—and theirs. If people smile and act happy, they do start to feel happy.[6] Interestingly, Botox's impact on facial muscles has been shown to both positively and negatively affect people's mood.[7] Smiling actually produces a biochemical change in the brain,[8] and you can seem more cooperative and reasonable by putting a genuine smile in your voice, on your face, and in your eyes.

A sincere smile includes crinkling around the eyes and can even be visible when someone's wearing a protective face mask. Without those wrinkles the smile can almost be a sneer. Organizations purposefully install mirrors in customer service cubicles to encourage employees to smile at themselves, so the smile will be sent through the phone line. Notice how you smile, relax, and feel better when other Americans smile, so use that emergency medicine to increase agreeableness.

Nervous about a political chat? "Fake it until you make it" actually is decent advice, since confident gestures, pace, and posture make people both appear and feel more confident. Behave in a confident way and check your speed, and you'll start to feel comfortable. Hopefully others will too.

Behaving as if agreement is possible makes us more likable, so even you don't feel the love yet, optimistically act like you expect other Americans will go along:

*"What should we try?"*

*"When can we start?"*

*"Let's do this much."*

Because recorded practice has helped many (including the New Yorker be less threatening and the manager bear bad tidings), try watching yourself on video to check and correct your nonverbal impact.

## PICK THE BEST COMMUNICATION CHANNEL

Should we disagree face-to-face, by phone, or via emails, texts, and printed material? It depends. Disagreeing agreeably usually happens face-to-face. Now, thanks to technology, we can see each other electronically even though it's not quite the same.

Written messages allow careful wordsmithing, feel safer for many senders, and are convenient. However, misunderstanding is a big risk with one-way communication, even with emoticons added.

Evidence also indicates written is less persuasive. People are more likely, 34 times more likely in one study, to comply with requests made in person than via email.[9] You may be able to reach someone via text or email who won't yet be willing to pick up the phone or meet you for lunch, however when others misinterpret a word or miss a nuance, a text-only exchange quickly and often sparks resistance without the sender even knowing things are amiss.

We're less agreeable and less inhibited the farther away we are. As the *America in One Room* participants (see chapter 4) confirmed, it's harder to hate up close. Hate mail and vicious, bullying messages are often sent anonymously. What people say behind your back, via tweet, or even over the phone is usually worse than what they will say to your face. People being fired feel less empathy via tweet than when the boss struggles to tell them in person.

Ear-to-ear communication supplies information from voice tone, inflection, pitch, and volume, while interacting face-to-face adds even more—eye contact, facial expressions, interpersonal distance, and posture. Most importantly, phone and in-person discussions allow us to clarify, convey feeling, and prevent a misunderstanding from escalating. Unfortunately, most of us overestimate the persuasiveness of our text-based communication or hide behind it.

Because face-to-face communication builds trust, it's considered essential for repairing strained relationships. Spend time together to bring people together. When the stakes are high, don't replace face-to-face. Of course, a phone or in-person conversation can be followed up or preceded by a written summary, so choosing a communication method is not an either-or situation. Want some guidelines?

## USE ORAL (FACE-TO-FACE, EAR-TO-EAR, OR INTERACTIVE VIDEO) COMMUNICATION WHEN:

- emotions are high
- you want to persuade or convince
- receivers are not particularly interested
- getting feedback is important
- receivers may feel judged
- discussion is needed
- receivers are too busy or preoccupied to read
- receivers can't read your language
- oral is more natural

## USE WRITTEN (EMAIL, TEXT, OR PRINTED) COMMUNICATION WHEN:

- you want a record for future reference
- receivers will be referring to it later
- messages are complex and require study
- messages include a needed step-by-step procedure
- a copy of the message should go to other people
- interaction delay is okay

## WATCH FOR WARNING SIGNS

Too often we get caught up in the situation and miss the warning signs that the discussion is going off track until far into the muck. To our demise, we don't catch they are looking away, interrupting, trying to change the topic, or getting increasingly emotional. Somehow we miss the glare, stare, shouting, pouting, and even pacifying behaviors. We fail to notice how long it's been since others texted or emailed back.

Daniel Goleman spread the word that "emotional intelligence"—the ability to read and regulate our own emotions as well as those of others—is vital to career, interpersonal, business, and political success.[10] EQ upstages IQ. A brilliant chief resident who couldn't get along with the team proved that to me.

The good news is that the four emotional competencies can be learned. We can get better at noticing our emotions, noticing others' feelings, reining in our reactions, and developing people skills (the bottom right quadrant) which include disagreeing without relationship damage.

|  | Self | Other |
|---|---|---|
| recognition | **Self awareness** | **Empathy** |
| regulation | **Self management** | **Social skills** |

Goleman

Watch yourself in the middle of a contentious interaction and see if a quick change is needed. Coach yourself by asking: How are they doing with my comments? What do they want to hear? What will make my ideas seem more compatible with what they think and believe? How can I bring that up another way?

## USE THOUGHT TRANSFERENCE AND INCOMPLETE SENTENCES

Socrates and Ferdinand Fournies, whose *Coaching for Improved Work Performance* sold more than a million copies,[11] used powerful questions to lead others to think the way they wanted. We can do the same.

Ask questions so that when people answer, *they* are saying the very thing you wanted to tell them. To get an idea from your head to theirs, use the right questions. When they respond, they'll be listening to themselves—not you—and be less likely to disagree with the idea.

With this thought transmission technique, you're spared having to point out something they may not like. For example, if your arrogant coalition partner Jack comes on too strong, spark that idea in his head with:

*"How did Karly respond when you said that?"* or

*"What was Karly's response when you said it that way?"*

Hopefully, Jack will realize Karly rolled her eyes, stiffened her body, and stopped listening, so he sees a reason to alter his message and/or delivery style.

When you'd like Emma to consider another view, ask:

*"What would someone from an urban area say if you suggested that?"*

*"How would a millennial take that recommendation?"*

*"What does that sound like to an American of Chinese descent?"*

Instead of you having to say "You'd be shot or written off," Emma will say it for you. Thought transference is a less risky alternative to direct feedback. However, if others sense you are trying to lead them, admit it so they don't feel manipulated:

*"What am I hoping you'll say?"*

*"What was I trying to get you to consider?"*

Incomplete sentences do essentially the same thing—encourage someone to say or think what you'd_____ . Trump has used this intimate, conversational fill-in-the-gaps style to his advantage. As linguist George Lakoff explains, finishing others' sentences for them is a natural part of conversation, especially for a New Yorker. With a raised eyebrow or a shrug Trump vaguely implies, thereby allowing his audience to reach their own conclusions. "People walk away from Trump feeling as though he were casually talking to them, allowing them to finish his thoughts."[12]

**"Thought transference"**

Your behavior irritates others

- "What happens when you do that?"
- "How did Mary react?"
- "What were the consequences?"
- "What effect did that have on the meeting?"

## APOLOGIZE

The relationship repair tool apology is mentioned again in this chapter, because many people won't hear you until you acknowledge a blunder. Just as a large number of Americans have never forgiven Bill Clinton for putting the country through impeachment proceedings over his scandal with Monica Lewinsky, a whole bunch wait for Trump to apologize for downplaying the pandemic and making scathing remarks about women, journalists, war veterans, people of color, and so on.

Political discussions today are ripe opportunities for making amends. When you realize an error or see you've come on too strong, these words might help:

*"I misspoke."*

*"I shouldn't have said that. I'm sorry."*

Admitting your position or tribe is less than perfect invites others to do the same.

*"Democrats can come across too concerned about political correctness."*

*"Republicans can seem like they dismiss science."*

## PRESENT YOUR VIEW AS AN ALTERNATIVE (BUT NOT AS "ALTERNATIVE FACTS")

Lack of trust and abundance of misinformation makes accuracy especially important these days. Be careful to have accurate facts from credible sources when disagreeing with other Americans, and encourage them to consider your different ideas with phrases like:

*"Here's another way to look at it."*

*"Here are the facts as I know them."*

*"Wondering about that, I carefully checked and found_____ ."*

For example, there is no evidence of widespread voter fraud that deprived Trump of the popular vote in 2016, but he made unfounded claims about it for months, talked about the possibility before that election, and devoted resources to try to prove his point. If the person you're speaking with raises that issue, you might delicately mention:

*"The Washington Post reported that by Trump's definition of fraud, one of his top aides Stephen K. Bannon, one of his daughters Tiffany Trump, and Treasury Secretary Steve Mnuchin would be guilty. In 2016 all three were registered to vote in two different states. I doubt the three of them were trying to manipulate the election by voting in both states. Most inaccurate voter rolls are due to deaths and failure to notify when people move, so I don't see it as an evil scheme to rig the system by a large number of illegal immigrants in the country."*

We can help America by appropriately digging for and reporting facts, even though we're up against confirmation bias discussed back in chapter 3.

## KNOW WHEN TO QUIT

When should you quit? Before it's too late, but that's not much of an answer. Quit on a positive note. Live to fight another day by leaving the relationship sufficiently intact and your cause unblemished. Disagreeing without being disagreeable may mean ending with:

> *"I'll give your perspective some thought."*
>
> *"We agree on_____ , and differ on_____ . Do we need to leave it there for now?"*

Sometimes you do.

## AVOID TRIGGERING DEFENSIVENESS

The biggest barrier that I've seen to relationships at home, work, or across the aisle is defensiveness. When on defense, people are too busy protecting themselves to understand others' positions, explore options, creatively converge on a good approach, or collaborate to get something implemented. With politicians and the media too often fanning the flames of fear and hate, reducing defensiveness has become urgent.

In his classic article, which profoundly altered my professional and personal relationships, Jack Gibb listed the behaviors that trigger defensiveness and described ways to create a supportive, non-defensive climate:[13]

| DEFENSIVE AROUSING | SUPPORTIVE |
|:---:|:---:|
| Evaluation | Description |
| Control | Problem Orientation |
| Strategy | Spontaneity |
| Neutrality | Empathy |
| Superiority | Equality |
| Certainty | Provisionalism |

On the left is relationship poison. On the right, the antidote and path to depolarization.

Most of us have evaluation anxiety and a strong dislike for being judged. We defend ourselves against sneers, labels like "loser," and people sitting as judge and jury. In contrast, **describing** with "I" language reduces emotional reactions. "I noticed it was 9:15 on the clock when the meeting began" sounds different than "You were late." Describe and report as a camera would. Cameras don't know if 9:15 was late for a 9:00 start or early for a 9:30 one. To agreeably lower defensiveness use description instead of judgment.

Being controlled inflames many of us Americans, so telling people, "You HAVE to" and restricting their choices generates pushback. Instead of forcing a position, what a difference when people adopt a supportive **problem-solving** stanch and ask, "How can this be solved?"

Attacking problems, not one another, is the path to reducing defensiveness and to principled negotiation. I've been pleasantly surprised to see how quickly the climate changes when the problem is written on a sheet of paper or flipchart and folks take aim at it instead of each other.

By "strategy" Gibb meant manipulating, and by "spontaneity" he meant being free of deception. We can't be totally spontaneous in this culture without getting arrested, but what we do and say can be honest. Being **genuine**, open, and transparent makes us trustworthy; deceit has the opposite effect. We work to defend and protect ourselves when we believe others are trying to trick us.

If you want to unnerve someone, act as neutral and unconcerned as a stone wall or robot. Your coldness, indifference, and disinterest signal how much you find them unimportant and how little you can be counted on. In contrast, **warmth and empathy** signal caring and draw people together. When someone is upset, a response that is too neutral inflames rather than douses emotions, because it comes across as unaware of the severity of the situation. It sparks a "I'll have to scream louder to impress you with the problem" response or a "You'll never understand" one. To show empathy and calm them down, begin with some intensity that almost mirrors or matches theirs, then gradually lower the emotional level, and hope they follow. Start where they are.

Acting condescending and superior quickly provokes others to defend themselves. In a supportive climate, people may not be identical in terms of knowledge or skill, but they are treated as worthy and **equally** valuable. Showing respect creates a non-defensive political climate. People want to be heard and taken seriously. I can more easily consider your views, if they aren't shoved down my throat.

Certainty, the final defensive-arousing climate factor, is like putting your hands over your ears. When we have strong opinions, remaining open-minded instead of dogmatic isn't easy. Gibb used the term **provisional** to remind us to hold our views open to revision and new information.

So, the recipe for defensive disaster is to be judging, controlling, manipulative, cold, superior, and closed-minded. When, instead, you want to be supportive, describe problems and differences in a genuine, warm, respectful, open-minded way, and you'll be hard to resist. Avoiding defensiveness is far easier than reducing it.

## BRIEF EMERGENCY KIT DIRECTIONS:

1. Start softly
2. Acknowledge
3. Clarify
4. Agree and side step
5. Shift with feel, felt, found
6. Use "I statements"
7. Remember "but" is an eraser
8. Say what you really want to say—about the issue

9. Add "because"
10. Repeat a concise point
11. Harness the power of positive words
12. Give in fantasy—"I wish"
13. Watch your nonverbal behavior
14. Pick the best communication channel
15. Watch for warning signs
16. Use thought transference and incomplete sentences
17. Apologize
18. Present your view as an alternative
19. Know when to quit
20. Avoid triggering defensiveness

Of all the ways to disagree without being disagreeable, these are my favorites:

- **Act like you like them**—"This relationship is important."
- **Point out agreement**—"We agree here and here."
- **Explain intentions**—"What I'm trying to do is_____ ."
- **Discuss alternatives**—"Here's another way to look at it."
- **Give in fantasy**—"I wish we saw it the same way."

Which will help *you* disagree without being disagreeable?

In the next chapters (Part Three) the focus shifts to you—how you can get off the defensive, cope with the stress of now, and find hope.

PART THREE

# Changing Ourselves

# CHAPTER 10 — Getting Off the Defensive

In politically charged conversations, most of us need more self-control and thicker skin so that we aren't adding to the problem. Fortunately with practice, people become more aware, and then better at keeping their cool under fire. For example, trained firefighters report that time on the job gives them a sense of which way to turn when entering a burning building.[1]

These days most of us need some PPE—personal protective equipment. Put some on.

Try this step-by-step sequence for managing your own defensiveness and be on alert because defensiveness is contagious:

**Getting Off the Defensive**
1. Recognize warning signs
2. Stop
3. Buy time
4. Analyze threat
5. Self-talk
6. Relax
7. Listen
8. Respond

## STEP 1: RECOGNIZE WARNING SIGNS

Pay attention to what you do, feel, and say when you are defensive. The amygdala has been called the brain's sentinel or smoke detector, standing guard and triggering an alarm that activates our physiological responses. Notice when it's on alert. These physiological and behavioral changes serve as warning signs protecting against harm, and learning to read them makes us emotionally intelligent. The sooner we detect our automatic fear reactions, the faster we can avoid being emotionally "hijacked" or saying something we'll regret later.

The body reacts instantaneously, readying us for action rather than thought. Blood pumps away from other parts of the body to our muscles, preparing us to attack or run with more strength and speed. Changes in breathing rate, blood pressure, heart rate, and blood sugars supply our bodies with extra energy in the anticipation of a battle or marathon flight. The body's blood clotting function actually speeds up to prevent excessive blood loss in case of injury.

When feeling threatened, some of us respond with dominance. We increase eye contact, focus, talk louder, lower the pitch, and tense our muscles in preparation to strike. Like lower animals, we posture, make ourselves bigger, stride farther, lean forward, and gesture loudly. Our breathing rate changes. We sweat. We use accusatory language, throw in "always" and "never," and stop smiling.

In contrast, some of us flee, withdraw, or even freeze. We speak quietly or not at all, look down, and seek to be invisible. Some of us flush, some fidget, some give in. Our submissiveness is another signal that we feel a need to defend and protect ourselves. You might show dominant defensiveness in some situations and submissive defensiveness at other times.

Others can read our behavior, and so can we, if we're mindful. Children astutely tell their siblings, "This isn't the time to bring this up with Mom," and co-workers give similar advice about approaching a boss or colleague. Typically, people who know us well can describe how we behave when our shield is out or sword is drawn. To become more aware of your defensive warning cues, ask them.

Like roadway signs indicating a sharp turn or rocks ahead, warnings help us change direction, slow down, and avoid catastrophe. Walking home after teaching a night class, at some level I sensed something was amiss. Each Wednesday that semester I passed a high hedge. This particular spring evening I walked farther from the bushes than normal, so when a guy jumped out and grabbed me, he didn't get a great hold. I whipped around, grabbed him back with every fingernail available, and in my loudest professorial voice demanded, "What do you think you're doing?!" I hadn't scripted that. Grad school had taught me to listen to my own internal warning signs, and thankfully that night I did.

Feelings and intuition are useful information, a type of "knowing before you know." Safety expert Gavin de Becker, author of *The Gift of Fear: Survival Signals That Protect us from Violence,* encourages people to trust their instincts that alert us to danger, because doing so may keep us from stepping into dangerous situations.[2] We need to trust our guts along with facts and guidance.

Fear is innate yet also a result of conditioning. Political topics are frequently paired with hostility these days, and just like Pavlov's dogs who learned to salivate at the sound of a bell associated with food, Americans tense at the mention of the Trump administration—especially if they don't know the political leanings of the other person. Pay attention to when you are readying for an attack. Defensiveness triggers defensiveness.

## STEP 2: STOP

The moment you recognize your defensive programming has taken over, stop doing what you're doing. People don't plan to be defensive—it's an automatic response to real or perceived threat. Information from our senses reaches the amygdala before arriving at the neocortex, the thinking brain. By noticing and interrupting the programmed emotional response, you give yourself a chance to compose yourself, think about what's happening, and select a course of action.

Some of my executive coaching clients heading into difficult meetings ask someone in the room to give them a time-out signal if they see defensive behavior. Others signal themselves to stop—by placing a ring on a finger that normally doesn't have one or a colorful, blank, post-it note on the table. Reminders to cease and desist are useful.

## STEP 3: BUY SOME TIME

Time helps settle us down and lets us think. Our brain's neocortex, which governs most emotional responses, has an on-off switch in the left prefrontal lobe, but it responds more slowly than the amygdala. We react first, think second. Having a habitual way of buying time, like a scripted coping response of what to say or do, can significantly decrease disastrous reactions.

In front of a large television audience presidential candidate Pete Buttigieg skillfully avoided getting hooked by answering, "I'm not a master fisherman, but I know bait when I see it."[3] No doubt he'd planned that reply. What are some other approaches you might have in your survival kit?

When someone pushes your buttons, push your own pause button, count to at least 10, and give yourself time to restore your emotional equilibrium. Mark Twain wisely said, "The right word might be effective, but no word was ever as effective as a rightly timed pause." Think of this as duct tape in your survival kit. Using a buying-time habit is like going on auto-pilot. And, with a practiced stalling technique, we get time to analyze the threat and coach ourselves to a good response.

Psychologically, it is easier to start an action than interrupt one. Keep yourself from saying something you'll regret by removing yourself—taking a break, rescheduling, or telling those on the other end of the phone or video meeting that you have a bad connection (which you actually do). Once you are calm, you can quickly and effectively connect again.

If temporary escape from Americans itching for a fight isn't possible, as it wasn't for Mayor Pete, buy time by taking a sip of water, blowing your nose, jotting down a note, or using my favorite approach—fogging.

## USE FOGGING TO COOL THINGS DOWN

The fogging technique is momentarily answering verbal attacks with calm, well-rehearsed *agreement*. It's a sidestep. Because most of us aren't great when caught off guard, it pays to have a ready response. Fogging phrases enable us to say something that won't escalate, and may even dampen, explosive situations.

Just as fog is cool and dense, you might appear as if you didn't understand their criticism if you calmly agree. That's ok for now. You got the attack but decided not to play that game. You're buying time. Fogging scripts are useful until you regain the capacity to deliberatively make a constructive response.

Once you detect you are feeling defensive, focus in and listen to what the other person is actually saying *on the surface*—not what they are implying. Find something they have said you can honestly agree with and choose one of three fogging scripts:

### FOGGING = CALMLY AGREE
- "You're right."
- "You may be right."
- "It could look that way."

- **Agree with truth:** *"You're right"* or *"Yes"* or *"That's true"* or *"You have a point there."*

- **Agree with possible truth:** *"You may be right"* or *"You might have a point"* or *"There could be some truth in that"* or *"That's possible."*

- **Agree with perception:** *"It could look that way"* or *"It could seem that way."*

Avoid denying, defending, and counterattacking.

Because foggers already know what words to use, the tool allows people to focus all their energy on sounding and looking reasonable. Though difficult, having memorized and practiced the script before, we more skillfully respond when the heat is on.

## FOR EXAMPLE

The *first fogging script* could be used if someone sarcastically shoots at you with, "You thought Trump should be impeached??!!" If you did, you can calmly say "Yes" then wait. Ignore the implied "Shame on you." If you're tempted to shout *"Any thinking person would!"* just count the number of seconds ticking past to keep yourself from getting baited into a contentious discussion. Calm down first, then respond in a way you can be proud of.

The *second type of fogging script*, agreeing with possible truth, is a better choice if the attack comes in this form: "No way should Trump have been impeached for investigating Ukraine corruption and Hunter Biden!" Use the script "You might have a point there." While you don't think their comment has merit, because you see Trump's behavior as having invited foreign interference to get himself reelected, they might have a point if what they were describing was the true situation. Give them the benefit of the doubt for a few moments, just to lower tension, and then, when everyone is ready, have a civil discussion about your differing views. Later is the time to say, "I see it differently."

To the attack "That's stupid!" you can slowly reply "That might be, because I *have* done some stupid things." The key is to avoid sarcasm and appear to be calmly listening while you deliver the scripted message. Fogging involves *acting* calmer than you feel. Again, fake it until you actually get back under control.

Use the **third type of fogging statement**—agree with perception—if you clearly are unable to agree with either truth or possible truth in the person's attack. "You're lying!" could be answered with the slowly delivered, coolheaded phrase, "Wow ... it *might appear* that way," or "It might *look* that way, I suppose." Please don't say, "It could look that way *to YOU!*" or "*to somebody with YOUR vision!*" which would amplify their defensiveness.

A senior executive mandated to get coaching from me yelled, "You're trying to ruin my career!" I couldn't answer his accusation with "That's right" or even "You might have a point," so I used the third fog *"Oh...,"* took a sip of water, and finished with *"It could seem that way."* Once under control, I could start to find out more and defuse with *"Help me understand why you believe that. I'd like to change your mind."* Buying time enabled me to eventually build the rapport crucial for a good coaching relationship.

## WHEN TO USE THE FOGGING TECHNIQUE

Most skills work better the faster you use them. Fogging is just the opposite. Pause, appear to be thinking about what they said, then deliver the script at a snail's pace. The goal is to slow things down. Use the time to choose your fog.

Designed to keep you in check until you are composed enough to answer well, fogging can also take the wind out of the sails of others. If they are baiting you, the expectation is you will defend yourself. Your sidestep will likely catch them a bit off guard. More importantly, it will keep your foot out of your mouth. Thinking you didn't understand, they may escalate the situation with another and stronger attack, but don't worry, you can fog again.

The time to use the fogging technique is when you need to rein yourself in. Fogging phrases are temporary coping responses. If you are sufficiently calm already, never mind fogging—just skip ahead to step #8 and respond effectively without the stall. If you aren't even ready to get out a fogging phrase, nod or take a sip of water to keep your foot out of your mouth for a moment.

## HOW TO FOG A QUESTION

Sometimes people will attack in the form of a question, such as the accusatory, "Why did you do that?!" Be ready. All you need to do is play volleyball—answer a question with a question—and set up the chance to use fogging.

If the critic asks, "Why did you do that?!" the scripted volley-ball response is a slow question back, *"You think I shouldn't have?"* to which the attacker will insist, "No, it was the wrong thing to do!" Now the attack is direct, which you know how to handle with a fog, so pick one of the standard phrases, such as *"You could have a point."* (You don't think they do, but they might.) The work of selecting a good volley has the benefit of tapping your thinking brain.

> **Set Up a Chance to Fog—Play Volleyball**
> - **Question: "Why?"**
> - **Volleyball: "You think I shouldn't have?"**
> - **Attack**
> - **Fog**

For maximum payoff, sound as if you are curious about their answer to your volleyball question. (Hopefully you *are* curious, because that

200

helps us find common ground, but you might be too upset at the moment to explore their thinking.)

Fogging works so well that even if someone knows you are fogging, it succeeds—as long as others believe your goal is to control yourself rather than manipulate them. A company's attorney hired me to help three aggressive, fifty-something brothers manage their frequent conflicts. They had inherited a family business from their domineering father and been pitted against each other since birth. I taught all of them how to fog.

In the middle of an argument, one brother pulled a 3x5 index card out of his suit coat. (I held my breath fearing he had reached for a gun.) Off the card he slowly read, "It could look that way," which got us all laughing. He was clearly working hard to stop himself from delivering his typically abusive remarks, and his fogging allowed us to tackle issues not people.

When someone hits your hot button, hit your fog button. All you have to do is choose which fogging button—one, two, or three. Because knowing what to do is not enough, develop some muscle memory. Like most things, skillfully buying time under fire requires practice, so find a buddy and run through the fogging phrases. Olympic and professional athletes practice and practice, so why do we think we don't have to?

Participants in my "Don't Take it Personally!" workshops rehearse a difficult, simulated exchange of Attack → Fog and Attacking Question → Volleyball → Attack → Fog. You might think about what triggers you, hand a buddy an attack script, and practice.

## STEP 4: ANALYZE THE THREAT

After you've (1) noticed defensiveness, (2) stopped, and (3) bought time, the fourth step is analyzing what put you on the defensive. No longer rushing down the wrong discussion path, you're ready to sort out what seems threatening.

Emotional hijackings include activation of the amygdala without triggering the neocortex (thinking) processes that usually keep emotions in check. What can we do? Neuroscientists have shown that simply naming an emotion activates our prefrontal cortex and lowers amygdala reactivity.[4] In other words, consciously recognizing emotions lowers their impact.[5]

Our associative, emotional minds react to the present as though it were the past, plus we respond to imagined threats as well as real ones. Though sometimes true and sometimes not, we might in the moment feel that others are mocking our beliefs, limiting our choices, and discounting our experience, because they have made those mistakes before. We become conditioned to expect a fight with a certain person or with people they remind us of. If that's the case, and if you planned ahead, you could have a constructive reply already prepared to use.

Determining the type of threat enables us to tailor our efforts. *Is the other person's behavior actually attacking or have you been stressed lately and hit the tipping point?* Are you hypersensitive, tired, and irritable, or are you facing a true jerk?

The Americans you encounter could either be accidentally or purposefully triggering defensiveness. Jack Gibb wrote the classic work on defensive communication, outlining six climates that arouse defensive reactions and six climates that have an opposite, supportive effect on relationships. Quickly examine if the person you're encountering is being (1) evaluative, (2) controlling, (3) manipulative, (4) indifferent, (5) superior, or (6) too certain. Awareness of their behavior can help. See the previous chapter "Disagreeing Without Being Disagreeable" for a more thorough description.

The more you know what sets you off, the more you can anticipate your reaction and have a ready response. If you determine stress is the culprit, quickly employ stress management techniques (chapter 11). If they pushed your low self-esteem button, the chapter

12 approaches for boosting your feelings of self-confidence and self-worth will pay off. If you are up against a know-it-all, use coping strategies for that specific type of difficult person.

We can vaccinate ourselves by some analysis and self-reflection ahead of time to be equipped when talking across the political divide. Diagnosing the type of threat should help you give yourself the right medicine. One prescription is positive self-talk, which is the next step.

## STEP 5: SELF-TALK, AKA "COGNITIVE RESTRUCTURING"

Now, at step five of the getting-off-the-defensive sequence, talk yourself down with phrases like: *"This too shall pass," "I'm ok,"* or *"Take it easy."* Cognitive restructuring entails getting off the defensive by changing your thinking, and this is something you have control over.

In the middle of a fierce debate, revise what you are telling yourself. Silently coach yourself to civility with the words that an objective judge, your best friend, or a wise mentor would tell you. You might find generally affirming self-talk does the trick or need a specific antidote to their poisonous words.

General self-talk statements that fit most defensive arousing situations include:

> *"Wait, find out if the person really meant that."*
>
> *"Hear them out first."*
>
> *"Remember, they may see things differently."*
>
> *"Keep an open mind."*
>
> *"Calm down."*
>
> *"Get curious not mad."*

Sometimes changing your thinking requires a custom-tailored coach strategy. When you perceive your self-esteem has been targeted, talk to yourself about your true value:

> *"I make mistakes sometimes, but I usually know what I'm doing."*
>
> *"Many people I respect think as I do."*
>
> *"I've competently handled_____ and_____ ."*
>
> *"My opinions are of value, even if they aren't understood yet.*

If facing know-it-alls, tell yourself:

> *"Focus, so you can paraphrase to prove you understood."*
>
> *"They aren't ready to hear you yet."*
>
> *"Remember they need to look good and are feeling threatened."*
>
> *"I should ask about their point of view, while I get back under control."*

Self-talk for hostile situations:

> *"Sidestep. They are probably better at being a bear than you are."*
>
> *"Avoid a direct attack. Divert, plan an escape."*
>
> *"Don't take them on alone."*
>
> *"Wait until you're prepared."*

Successfully managing interactions typically begins with managing ourselves. No doubt you've seen that taking things personally and reacting too strongly for the situation costs people credibility and influence. Explore Appendix 7 for additional self-talk statements and strategies. Better yet, you may find planning your own phrases works best.

## STEP 6: RELAX

While the fifth step calls for changing your thinking, this sixth one involves purposefully changing your body to get off the defense.

Both mental and physical strategies work, especially when used together.

Teach yourself to relax on demand. By pairing a perfume fragrance with repeated practice of progressive relaxation exercises, a client of mine taught herself to cope with hostile, heckling audiences. She spent hours listening to a relaxation tape and practicing the exercises with the scent of her favorite perfume in the room, so when verbally assaulted later, she could simply move her wrist to her nose, trigger her conditioned self to calm down, and constructively confront the audience's issues.

Since it is impossible to simultaneously be relaxed *and* defensive, breathe—deeply. Breathing has been called the natural, always available tranquilizer.[6] Focusing for even just a few minutes on inhaling and exhaling from the diaphragm in a smooth, even rhythm allows people to handle intense situations more effectively.

The good news is that relaxing lowers anger—and blood pressure. I wish more of us adults had learned this calming technique from Mister Rogers and Daniel Tiger's Neighborhood: "Give a squeeze, nice and slow. Take a deep breath, let it go."

If you can exit, take a walk and shake off your anger. You might escape to a restroom and relax there by doing jumping jacks, tensing and relaxing muscle groups, stretching, or sighing deeply. (Sighing in front of those you disagree with, however, could appear condescending.) The goal is to relax and slow down.

## STEP 7: LISTEN

To break the defensiveness cycle, get busy with actions that prevent further defensiveness. Start paying keen attention to what others are saying, because when you are actively listening—using the skills of encouraging, echoing, paraphrasing, clarifying, and checking your perceptions—your thinking brain is working. Knock yourself out to understand and find common ground.

Unfortunately, and particularly when defensive, most of us plan our attack rather than listening carefully to theirs. When Americans doubt you have heard, understood, or taken them seriously, they usually ratchet up an attack. That's the time to point the microphone in their direction and let them talk. Used well, all of the following listening tools can make you better at hearing, showing respect, and defusing the attacker's wrath:

- Encouraging = nodding and inviting them to continue.

  *"Oh..." "Tell me more." "That's interesting!"*

- Echoing = repeating exactly what they said using their words. To their statement "That won't work!" say *"That won't work?"* with interest but without sarcasm or too much intensity, so they continue.

- Paraphrasing = summarizing to indicate comprehension.

  *"If I've understood correctly, you said_____ ."*

- Clarifying = checking their meaning.

  *"Do you mean_____ or_____ ?"*

- Checking your perceptions = explaining what you've concluded from what they have said.

  *"It seems to me that you believe_____ , right?"*

Belittling or disrespecting views triggers people to defend their position. When Americans believe you are considering their perspective, they can lower their swords. (For more ideas, see the chapters on empathy, managing differences, and overcoming resistance.)

## STEP 8:  RESPOND

Now that you have gone through steps 1–7—noticed your defensive reaction, stopped, bought time, analyzed the threat, coached yourself, relaxed physically, plus listened—you're closer to answering the way you really want. This is the time to say, "I have had a different experience" or "I reached a different conclusion." Tell of your life experiences and walk others through how you arrived at your perspective. Your story may pry open their hearts.

Many good responses can be prepared and rehearsed ahead of time. Skilled impromptu speakers actually pull stories, facts, and phrases from previous conversations and presentations. They have 30-second and 2-minute versions of the same point. Like them, plan ahead, so you can execute. Please don't sound canned or come across as insincere. Be in the moment—nervous perhaps about their response, but genuine with yours.

## SHORT CUTS ARE POSSIBLE

With practice, you can skillfully defuse a situation and even skip a defensive sequence step or two. If you realize that your voice has gotten louder and has an edge in it, you might quickly fog and then ask a question to get them clarifying, while you regain control and listen.

You may have heard a certain argument before, allowing you to jump from noticing your reaction (step 1) to analyzing (step 4) to a good, practiced answer (step 8) such as *"I thought that too. When I learned_____ , I changed my mind."* (See more in the previous chapter about how to disagree without being disagreeable.)

When no longer defensive, you and fellow Americans can explore differing views and ideas with respect and curiosity. Be careful, though, that others feel they are sufficiently heard. Duct tape is mighty useful. Listen twice as much as you speak.

## PUTTING IT INTO PRACTICE

1. **Recognize:** What do your family members and friends notice when you are defensive?
2. **Stop:** How can you stop yourself? Who might give you a time out cue when they notice you are taking something

personally? What signals could feedback providers use to stop you from defensively barging ahead?

3. **Buy time:** Think of a difficult situation that failed to go well. What approaches might have helped you stall and restore your equilibrium if someone sneered, "That's what you believe?!" What fogging script could you use? Imagine an attack someone might throw at you and plan a fogging answer or two.

4. **Analyze the threat:** What made you feel under attack?
   High stress level—therefore irritable and easily triggered
   Low self-esteem—doubts about worth and competence
   Other's behavior
   - Evaluative and judgmental
   - Controlling and aggressive
   - Manipulative and deceitful
   - Indifferent and uncaring
   - Superior and condescending
   - Dead certain and close-minded

5. **Cognitive restructuring self-talk:** What would a good coach whisper in your ear?

6. **Relax:** Which techniques work best to relax you?

7. **Listen:** Which listening techniques should you be using more often? Think of a difficult conversation and what you would actually say, if you were using the listening skills.

8. **Respond:** What key points (maximum three) you would like heard and considered? How can you keep your planned nuggets short and simple for maximum impact?

Congratulate yourself for getting off the defensive and not taking things personally!

## CHAPTER 11

# Coping with the Stress of Now

S tressed by national intolerance, whiplashed by reports that Covid-19 is and isn't serious, terrified by the economic aftershock? Isolated by social distancing and frightened that a loved one or job is at risk? Stunned by American cities burning? Americans are wounded, wary, and weary.[1]

You might be thinking, "I used to have a handle on life, but now it fell off." Riots and a health disaster came on top of us already being anxious about the environment, school shootings, the refugee crisis, and North Korea, Syria, and Iran. Scared or overwhelmed? You have a right to be.

Previous chapters zeroed in on how to change the situation we're in. Here the focus is on *you*.

## ADJUSTMENT DEMAND

Stress is a reaction to threat—what psychologists call an adjustment demand. Unprecedented times require coping. We're in a worldwide crisis of monumental proportion without a competent leader. The far right is accusing infectious disease expert Anthony Fauci—who has advised six presidents and bravely told the truth about the virus—of trying to take Trump down. Saving lives and concern for country is taking a back seat to party loyalty or the cult of Trump. This can't be happening.

Hans Selye used the term "general adaptation syndrome" (GAS, which I find is a great acronym) to refer to our body's three-stage stress response—alarm, resistance, and exhaustion. Many are recognizing those stages in themselves right now. However, not everyone is experiencing the same level of stress in these tumultuous times because appraisal of whether or not something is threatening is highly subjective.

### Stress— Too little, too much

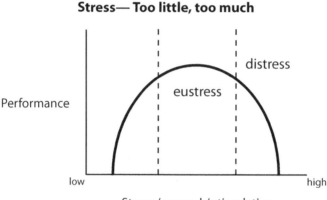

Stress / arousal / stimulation

Stress can be positive or negative, and both a hectic day and a monotonous one make people weary. Just as euphoria is a positive emotion, "eustress" refers to the right amount of stimulation, when we are positively challenged and performing at our best. Too little leaves us bored and dispirited. However, the right amount for me isn't the right amount for everyone.

Too much alarm, pressure, and fear—"distress"—triggers the release of cortisol and other hormones, depresses our immune system and, if prolonged, damages our mental and physical health. Like a string on an instrument, we need some tension but snap with too much.

"This morning I had one nerve left—
and now you're getting on it."

You know the stress symptoms—headaches, insomnia, neck and back pain, GI disturbances, fatigue, difficulty concentrating, irritability, anxiety, confusion, procrastination, lethargy, and depression.

Referred by his dentist, a teeth-grinding client of mine told me not to advise him to quit his job. He acknowledged that he drank heavily, worked more than 80 hours a week, was being threatened with divorce, and didn't know how to relate to his son who was just caught using drugs. Blind to more options, he thought he only had two choices—live exactly as he was or quit the job he loved.

Be careful of tunnel vision like his. When stressed, we are less able to see alternatives, think clearly, use information, solve problems, and master new tasks, so we make poor decisions. That sends our stress levels even higher. Exhausted, we forget, delay, and want to escape.

**LESS ABLE TO**
- **See alternatives**
- **Think clearly**
- **Use new information**
- **Solve problems**
- **Master new tasks**
- **Make good decisions**

Making things worse, brain research shows that chronic stress shrinks the volume of gray matter in the areas associated with self-control.[2] So? Distress actually makes it more challenging to deal with future stress. Yet, there is positive evidence that some *intermittent* stress prompts our brains to grow.[3]

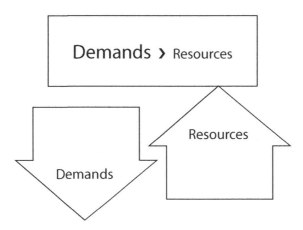

## PERCEIVED DEMANDS > RESOURCES = DISTRESS

Richard Lazarus explained that we experience distress when we perceive that the demands we face exceed our resources to handle them.[4] Consequently, managing stress involves lowering stressors, increasing our resources, and better yet, doing both. The trouble is we often fail to perceive situations accurately, especially under pressure. When we have a lot to do *and* realize we have a lot of resources, we get tired but not alarmed.

Handling stress involves (1) changing reality and/or (2) changing our appraisal of it. Because our bodies respond to perceived threat as if it were real, what needs altering may in part be how we view our unprecedented times—rather than the actual demand or real supply of resources. Watch a scary movie and your body reacts with changes in breathing, muscle tension, etc., as if you actually were in that frightening movie. Believe that a family member is about to be deported, and you will respond physiologically, whether or not that is true.

Times are bad. So are our attitudes. Anxiety is contagious and being fueled, so what can we do about it? Diagnose then treat.

## SORT OUT THE CAUSES OF YOUR STRESS

- Big stressor = big stress reaction. The need to cope depends on the **intensity of the stressor.** For example, extremely loud noises are more stressful than noises that are simply loud.

- The **importance** of the demand makes something stressful. You may have only one concern, but if that worry is about getting coverage for your child's expensive life-saving medical treatments, your only sibling writing you off because of your political beliefs, or preventing damage to your water source as climate change legislation is rolled back, you will be stressed.

- Ongoing problems—demands of **duration**—drain our energy and resources. The longer people have to deal with a serious illness or political argument, the more resources are used. Because relationship wounds and unfinished business keep us anxious and angry, tackling problems instead of letting them drag on pays off.

- The closer or more **imminent** the demand, the greater the stress. People frequently become more agitated the nearer another car is to hitting them, as a deadline approaches, and when caught surprised.

- In **unfamiliar** situations, doubt and fear erupt. We question our ability and judge—sometimes appropriately and sometimes not—our resources to be insufficient. Novice parachute jumpers are more stressed than experienced ones, and so are drivers handling traffic on new routes compared to familiar streets.[5] The good news is that training, practice, and familiarity can make yesterday's disaster quite routine or even delightfully challenging.

- Similarly, events are usually experienced as more threatening when they are **unpredictable**. Not knowing what is coming, we must vigilantly be on guard. No wonder we are seeing articles titled "Donald Trump's doctrine of Unpredictability has the World on Edge."[6] Just a little uncertainty lights up the amygdala.

- Again and again scientists have found **lack of control** is crucial to the amount of stress we experience, and the more stress, the greater the need to control. We get frustrated and tense if we perceive that we cannot get where we want to go, finish a task, or make something happen. Imagine the stress our emergency workers are under having to fight the novel virus without adequate data, supplies, and hospital equipment.[7]

  While perceived control decreases stress, control *plus* responsibility intensifies it. Greater control is actually associated with *increased* stress for those, like Republican senators, who fear how others will judge them. In demanding situations, people avoid, disavow responsibility, and insist, "He's not my President" or "Trump's behavior was wrong, but not impeachable." Powerlessness elevates stress, except when it takes us off the hook.

- Stress is cumulative, so reduce the **number of stressors** in your life—real or perceived. Have fewer responsibilities, a limited number of causes you champion, and less on the "To-Do" list. Prioritize. With too many concerns (and there are many deserving our attention) resources become depleted. When exhausted, it is easy to get stressed out by misjudging ourselves unequal to our plentiful tasks. At that moment, the camel can't take any more.

## STRESS FACTORS

- **intensity**
- **importance**
- **duration**
- **imminence**
- **unfamiliarity**
- **unpredictability**
- **lack of control**
- **number of other stressors**

## STRESS PRONE DOES NOT EQUAL STUCK

Both biology and life events affect how stress prone we and other Americans are. Some of us are born more emotional and easily triggered, while others are calm by nature. Some of us quickly recover from emotional "hijackings." Those who don't are at greater risk for health problems.

In the University of Wisconsin neuroscience lab, Richard Davidson is studying people's different left-to-right ratios of prefrontal brain activity.[8] Measured when we're just resting, this ratio accurately predicts the typical range of our moods. When people feel enthusiastic, energetic, and engaged, the left prefrontal area is active. Those of us who typically have more activity on the left than right tend to have more positive emotions. The right prefrontal area shows lots of brain activity when we've emotionally "lost it." While most of us fall in the middle of the ratio spectrum, those with extreme left-to-right ratios rapidly bounce back from setbacks.[9]

According to Davidson, the good news is that *we can influence our biology.* With mindfulness training, for example, we can shift our emotional set point and strengthen our vagal nerve tone—enabling us to cool down, sleep better, and guard against damage from chronic arousal. The vagal nerve regulates heartbeat, and better vagal tone increases both our ability to arouse ourselves to meet a challenge and to let go. Like Buddhist monks, we can train ourselves to be less reactive.

*Life experiences* also affect whether we are flexible and adaptable or more structured and rigid. For individuals who have had fewer experiences, confronted less change, not had responsibility, or been overprotected, demands tend to loom larger than their perceived skills and abilities. Some people haven't learned many coping techniques. Less practiced at adapting, these Americans encounter a lot that is unfamiliar without having the benefit of the confidence that comes with multiple successes. In political conversations, don't expect them to be unflappable.

People lacking a **support system** are at risk. More stress prone, too, are those lacking the belief they can control situations—they have an external rather than internal locus of control described in more detail in the next chapter. They simply are not as resource full or as hardy. Yet, with effort, people can alter the belief that what happens is out of their hands, develop supportive friendships, and become skilled at coping.

## THE HARDY PERSONALITY

Who is more resilient, stress-adept, and hardy? Comparing high-stress executives who remained healthy with those in similar situations who became ill, Suzanne Kobasa and Salvatore Maddi found the "hardy" executives had more commitment to well defined goals, felt more in control over what happened in their life, and had bigger appetites for challenge and change.[10] [11] [12]

I'd like to immunize Americans with some commitment, challenge, and control to help defend against the stress we face. As Henry Ford said, "Whether you think you can, or think you can't—you're right." Let me start by recommending again Holocaust survivor Viktor Frankl's book *Man's Search for Meaning*.[13] Stripped of everything, Frankl found power in purpose—something he *could* control—and his profound words are inspiring. Martin Seligman's empirically sound *Learned Optimism*[14] provides fascinating anecdotes and practical strategies that should also help you feel more in control.

Can't change a situation? Turn it into a challenge. My clients who faced irate customers 8, 10, or 12 hours a day, depending on their work schedule, did just that.

Knowing every phone call would bring verbal abuse, they managed their difficult job by treating the encounters as a challenge. When picking up the phone, they stood in their cubicle and signaled to their coworkers the number of minutes they estimated it would take to calm this particular customer down. Ten fingers meant ten minutes to resolution. They also awarded trophies for handling the worst customer of the week. Motivated by specific challenges, department turnover dropped.

## STRATEGIES FOR MANAGING STRESS

Managing stress is complex. If stressed by lack of stimulation you need to get going, not relax. Americans bored by the familiar need more novelty, but those distressed now by the unprecedented require more normalcy, rest, and resilience. We're worn out.

You may have been encouraged to vent, but **distraction** yields better outcomes than rumination.[15] A diet of news, talk shows, texts, tweets, and emails about current political happenings feeds anxiety and anger. Find outlets and control frustration, because perpetual outrage will harm your health. Chronic stress makes things worse—triggering more anxiety, faster fear-conditioning, and slower habituation.

A well-equipped stress management kit includes strategies to both (1) alter the real demand/resource ratio and (2) modify our perception of it. Too frequently we fail to recognize that we have choices—choices that can minimize demands, add resources, and make us more resilient. So, we suffer rather than use mental and physical relaxation techniques to help us cope or recover.

Pick some survival strategies from the list below, remembering what works in one situation or for one individual will not for others.

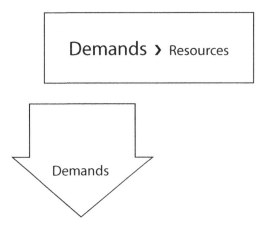

## LOWER YOUR STRESSORS!

Bring demands into line with your resources.

- **Minimize change**

    In the midst of American chaos, let successful routines provide some solid footing. Keep in place the parts of your life that are working for you. Now is not the time to change your good sleeping, eating, exercise, and work habits, if you have some.

- **Get information and clarification**

    Reduce the intensity of your stressors by finding out if those demands are as big and awful as you think. If you worry about security, learning that an American has a 1 in 3.64 billion chance of being murdered in a terrorist attack caused by a refugee and 1 in 10.9 billion in an attack perpetuated by an illegal immigrant might help calm your fears.[16] Find out a project's required elements, steps, and deadlines, so you don't sweat unnecessarily. Analyze what is and is not needed, and determine the "givens" and "controllables."

- **Reduce uncertainty**

  Get information, because information reduces stress. You might be worrying needlessly. If you are anxious about your elevated cholesterol, ask your doctor to calculate the probability of a heart attack in the next 10 years. Investigate the impact of proposed healthcare changes on access to treatment and your pocketbook. Inquire whether your department does have to lower head count as rumored or if loans are available to you. Turn off the alarms caused by ambiguity and uncertainty.

- **Check your perspective**

  See if what you are telling yourself is both true and helpful.[17] Compared to the rest of the world, how are you and our country doing? Don't get me wrong, denial will only temporarily delay the stress reaction and possibly prevent you from acting soon enough, but overreacting is harmful too. Refute your irrational thoughts and take a bird's eye view. Life looks different when we realize that unlike so many, we have food on the table, freedom of expression, water, access to information, clean air, or a place to sleep. See Appendix 7 for specific self-talk ideas.

- **Prioritize**

  Ask yourself, "In light of the greater cosmos, how important is this?" Focus on people, issues, and actions that are highly important to you, and then give yourself permission to let go. Divvy up tasks and set boundaries on how much time you can devote toward a particular target. Keep your demand level in line with your resources while you work to make a difference.

- **Anticipate**

We can benefit from the "work of worrying"—anticipating and doing some contingency planning—for military deployment, hip surgery, or difficult family situations. Think ahead and visualize yourself coping with a tough political conversation, because our brains and nervous systems remember and record imagined events.

A year after pianist Liu Chi Kung took second to Van Cliburn in the Tchaikovsky Competition in 1958, he was imprisoned during China's Cultural Revolution. He spent seven years without being able to play a piano. Stunned that he was back on tour better than ever soon after being released, critics asked, "How did you do this? You had no chance to practice for seven years." Liu answered, "I did practice, every day. I rehearsed every piece I had ever played, note by note, in my mind."[18] Similarly, injured athletes profit from using mental rehearsal until they can work their limbs and muscles.[19]

- **Delegate**

Reduce stress by offloading some demands to competent others. Who else might host the next fund-raiser or chair the upcoming meeting? Could your children prepare dinner tonight? Could your partner get groceries this week?

- **Chunk**

Cut projects into manageable bites. Instead of expecting to persuade everyone in town or in the opposing political party, reducing the tribalism in two neighbors or being able to talk constructively with one additional family member may be enough for now. Start small.

- **Lower your standards**

Would 90% be good enough? What will the final 10% get you? Are you demanding too much of yourself or others?

Psychologists distinguish between "satisficing"—satisfying sufficiently—and "maximizing"—seeking the best or perfection.[20] As you probably guessed, satisficers are happier, and so are the people around them.[21]

- **Shorten stressor duration**
When possible, don't put up with things that don't work. Because stress is cumulative and draining, replace the leaky tire on your car and complete items hanging over your head, so you'll have resources for what comes next. Tackle your demands. Repair that strained relationship.

- **Unplug**
Detach from emails, stop looking at your phone 96 times a day,[22] and put your brain and emotions on a healthy diet. Allow yourself only a limited number of news articles, talk shows, social media sites or hours of exposure, otherwise you'll need a side order of blood pressure medicine. Stay informed, but tune out too.

- **Take charge of what you can control**
Though you cannot add more hours to the day, you can manage your time better. You may not be able to stop Trump from rolling back climate change legislation, but you can control your attitude, prepare a list of climate change facts to share with your Congressional representative and neighbors, sign a petition, march, or distract yourself with a good book. Recognize your choices, and act to shift the demand/resource imbalance. Choose not to remain stuck.

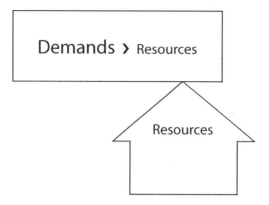

## GET MORE RESOURCES!

Being stronger and feeling happier helps manage the stressors you face. How? There are lots of ways.

- **Develop competencies**

  Acquire the skills, knowledge, and training you lack to meet the demands you're up against. Learn what you need to know for your job—and for this political climate. Perfect communication, conflict, and influence skills (see chapters 4–10), so you can constructively solve problems and discuss ways America can pull together.

- **Find thought partners**

  Scrutinize your perceptions and take wise advice. Because stressed minds become more rigid and less creative—preventing us from seeing alternatives—ask others to check your thinking as you analyze the gap between where you are and where you want to be. There is a danger you are undervaluing your abilities and failing to recognize resources you have. Coaches, mentors, friends and spouses can help brainstorm options and uncover successful strategies you and others have used. (Some appreciative inquiry techniques are in Appendix 8.)

- **Join forces**

  Seek support, encouragement, and extra hands. In stressful times, the presence and proximity of others helps, and Americans trying to heal this nation and preserve our democracy need the power of numbers. Find others with your concerns and be there for them. Gather in political "salons," local Indivisible groups, and "Thrive Tribes" to share the load and get energy, ideas, and inspiration to combat Trump era stress.

- **Relax mentally**

  Increase your thinking capacity by taking a mental vacation. Your body relaxes at imagined spas just as it mobilizes to imagined threat, so visualize yourself on a beach or in an alpine cabin and mentally savor the sound of the sea or the smell of logs in the fireplace.

- **Take breaks**

  Manage your stress with some R & R. Long before organizations were required to give employees breaks, many companies realized that workers who took a breather returned refreshed and more productive. We're wired to respond to change. Renewal data shows breaks every 90 minutes yield a higher level of focus,[23] [24] and those who take breaks report an increase in health, well-being, performance, and ability to think creatively. [25]

- **Be uplifted**

  We benefit from a chance to talk about our stressors and commiserate with colleagues, but not from repeatedly ranting and raving.[26] Our brains need to recover from high arousal just as our bodies do. Surround yourself with uplifting people and music, the laughter of children, and the beauty of nature, plus restore your equilibrium with inspiring books, sermons, or podcasts. Spend time doing what brings you joy.

- **Relax physically**

  You cannot be both stressed and relaxed at the same time, and the evidence about health benefits from relaxation via meditation and yoga, for example, is plentiful.[27] Taking control of your breathing is a powerful way to relax and feel more in control. Shift from revved up to relaxed by meditating, strolling, napping, and soaking in a tub. Rid yourself of tension by walking briskly, swimming, jogging, biking, dancing, running, and gardening. Get healthy, therefore more resourceful, with Tai Chi, good nutrition, biofeedback, exercise, and that precious commodity sleep.

- **Touch**

  When appropriate, touch—even just someone's forearm. Physical connection provides comfort, reduces pain, makes you more persuasive, and releases oxytocin, the relationship bonding hormone.[28]

- **Laugh!**

  You probably have not been giggling enough lately. Norman Cousins, newspaper editor and UN Medal of Peace recipient, astounded the medical community with his recovery from a degenerative disease. Given little chance of survival, he checked himself out of the hospital and into a hotel where he watched hours of humorous films and TV shows. His discovery that ten minutes of belly laughter outperformed morphine in giving him pain-free hours of sleep sparked research on humor therapy.[29] Follow his example. Humor is a wonderful buffer against stress, so laugh, guffaw, blow bubbles, and be silly.[30]

- **Have fun**

  You can intentionally increase your happiness and resilience—affecting not only you but those around you by creating an "upward spiral of positivity."[31] [32] When we explore and play, we actually discover new ideas and actions, thereby building our resource side of the demand/resource equation. There is utility in fun.

Positive emotions broaden our thinking and flexibility—the opposite of the brain under stress. And, not only do positive feelings help us feel good at the moment, positive experiences accumulate and help us feel better in the future. Start having some.

- **Count your blessings**

Because you may not be noticing positive experiences these days, change your perceptions by practicing the highly effective, simple Three Blessings exercise. My grandmother always told me to count my blessings, and now research proves how right she was. Our perceptions are resources.

In the evening think about three positive things that happened during the day and why you believe they happened. Participants doing so for one week benefited with increased happiness and decreased depression for months.[33] Contemplating what we're grateful for activates the brainstem region that produces serotonin, plus reduces the stress hormone cortisol.[34]

Newer research suggests that this powerful gratitude exercise may actually be more effective if done less rather than more frequently over a longer period of time, so try it a couple of times a week and even write down the blessings so you'll be on the lookout for them.[35]

What blessings? Blessing number one could be that Americans agree that social distancing saves lives. Number two that people aren't following Trump's suggestion to ingest cleaning solvent. Number three that Americans concur that no one is above the law. Train your brain to see the positive.

Decades of research have found that positive emotions boost the immune system, counter depression, lower blood pressure, and help control weight and blood sugar. Studies of people with Type 2 diabetes, AIDS, and chronic illnesses even show a link between positive feelings and longer life. With the primary focus on living better with the stress of an incurable disease, researchers are testing the value of practicing at least one of eight positive skills every day:[36]

1. Recognize a positive event each day.
2. Savor that event and log it in a journal or tell someone about it.
3. Start a daily gratitude journal.
4. List a personal strength and note how you used it.
5. Set an attainable goal and note your progress.
6. Report a relatively minor stress and list ways to reappraise the event.
7. Recognize and practice small acts of kindness daily.
8. Practice mindfulness, focus on now rather than the past or future.

Gratitude has been shown to yield amazing benefits for children and adults—increased optimism, health, social connection, well-being, creativity, and altruism. Gratitude is linked to decreased envy and materialism, which means appreciating what we have even makes us less insecure about what we don't.[37] Let's start counting those blessings and feeling better.

- **Do something for others**
Altruism is strongly linked to happiness.[38] When stressed and depressed we become more self-centered, but the best way to make yourself happy is to make someone else happy. As St. Francis highlighted, "It is in giving that we receive." I'm

not sure who benefited most when my dog and I visited nursing home and hospital patients as a pet therapy team.

Focusing on others has provided meaning for parents grieving the loss of their children to car accidents, shootings, or disease. People who gave their time to help others through community and organizational involvement had greater self-esteem, less depression, and lower stress levels than those who didn't.[39] And, their giving stimulated their mesolimbic pathway—the reward center in the brain—releasing endorphins and triggering what is known as the "helper's high."[40]

- **Express gratitude**

In addition, let other Americans know you are grateful for their efforts and actions, because almost no one gets enough thanks. Our first responders, helpful colleagues, and patient relatives deserve tons of appreciation. Elected officials also need praise for doing what's right, especially when those actions aren't popular.

Be generous with the phrases "Thank you," "Thanks for hearing me out," and "Thanks for telling your neighbors about this." The more specific the feedback, the more genuine it seems and the more helpful in guiding future action. "Yesterday's call boosted my spirits" and "That funny video you emailed was just what I needed" are likely to get you more of the same.

As you know, people do what they get rewarded for doing and act in line with their self-image. You can help people see what they are contributing by appropriately labeling them as "dedicated warriors" and "faithful servants." Unfortunately, too often we forget that praising others' efforts will make us all feel good. Let's help others see themselves as blessings.

## HOW *CAN* WE MANAGE OUR MOODS?

Stress affects our health and our moods, and we can act to influence both. Years ago Robert Thayer's team researched how often and how effectively Americans regulated their own moods.[41] The most common strategies used

*To eliminate bad moods*:

- calling, talking to or being with someone (54%)
- controlling thoughts (51%)
- listening to music (47%)
- avoiding the thing causing the bad mood (47%)
- and trying to be alone (47%)

*To reduce tension*:

- calling, talking to, or being with someone (59%)
- controlling thoughts (58%)
- listening to music (53%)
- exercising (44%)
- using relaxation techniques (44%)
- and resting, napping, or sleeping (37%)

What was judged ***most effective***? Exercising was the most effective self-regulating strategy for eliminating bad moods but was only used by 37%. Most effective for reducing tension were engaging in religious activity, listening to music, and exercising. Thayer suggested that exercise, because it both increased energy and reduced tension, was probably *the* most effective overall.

Now, some 20 years later, a strong link between exercise and mood has been found—in both correlational and experimental studies. And, the result is quick. "Usually within five minutes after moderate exercise you get a mood-enhancement effect."[42]

Exercise is generally comparable to antidepressants for patients with major depressive disorders and helpful in preventing relapse. It's beneficial for sleep, cognitive performance, weight loss, and anxiety reduction. Exercise also helps increase blood flow, make the brain's white matter more fibrous, lower cholesterol, prevent diabetes, and lengthen life.[43]

Though greater amounts of exercise will provide greater health benefits, even small amounts of physical activity in short periods throughout the day help.[44] However, according to the Centers for Disease Control and Prevention, some 25% of the U.S. population reported zero leisure-time physical activity in 2008, the last year data was available.[45] Maybe the need to get outside after sheltering at home will change that.

## TAKE CARE OF YOURSELF

Remember how flight attendants tell us to put on our own oxygen masks, so we can help others? Take care of yourself so you can make a difference healing your family, neighborhood, and country. You're urgently needed.

Demands (either real or perceived) exceeding resources (either real or perceived), cause distress. In these unprecedented times, alter your demand/resource ratio. Change reality *and* perceptions.

This chapter was stuffed with more than 20 strategies for managing stress—ways to lower demands and increase resources. I'm not suggesting this is easy, but my guess is several would help you get out of the cycle of stress, depression, outrage, and contempt. Get moving and start coping.

Find more ways to become resilient in the final chapter about courage, confidence and hope.

# CHAPTER 12 Having Courage, Confidence, and Hope

P lease pick some tools, maybe one or two from each chapter, and get to work because tools only mend fences and build bridges when someone uses them. Healing America hinges on courage, confidence, and hope—the belief that things can change. Wayne Gretsky is often quoted for saying, "You miss 100 percent of the shots you never take."

We need resilience—the ability to recover quickly. We need nerve to overcome fear that our finding common ground efforts will be in vain or, worse yet, harmful. Turning Americans into friends won't be easy. We know we could be ridiculed, bullied, and ostracized for challenging others' positions and/or modifying our own. We need perseverance.

## KEEP YOUR EYE ON THE PRIZE

Bright visions keep outstanding performers, survivors, and hardy personalities committed, so stay focused on the goal of America as caring, moral, and inclusive. Imagine conversations and communities where people hold different positions without being considered fundamentally bad people.

We citizens have the job to fight for freedom, justice, equality, and even kindness because this republic's well-crafted Constitution can't defend itself. Take heart that many along the political spectrum share this crucial concern.[1,2]

Returning after brain surgery to inspire us all, Senator John McCain said, "Merely preventing your political opponents from doing what they want isn't the most inspiring work."[3]

He took some of the blame as he told his fellow senators:

> "Sometimes I've let my passion rule my reason. Sometimes I made it harder to find common ground because of something I said to a colleague. … We're not getting much done apart. I don't think any of us feels very proud of our incapacity."[4]

As McCain urged, let's respect differences without allowing them to prevent us from reaching agreements. Similarly, Michelle Obama spoke fondly of the warm relationship she forged with George W. Bush, "We disagree on policy but we do not disagree on humanity. We do not disagree about love and compassion."[5]

## WHAT WILL KEEP YOU MOTIVATED?

What we believe affects what we do. The practical "expectancy theory" of motivation explains why Americans don't do what they could—they either don't expect their effort will be successful or they don't expect that completing the task will be worth it.

We'll put in effort to develop a vaccine, build a voice-activated device like a smart phone, or get along with our political opposites, *if* we believe our effort will get the job done *and if* we believe that performance will lead to outcomes—saving lives, making money, peace—that we value.

We need *both* expectations—that we can and that it's worth it. For action, our belief in success need not be 100%, but we must be convinced of a decent chance that:

**Effort will lead to performance**
**Performance will lead to valued outcomes**

Highly successful people "begin with the end in mind."[6] Like them, start with a reason to put in effort—preserving relationships, protecting democracy, or feeling better—then expect that your effort will make a difference.

What convinces us we can do something? Actual or observed experience in a similar situation is crucial. Plain and simple, both (1) a history of positive experiences and (2) seeing others succeed affect what we predict.

Swimming too far out in the Pacific Ocean when the tide changed, a teen survived by treading water and floating for more than 13 hours, waiting for the tide to change and return him to shore. When debriefed, he explained that several factors kept him going.

He figured his death would devastate his parents and place too much burden on his younger brother whom he loved, so he had a reason to try to live. He inventoried his strengths (youth, health, and stamina) and reminded himself of his past successes ("I've made it through ____ and ____") and his heritage ("I'm a ____," where I'd fill in my Viking background). His conclusion was if anyone could survive that long in the ocean, he could. We need to survey our strengths and achievements and label ourselves as survivors.

For inspiration, also examine others' accomplishments. While studying for the orals for my doctorate, I learned something wonderful—a less than stellar guy, let's call him Frank, had passed the exam. Deep in my soul I knew that if Frank could, I could. His surprising achievement tempered my anxiety, gave me hope, and made me more willing to devote the effort needed to prepare and pass. I kept telling myself, "If Frank can, I can."

## WATCH OUT FOR LEARNED HELPLESSNESS AND *EXTERNAL* LOCUS OF CONTROL (LOC)

When past efforts haven't led to accomplishment, people start to predict failure. Positive psychologist Martin Seligman first studied learned helplessness, how people become conditioned to perceive themselves as powerless. Those with an *external* "locus of control" believe outside factors are in charge. When people think they are unable to control aversive events—like stopping a loud, obnoxious noise—they give up and don't try.

Not all of our reaching-across-the-divide attempts will go well. When they don't, we can attribute failure to the problem itself being unsolvable or consider ourselves as the ones unable to fix the situation. Both dampen effort. An important buffer against discouragement is an *internal* locus of control—the belief that our actions (not fate or luck) influence outcomes.

People with self-efficacy think "I can." They have an *internal* locus of control. They see themselves changing their tone, respectfully listening, and speaking carefully. It's when caught surprised by failure, that confident people attribute most of their defeat to outside factors, like too little sleep, hyper-partisanship, or disinformation campaigns, instead of themselves. Concluding the situation was to blame, they remain self-assured and optimistic. This appropriate self-confidence helps us succeed. Of course, *over*confidence or inability to admit mistakes doesn't.

Views of our ability and predictions of success change with experience—and even vary with the specifics of a situation. For example, people may consider themselves smart in general but completely dumb about political activism. They see themselves likely to fail at talking politics, until they see their efforts succeeding.

## HOW TO BUILD SELF-EFFICACY

*A pattern of success* gives us a belief that success is possible and that our failures are simply a "fluke." Because high achievers take calculated risks, they do fail, but they don't quit. When blocked they work harder because they expect to eventually achieve as they have before. People can be helped to appreciate their past accomplishments and also identify strategies that worked for them. What has helped you make things happen? How can you use those tactics now? (See Appendix 8.)

***Read your "mother file."*** Start collecting tangible evidence—thank yous, attaboys, performance reviews, reference letters—of your success, skills, and worth. Just as your mother saved your school grades and art projects. Put those treasured mementos in an easily accessible file for whenever you need extra oxygen. If the file is empty, ask supportive family and friends for some entries about when and how you have made a difference, and then recharge by immersing yourself in the data.

Instead of having the bar too high, ***gradually raise expectations*** for yourself and those in and out of your tribe. Operate in the sweet spot of appropriate challenge—neither overwhelmed nor overprotected. Children achieve when encouraged to do things on their own and when given challenging tasks that can be mastered. Once kids discover they can, they want to do more, and they start with baby steps. We should too.

***Find evidence that effort → performance → valued outcomes.*** Again, just understanding that we can discuss politics with unfriendly neighbors, call our senators, and vote is not sufficient to get us to do so. Unless we *expect* those actions to make a difference, we won't invest the effort.

Of concern is what our politicians' failure to pass gun safety measures teaches teens like those from Parkland, FL. Don't give up on holding those in Congress and the White House accountable. Remember that Americans' protests helped children separated from parents at the border.

Early in my career, IBM asked me to write a detailed proposal for a weeklong training conference. Thrilled with the project, I pulled an all-nighter to include some new ideas that prompted last minute design changes. The next day as I handed the lengthy document to the IBM leader who had requested the proposal, he sheepishly said before glancing at it, "Andrea, I don't know how to tell you this, but the conference has been cancelled. I'm sure your plans are great, and I look forward to using them sometime in the future." Many of those ideas were used later, but how many times in the next year do you think I stayed up all night writing proposals? Zero. It hadn't paid off. We have to believe that doing something has a reasonable chance of leading to a desired result.

Our expectations influence which challenges we take on and how well we perform, so in addition to your mother file, collect and spread success stories. Remind discouraged Americans that we can improve and *will* heal.

Need some examples? Decades ago Los Angeles air quality was among the worst in the whole *world,* and a 1943 smog event was so bad residents worried it was a chemical attack.[7] Cigarette smoking among U.S. adults has reached the lowest level ever recorded,[8] cigarette butts have disappeared from our streets, and seat belts have reduced the risk of death by 45% and cut the risk of serious injury by 50%.[9] Positive change is possible. Marriages on the brink of divorce heal. People have civil conversations about tough issues.

## BE COURAGEOUS

Americans need courage. As Churchill told us, "Fear is a reaction. Courage is a decision." Decide to help Americans get along better. Decide to respectfully and productively hash out political differences. Decide to reduce contempt.

No doubt you remember former president Obama rode to the White House on the slogan, "Yes, we can!"—a hope that captured the hearts of many, while probably setting unrealistic expectations for his presidency. The changes he represented required more time and support than he had, yet he bravely tackled healthcare and climate for which he received the JFK Profile of Courage award.

As he accepted the honor, Obama said courage often begins "with the story we tell ourselves about our own capacity to make a difference."[10] He told America:

> "We need courage to stand up to hate ... to believe that together we can tackle big challenges like inequality and climate change ... to listen to one other and seek common ground and embrace principled compromise ... put personal or party interest aside when duty to country calls or when conscience demands."[11]

## THINK LIKE A REALISTIC OPTIMIST

While studying learned helplessness, Seligman was intrigued by the people who didn't give up. Their habit of interpreting setbacks as (1) temporary—"It won't last long," (2) specific—"It's just this one situation," and (3) changeable—"I can do something about it"—suggested how people might be immunized against helplessness, anxiety, and depression. As Seligman explained:

---

**"**

**Finding temporary and specific causes for misfortune is the art of hope. Finding permanent and universal causes for misfortune is the practice of despair.[12]**

---

Need some hope? Change what you tell yourself. This takes practice, so see Appendix 9.

## LEARN RESILIENCE

Resilience can be learned. The University of Pennsylvania's resiliency program for young adults and children has been replicated in 21 different school settings across the world, and similar programs have been developed for the U.S. Army, business professionals, and teachers. Participants learn how to build resilience in themselves and teach the techniques to those around them.

Insights have come from examining why high-risk adolescents, schizophrenics, cancer patients, military prisoners, and other survivors have beaten the odds. CEO Dean Becker highlighted the importance of resilience:

> "More than education, more than experience, more than training, a person's level of resilience will determine who succeeds and who fails. That's true in the cancer ward, it's true in the Olympics, and it's true in the boardroom."[13]

MRT, master resilience training for drill sergeants and other leaders, begins with Albert Ellis' **ABCDE model**. The soldiers learn that emotional consequences (C) are not directly caused by adversity (A) but instead from one's beliefs (B) about the situation, and they practice dispelling (D) and refuting the negative beliefs.

Failure doesn't make us depressed. What we Americans tell ourselves about the failure does. Replace "It's hopeless" with "I failed to finish this three mile run today. I need to get in better shape," or "I learned that telling my siblings they were stupid for supporting Trump doesn't work. I need to approach them differently." When we use loss and failure as learning lessons, the emotional and cognitive effects (E) are positive.

Our tendencies to ignore the positive, overgeneralize, and jump to conclusions (described in chapter 3) require confronting. There are many ways to untwist our harmful, negative thinking. Boost self-esteem and manage moods by examining the evidence to determine if what we are telling ourselves is accurate.

Many depressed, discouraged, and unmotivated Americans benefit not only from pharmacology, but also from psychology— changing their thinking and their behavior. Disputing negative thoughts and distracting ourselves from pessimistic thinking both work. According to Seligman, the combination—stopping *both* negative thinking *and* rumination—works best.[14]

*"What evidence do I have for that?"*

*"Let me be more precise."*

*"See the whole picture."*

*"Oops, look for the positive."*

*"Wrong. Cancel that."*

*"That's ridiculous."*

*"No absolutes—quantify exactly."*

*"What else could that mean?"*

*"Why assume the negative?"*

*"If_____ made it, so can I."*

Let me be clear. While optimism is linked to health, success, and happiness, some realism avoids disaster. Let's refrain from burying our heads in the sand. In her first-rate article, "How Resilience Works," senior *Harvard Business Review* editor Diane Coutu emphasized three important characteristics that make us resilient:[15]

1. a staunch acceptance of reality
2. a deep belief that life is meaningful
3. an uncanny ability to improvise

America needs to have all three as we struggle to protect health and wealth.

## ACCEPT REALITY

*Good to Great* author and business consultant Jim Collins found resilient people and companies do not ignore the sober facts essential for survival. He was initially surprised to learn from Admiral Jim Stockdale, a Hanoi Hilton captive tortured by the Vietcong for eight years, that the optimists were the ones who did NOT make it out of the camps. Those prisoners said they were going to be out by Christmas, then Easter, Fourth of July, Thanksgiving, and Christmas again, but weren't. Stockdale told Collins, "I think they all died of broken hearts."[16]

Collins coined the term "Stockdale Paradox" to refer to "perseverance with unwavering faith that you will prevail, while still having the discipline to confront the brutal facts of your current reality."[17] We have to face trouble and keep going.

Instead of denying reality, prepare for it. Morgan Stanley, the financial company that was the largest tenant in the World Trade Center on 9/11, lost only 7 of its 2,700 employees that day, because they started evacuating the south tower only a minute after the first plane hit the north one. Following the earlier World Trade Center attack in 1993, the VP of security who was a highly decorated, resilient Vietnam vet had assessed their vulnerability, prudently developed a catastrophe plan, and even drilled it.[18]

We need to know the truth and be ready. The truth is we have a lot of divide to overcome in America. Emulating the resilient, let's accept, anticipate, and act—accept that people have widely differing perspectives, anticipate how conversations can run amuck, and act to prevent and handle harmful interactions.

## FIND MEANING

Corporations, religious groups, political movements, and the military are propelled by core values and the power of purpose. A big enough reason will move us from complacent citizens to active Americans and from silently seething neighbors to working across the divide. What's your big enough reason? Mine is a country for my kids and grandkids where Americans treat each other better.

Mike Eskew, Chairman and CEO of the delivery company UPS, believes that his company's "Noble Purpose" helped them rally after a difficult, heated strike in 1997 likened to a family feud.[19] Despite big differences, UPS folks on both sides shared a common set of values. Americans share basic values too. Revisit the list of American values (Appendix 3), recall the team challenge that got Americans to the moon, and envision Americans from all parts of our country united for common good.

Resiliency relies on a deep involvement with life. The Army's resiliency program includes a spiritual fitness module, which refers not to a specific religion but to belonging to and serving something larger than the self. Soldiers work on building a "spiritual core" with self-awareness, a sense of agency, self-regulation, self-motivation, and social awareness.

Resilient individuals have strong beliefs that keep them from feeling like victims, plus a strong vision of what they want to achieve. Life matters, if you have the same religious orientation I do. Tap the spiritual and be purpose driven. Get involved. We Americans shouldn't just adapt to a divided, uncivil America.

## BE FLEXIBLE AND IMPROVISE

Both resilient organizations and individuals demonstrate plasticity and adaptability. Neither chaotic nor unbridled, they still ask "What else can we do?" and "What haven't we thought of?" In the face of uncertainty, they improvise and innovate, and in the face of adversity they bounce back. Holocaust survivors hoarded pieces of string and wire, thinking they might be useful for something, and as a result later kept shoes on in sub-freezing temps.

Be the kind of American who looks for ways to go over, under, around, or through obstacles. When damaged, our brains build new pathways. Look for opportunities and, pardon the pun, think outside the box like the UPS drivers during Hurricane Andrew who sorted packages at a diversion site and made deliveries to people stranded in their cars.

## FIND ROLE MODELS

It's hard work to mend fences, manage differences, and influence positive change. When you need a boost, find heroes and heroines to emulate. Besides supplying hope, role models provide a lead worth following and tips worth using. What *looks* effortless is the result of a huge amount of dedicated practice and persistence.

Take inspiration from Medal of Honor recipients and stories of Malala Yousafzai, Rosa Parks, Abraham Lincoln, and Susan B. Anthony. Don't forget Thomas Edison who learned 10,000 ways not to make a light bulb before his persistence paid off with one. A failed experiment or conversation is a learning opportunity. For inspiration, open the pages of some of the books on the list of recommended readings.

## COUNTER NEGATIVITY BIAS

Remember our negativity bias? Positive things have less impact than something equally emotional but negative. This tendency to remember loss and criticism more than praise and reward probably served our species well by keeping us alert to danger. However, it robs us of confidence and hope if we aren't careful.

Because it takes more positives, at least 3, 4, or 5 of them, to counter every negative, continue to count blessings, look for good, catch people doing something right, and pass out compliments. It's worth it.

## TAP YOUR SUPPORT SYSTEM

Surround yourself with positive people. Coaches, colleagues, family, and friends who believe in us, even when we don't, infuse us with energy. They encourage us to take risks. And if we fall short, their support—coupled with honest feedback and astute analysis of our roadblocks—helps us try again.

However, carefully drink from the support cup. Misery not only likes company, misery likes miserable company.[20] When scared or down, being with others who are in *similar* spots and understand our pain provides comfort, as long as we don't get stuck ruminating. Check whether being with people who share your political positions is encouraging you to work for peace or deepening the divide. De-polarization within may be required.

When we're at our lowest, we may encounter an always optimistic Pollyanna who can appear insensitive and make us feel worse. Their positivity is a "disconnect" from our despair. We're depressed, and now we have a second, additional reason to feel down—people are telling us we shouldn't be depressed but we are. Empathetic folks who aren't absorbed by our emotions will ideally start alongside us in the tunnel and gradually help us see the light at the end—that this president and the pandemic too shall pass.

## BUILD CONFIDENCE BY EXTENDING YOURSELF

Self-worth and self-confidence rise when we reach out, volunteer, and help someone. Similarly, learning a new language, instrument, or craft promotes a sense of achievement and mastery. You can help the country and yourself by developing the skills needed for improving relationships, handling conflict, and managing emotions. Every skill is a resource—a way to shift your demand/resource stress ratio, increase self-confidence, and keep hope afloat.

## BRINGING AMERICANS TOGETHER TAKES DETERMINATION

Remember, Garfield found peak performers differed in many ways, like skill and personality, but the one element clearly shared by all of them was a "virtually unassailable belief in the likelihood of their own success."[21] Not naïve, just incredibly determined. Like all of us, outstanding performers question whether they have it in them, but then commit and consciously use forward motion as the antidote to doubt.

As you think about making a difference, which of the following did Garfield's study of over 1,500 successful people find to be TRUE about those performers?

_____  Have a mission

_____  Use foresight to help plan strategically

_____  "Stretch" to attain specific goals even if it means taking risks

_____  Have extremely high self-confidence and sense of self-worth

_____  Have a significant need for responsibility and control

_____  Take credit for their own good ideas

_____  Know how to mentally rehearse key situations as preparation

_____  Learn from their mistakes and from the past

_____  Believe in their own ability

_____  Fully utilize their time and capacities

_____  Flourish even when other people don't understand their contributions

_____  Are innovators

_____  Know how to work with other people

_____  Act decisively when opportunities present themselves

_____     Anticipate and adapt to change by growing along with it

_____     Regularly check to see that they are on course with their mission

_____     Never rest on their laurels

All of the above!

## KEEP GOING

Meaningful missions may not be permanent, but peak performers never stop learning or searching for the next place to put their skills to work. Today it may be healing the political divide within your family and voting in competent leadership. Tomorrow it may be the environment, national debt, feeding the poor, or inspiring children to lives of service. Keep looking for where you are needed, then jump in.

> **Peak performers persevere because**
> **they believe in their vision**
> **and in their ability to carry it out.**
> **Have hope.**

Take comfort in the positive actions of your fellow Americans. For example, in February 2017 at the annual National Campaign for Political and Civic Engagement conference organized by Harvard's Institute for Politics, over 70 student ambassadors from more than 28 colleges and universities worked to create concrete community-based action plans for addressing what they saw as the root causes of national divisiveness.

Bridge-building groups like Braver Angels, Living Room Conversations, Convergence, and Village Square are there for you. Across the country, people are standing up, not down—working for Covid containment and science, staying home to protect the health care workers who stay on the job to protect us, and fighting for equality across income, gender, race, and preference. We *are* all in this together.

We can get along. America has a decent success record, which should build our belief that "we can." Though we still have a lot to do, America made it through the Civil War, the Great Depression, two world wars, and McCarthyism. We fought each other over Vietnam and civil rights and then elected a black president—twice—and almost voted in a female, a Mormon, a gay, and a Jewish leader.

There are hopeful signs for the future. "We were able to beat back slavery, women won the right to vote, and America has lived through racist presidents before," says Reverend William Barber, of North Carolina's "Moral Monday" civil-rights protests.[22]

Recognizing the pain and history of horrible racial injustices, the thousands, who peacefully demonstrated to protest George Floyd's killing at the hands of police officers, represented a broad coalition of Americans. Never give up on the heart of this democracy. Barber says he won't. He wants us to be the "moral defibrillators of our time and shock the heart of this nation."[23]

We're in a crisis, so use this proffered emergency kit for finding common ground. It's urgent that we heal. Together let's make America a caring, "heart healthy" country.

## CONCLUSION  **Putting It All Together**

Strengthening our democracy requires the will and stamina of marathoners. Take care of yourself so you can make a difference healing your family, neighborhood, and nation. America needs you—urgently. In her article, "How to Get Out of the Cycle of Outrage in a Trump World," HuffPost founder Arianna Huffington advises:

"So whatever you do, don't just let yourself get stuck in the outrage storm—that particular weather pattern is likely to be here for a long time. Remember, you have the power to step out of the storm, think carefully about how best to channel your valuable energy, and then take action. And there are so many ways to do that."[1]

See Huffington's article and Joel Berg's *America, we need to talk: A Self-Help Book for the Nation* for groups you can join and specific causes that will help our nation.[2] Be an inspiration, a role model, a peak performing American with grit. Take constructive action by yourself and with others.

From Part One I hope you better understand other Americans' views, biases, and values. In Part Two's chapters I hope you found specific skills for managing differences, repairing strained relationships, influencing, and dealing with resistance. And, from Part Three I hope you're taking specific strategies—ways to not take other Americans' comments personally, how to cope, and reasons to hope. I hope you're better equipped with words and phrases for constructively disagreeing, collaboratively reaching decisions, and working along side other Americans.

Find common ground and get engaged with and for America. The lower productivity of actively disengaged U.S. workers is estimated to cost our economy about $450 to $500 billion a year. Disengagement from America can cost us our democracy.

Please act on some ideas from this American survival guide—alone and with other Americans. Let's un-divide. If you help just one person or one family or one neighborhood or one cause, what a difference we'll make.

Collaborate, cope, and care so we survive and thrive.

# Why all the Fuss About Competence and Fitness?

## DUTY TO WARN

### LEADERSHIP COMPETENCIES

Along with intelligence, industry knowledge, and experience, what should we look for in a leader? Leadership selection and development focus on these competencies:

- **Intrapersonal skills:** self-awareness and self-control, emotional maturity, integrity, trustworthiness, curiosity, ability to learn from mistakes, grit, resilience, taking initiative, accepting responsibility
- **Interpersonal skills:** empathy, communication, social skills, relationship development, collaboration
- **Leadership skills:** ability to chart a course, inspire and motivate, role model, engage and influence, build and maintain a functional team, assume and share authority
- **Execution skills:** ability to plan, organize, use and monitor processes and resources

Not one of us will be an outstanding person for *every* position—or even successfully grow into a job. To predict who will be an effective leader, look for emotional competence[1] and learning agility.[2] Look for someone with character, competence, and coachability.

## NOT EVERYONE IS FIT FOR THE OVAL OFFICE

Before the 2016 election, fifty of the nation's most senior G.O.P. national security officials, signed a letter saying Trump lacked the qualifications—character, values, temperament, and experience—to be president and would put our country at risk.[3]

The officials warned Trump would be dangerous to our national security and well-being and be the most reckless president in history.[4]

Mental health professionals agreed. Early in Trump's term and despite the Goldwater gag rule, over 70,000 psychologists, psychiatrists, and mental health professionals signed a petition declaring Trump "psychologically incapable of competently discharging the duties of the President of the United States."

A letter voicing concern was written to President Obama immediately after Trump's election,[5] and books like *The Dangerous Case of Donald Trump* from esteemed clinicians were quickly published.[6] Hearing the call, a congressional bill was written requesting that a panel of physicians and mental health professionals—a Presidential capacity commission—be established to examine his mental health and that of all future presidents.

Three years into Trump's administration, esteemed Marine general and former defense secretary James Mattis felt compelled to break his silence about Trump's lack of mature leadership. Mattis denounced Trump for deliberating attempting to divide us, endangering our country, and threatening the Constitution.[7] Quickly, in an unprecedented move, other senior military officials endorsed Mattis' position.[8]

Military leaders, lawyers, scientists, civil rights activists, historians, and economists worry about a second Trump administration for many reasons. My perspective is psychological—and performance based.

## DUTY TO WARN

Psychological professionals spoke out in 2017 at risk of being accused of violating our ethical code, because linked to our licenses is the *ethical duty to warn the public of potential harm*. We are duty bound to use our professional judgment.

Though I can't ethically give Trump the diagnosis of narcissistic personality disorder—I'm doubly trained as a counseling and organizational psychologist, not a clinical one, and I've never met him—the NPD description seems to fit. The extreme danger of a president with an excessive need to maintain his self-image was, and is, alarming.

Our conclusions that Trump is unfit are based on thousands of tweets and hours of video available to everyone—far more than a diagnostician would typically have. If you examine the nine characteristics of the narcissistic personality disorder below and consider Trump's behavior, you'll probably understand our concern. "The hallmarks of narcissistic personality disorder (NPD) are grandiosity, a lack of empathy for other people, and a need for admiration."[9] Narcissists, psychopaths, and Machiavellians share some characteristics but are different.[10]

## CHARACTERISTICS OF THE NARCISSISTIC PERSONALITY DISORDER

According to the DSM-5, the standard diagnostic manual for mental health professionals, to warrant the label narcissistic personality disorder **only five of the following** (barely more than 50%) are required:[11]

1. Has a grandiose sense of self-importance (e.g., exaggerates achievements and talents, expects to be recognized as superior without commensurate achievements)
2. Is preoccupied with fantasies of unlimited success, power, brilliance, beauty, or ideal love

3. Believes that he or she is "special" and unique and can only be understood by, or should associate with, other special or high-status people (or institutions)
4. Requires excessive admiration
5. Has a sense of entitlement, i.e., unreasonable expectations of especially favorable treatment or automatic compliance with his or her expectations
6. Is interpersonally exploitative, i.e., takes advantage of others to achieve his or her own ends
7. Lacks empathy: unwilling [or, often unable] to recognize or identify with the feelings and needs of others
8. Is often envious of others or believes that others are envious of him or her
9. Shows arrogant, haughty behaviors or attitudes

## SEE FOR YOURSELF

Instead of relying on a Fox reporter or CNN's description, encourage others (better yet sit with them) and actually watch footage of this president and read his tweets. Faithful Trump supporters smile that he has been "shaking things up," but what we are seeing is *not* normal. U.S. presidents do not call a past president a "sick dude," repeatedly bring up that they won the last election, or say they have the "biggest brain."

Not only would most Americans not allow their children to behave the way he does, his need for attention is excessive by psychological standards. Far more extreme than a typical politician seeking center stage, his self-aggrandizement casts serious doubt on the veracity of what he says.

Journalists and psychologists alike have learned that what someone brags about is a sign of what the person is lying about. All Americans should especially start digging when they hear, "Believe me." That phrase, which Trump uses frequently, suggests what is being said is baseless or won't sit right with the audience.

In research studies when asked made-up questions like, "Have you ever heard of_____ " and given a made-up name, narcissists answer, "Yeah, of course I've heard of him." Just like Trump, they mislead and avoid the truth plus react to contrary viewpoints with anger, rage, and self-righteousness. Protecting yourself from charismatic narcissists merits consideration.[12] [13] [14] They thrive in chaotic times.

## LIES

Politicians aren't pure, but since taking office Trump has clocked more than 18,000 lies and misleading statements, averaging 15 per day,[15] plus repeated them after they were disproven.[16] Trump isn't merely exaggerating.

There is a behavior pattern here—something psychologists and investigators look for. When confronted with the lack of evidence for his outlandish statements, Trump refused to back down about Obama's birth certificate, 3 to 5 million illegals costing him the popular vote, size of his inauguration crowd, and Russian election meddling.[17] It took him months to admit Covid-19 was a world-wide public health crisis not a hoax.

Continuing with untruths after being informed of the truth indicates either (1) an inability to accept what is real, or else (2) the deliberate, immoral repetition of falsehoods to create a new narrative. Both are unfitting of our highest office. America cannot effectively function when we must seriously doubt what its president says. Sharpiegate—his false, Hurricane Dorian emergency weather map—was unacceptable. The deaths from his coronavirus inaction were catastrophic.

Years before Trump was elected and writing about narcissists in general, clinical psychologist Leon F. Seltzer explained that when narcissists are

> "asked a question that might oblige them to admit some vulnerability, deficiency, or culpability, they're apt to falsify the evidence (i.e., lie—yet without really acknowledging such prevarication to themselves), hastily change the subject, or respond as though they'd been asked something entirely different."[18]

You've seen Trump repeatedly do exactly what Seltzer described, if you've watched Trump fielding questions.

What clinical experts like Lance Dodes[19] try to highlight is that the manner in which Trump lies (not only to scam or brag) suggests he even **believes** some of the lies he tells, which actually makes him more persuasive initially but highly dangerous for the nation.[20] Trump appears to be convinced of facts that praise or favor him— which he cites again and again—and to make up reality to suit his self-image.[21] Years before Trump's administration, Seltzer warned, "No one equivocates or dis-informs with greater conviction than the narcissist-politician, whose blatant disregard for facts can at times be mind-boggling."[22]

While many Americans are numb to Trump's flagrant misbehavior, others rationalize his actions by telling themselves we all make mistakes. We do, but not of this magnitude and frequency— especially without owning them.

## WHAT ABOUT IMPEACHMENT?

Speaking under oath at risk to their careers, the House impeachment witnesses referred to Trump's behavior as a "drug deal" that many were in on. Impeachment wasn't about overturning his election—it was holding Trump accountable for his un-American actions *while in office.*

What are the basic facts? Only the third president in history to be impeached, Trump asked the Ukrainian government to investigate a political rival, which makes his misconduct more egregious than Nixon's and exactly what our founding fathers worried about. And, by withholding vital aid which Congress had approved, he left a NATO ally at war with Russia high and dry. What's a logical conclusion? He attempted to cheat to be re-elected with the help of foreign assistance.

Because 53% of Americans said Trump was not telling the truth about Ukraine,[23] and the majority (75%) wanted witnesses and documents at the Senate trial to settle the case either way,[24] failure to provide them smelled like a coverup.

Shrugging shoulders and saying "That's just Trump" moved to where the majority of the country favored an impeachment inquiry and wanted impeachment trial witnesses. We split on removal. Elected Republicans refrained from defending Trump's actual behavior, decided not to run again, and accused Democrats of just hating the man. It's Trump himself who branded questioning as "witch hunts," tweeting that term approximately every third day.[25]

## ABOVE THE LAW?

You don't need psychological or legal training to see the danger of an emboldened president believing and bragging, "I can do anything I want" and "I have total authority." In addition to blatantly asking for China and Ukraine's investigation of his rival, Trump has called for an opponent to be "locked up," labeled Congressional representatives who disagree with him "crooks," and promised to uncover the identity of a whistleblower which is blatantly against the law. In six weeks, in the middle of the coronavirus crisis, Trump fired six internal watchdogs—inspectors general—whose role is oversight.[26]

Former federal prosecutors pointed to Trump's behavior during the trials of Paul Manafort and Michael Cohen saying that the president repeatedly dangled pardons and posted threatening tweets to try to sway former associates from working with the special counsel's office. Prosecutors concluded, "...if he weren't in the White House, President Trump would be charged with serious crimes. This isn't even a close case."[27]

With parallels to a mob boss or bully, Trump's tweets about the sentencing of his convicted buddy Roger Stone threw the president's own Department of Justice into disarray. Prosecutors quit in protest, their replacements argued for stiffer sentences, and more than 1,100 former DOJ officials called for Trump's hire—Attorney General William Barr—to resign.[28]

Because Trump has badmouthed so many, his three-year silence about former National Security Advisor Michael Flynn has been noteworthy along with his refusal to release his taxes. Trump had been warned by the Obama administration not to hire Flynn.[29]

Retired lieutenant general Flynn pled guilty under oath in late 2017—to a felony false-statement charge brought by special counsel Robert Mueller.[30] Trump announced he fired his National Security Adviser Flynn because Flynn had lied about his conversations with Russia's ambassador.[31] Trump fired Flynn not after he knew he lied, but after the news went public.[32]

We have to dig to get facts and be careful of revisionist remarks from the White House. Again, people see the same thing very differently, but a federal judge already ruled the FBI did not entrap Flynn.[33]

Opposition to Trump is unprecedented because his actions are. Americans are appropriately concerned about the rule of law—a bedrock of democracy. No president is king, has total power, or can shoot someone on 5th Avenue with impunity.

## DANGER?

It is not uncommon for people deserving the narcissist diagnosis to rise to positions of power and amass fortunes, while having fragile egos and ever-vigilant defense systems extraordinarily easy to trigger.[34][35] Lots of money, power, and attention are their desires.

Despite Trump's popularity with his base, there is real danger.[36] Americans' anxiety is warranted when their president encourages aggression—"liberate Michigan"—and is easily provoked. Punch Trump and he's proud to punch back harder, which is why many fear him having the nuclear codes.[37] Within days of taking office, he hung up on Australia's leader and threatened to send troops to Mexico. Now he has threatened to withhold aid to states who allow voting by mail for safety during a health crisis.

Refusing to wear a mask and taking potentially harmful medication against medical advice set a dangerous example for other Americans. He ignores federal guidelines, plus dismisses science and advisers—saying, "My gut tells me more sometimes than anybody else's brain can ever tell me."[38][39]

When researchers give narcissists a question, ask them how confident they are in their answer, and have them bet a certain amount based on how confident they are, the narcissists are always *extremely* confident, not just optimistic. They lose a lot in those situations because they think they're smarter than they actually are.[40] Trump went through six bankruptcies.

## BRAGGING BOSSES V. OUTSTANDING LEADERS

Like the mental health professionals, organizational psychologists who evaluate job candidates and develop leaders saw Trump unfit for the Oval Office based on his behavior and bankruptcies. Not sounding an alarm would have been professionally irresponsible.

Bragging bosses are very different from outstanding leaders. Exceptional leaders are the first to own up to mistakes and the last to take credit for success. Those who have taken companies from good to great have been known for their unique combination of humility and fierce resolve.[41] Leaders with emotional competence succeed.[42]

In sharp contrast, problem performers overrate their performance. Those who are prone to exaggerating their accomplishments and downplaying the contributions of others reject crucial feedback. They create toxic environments, hurt productivity, harm profitability, get into legal trouble, and accrue debt.[43 44 45 46 47 48] Prior to our economic disaster Trump bragged he loved debt, and in his first two years—*before* the pandemic and during a *bull* market—our nation's debt ballooned to $23 trillion, a record high.[49]

## CHARACTER, COMPETENCE, AND COACHABILITY

When selecting a candidate for a leadership position, you look for character, competence, and coachability—that ability to seek out what the person does not know and profit from the wisdom of others. One who owns his/her actions and can learn from them. One who is respected. One who gives people the plain hard truth plus needed reassurance. We don't have that kind of POTUS, whether Trump is a narcissist or not.[50]

A major obstacle to a good prognosis both for ineffective leaders and for narcissists in general is their perception that problems are caused by others not them, making self-improvement unnecessary. According to Trump, pandemic blame rests with the World Health Organization, the Chinese, bad masks, but certainly not him. In comparison, effective leaders realize they benefit from briefings and from devil's advocates who challenge their thinking.

If the country had begun locking down cities and limiting social contact on March 1, two weeks earlier than most people started staying home, 50,000 fewer would have died."[51] A week would have saved tens of thousands. The buck stops with the president.

People with the narcissistic disorder routinely put their needs ahead of everyone else's and view others as existing to serve them. Why is this important? Failure to consider human needs has been found highly damaging to morale.[52] [53] Bullying matters.[54] [55]

In short, Trump's conduct falls below appropriate performance standards for the leader of the free world. He has shattered our norms, accepted Russian and Saudi denials over his own intelligence agencies' data, lied often, cost Americans their lives, and threatened the Constitution. Read what the world says about him.[56] [57] His alienation of allies comes at a time when we may most need them.

From my perspective, Trump is not the right medicine for our economic, health, and racial emergency. If you believe he is, I wish we could have a conversation with both of us using the skills in this survival kit to manage our differences and disagree without being disagreeable.

It is my ethical duty to warn. America deserves a better leader.

# Basic Differences Between Left and Right

B
elow you'll find two guides to understanding how Americans on the left differ from those on the right—adapted from Kevin Wilhelm and Natalie Hoffman's *How to Talk to the "Other Side"*[1] and Dennis Prager's opinion piece on the conservative site *Townhall.com*.[2]

Purposefully pointing out differences, the comparisons have an "us v. them" feel, unlike the list of shared core American values in Appendix 3 and the descriptions of our shared biases and values in this kit's third chapter. To get Americans united, both understanding differences and finding similarities can be useful.

These lists outlining differences might be a starting point for talking across the divide, as long as we carefully remember:

- most of us have views more nuanced than these end points suggest
- most of us are more similar than what gets depicted by the media
- all Reds and Blues don't agree with these descriptions—or with each other
- within the tribes there's a lot of variation, especially on certain issues
- we can hold some views on the right, on the left, and anywhere in between

Our challenge is to become one tribe—to explore differences, work for common good, and get along. Hunt for commonality not extremes. For example, we may share interests, goals, and even the same religious faith. People ask, "How you can be a Christian and support Trump?" and "How can you be a Christian and not support Trump?" "What would Jesus do for immigrants, the environment, the sick, and the poor?"

As I say, "In God I trust," let me gently remind all of us that the framers of our Constitution sought separation of church and state plus freedom of religion but not freedom from religion. When claiming independence, our forefathers declared people are created equal with the right to liberty and pursuit of happiness. America has amended the Constitution 27 times to reflect this need to protect rights and equality, and since 1789, over 11,000 amendments have been introduced.[3] We continue to struggle with how a citizen can exercise freedoms without putting another—or our country— in danger.

How can we stop demonizing? How can an evangelical treat an atheist, deist, agnostic, Jew, or Muslim as an equal? How can an atheist, deist, agnostic, Jew, or Muslim treat an evangelical as an equal? Being a Christian doesn't make someone a Republican, just like being black doesn't make someone a Democrat. No doubt you know people outside your tribe who are exceptions—and exceptional.

Sincerely seeking to understand one another helps people get along better. As you know, stereotypes and generalizations don't actually tell you anything about the person sitting across from you.[4] A meaningful exercise in the Braver Angels Red/Blue workshops involves participants uncovering misguided stereotypes and wrestling with the kernel of truth in them.

Because the more we define ourselves as part of a group, the more we like that group and its members,[5] what a difference it would make if we first identified as Americans, not Red, Blue, or Purple.

With curiosity examine Wilhelm and Hoffman's and Prager's guides in the following tables.

You'll probably find something below you disagree with, and that's the point. "Each side might be surprised at their similarities if they took the time to discover them."[6]

| DEMOCRAT/ PROGRESSIVE | REPUBLICAN/ CONSERVATIVE |
|---|---|
| Pro-choice | Pro-life |
| Believe higher taxes are needed on wealthy and big business | Want minimal taxes |
| Value people over economy. Stop Covid-19 spread or economic pain will be much worse | Covid-19 cure must not be worse than virus |
| Socially progressive, more accepting of diversity | Socially conservative, traditional, isolationist |
| Trust scientists | Skeptical of scientists |
| Pro-immigrant rights—we are all immigrants | Anti-immigration—don't want open borders |
| Pro-government to take care of less fortunate, regulate corporations because they work in their self-interest | Anti-government, less regulation, free market better than government at solving problems |
| Pro-environment, climate change advocate | Anti-environment, climate change skeptic |
| Gun control advocates | Gun rights advocates |
| Atheist | Religious |
| Freedom = equity + opportunity | Freedom = individualism |
| Distrustful of authority and police | Respect authority, prefer law & order |

Adapted from Kevin Wilhelm and Natalie Hoffman's (2020) *How to Talk to the "Other Side."*[7]

| ISSUE | LEFT | RIGHT |
|---|---|---|
| **Human Nature** | basically good— society is primarily responsible for evil | not basically good— individual is primarily responsible for evil |
| **Economic Goal** | equality | prosperity |
| **Primary Role of the State** | increase and protect equality | increase and protect liberty |
| **Government** | large as needed | small as possible |
| **Family Ideal** | any loving unit of people | a married father and mother, and children |
| **Good and Evil** | relative to individual and/or society | based on universal absolutes |
| **Ideal American Identity** | world citizen | American citizen |
| **How to Make a Good Society** | abolish inequality | develop each citizen's moral character |
| **Greatest Threat** | environmental catastrophe (currently global warming) | evil (currently radical Islamist violence) |
| **Guns** | ideally abolished except for police, armed forces, registered sportsmen | ideally widely owned by responsible individuals for self-protection and the protection of others |
| **View of Illegal Immigrants** | welcomed guests | illegal immigrants |
| **Nature** | intrinsically valuable | made for man |

Adapted from Dennis Prager's *A Guide to Basic Differences Between Left and Right*.[8]

Though not readily apparent, we *can* find common ground, and we urgently have to. Let me encourage you to spend time with Chapter 4, "Starting with Empathy—for Both Sides."

# Appendix 3

# Ten Core American Values[1]

1. **individualism**
   - belief that each person is unique, special and a "basic unit of nature"
   - emphasis on individual initiative
   - stress need for independence
   - premium on individual expression
   - value privacy

2. **equality**
   - open society that ideally treats everyone equally
   - little hierarchy
   - informal
   - directness in relations with others

3. **materialism**
   - a "right" to be well off and physically comfortable
   - judge people by their possessions

4. **science and technology**
   - values scientific approaches
   - primary source of good
   - major factor in change

## 5. progress and change

- belief in changing self and country
- "Manifest Destiny"
- optimism—nothing is impossible

## 6. work and leisure

- strong work ethic
- work is the basis of recognition, power
- idleness seen as a threat to society
- leisure is a reward for hard work

## 7. competition

- aggressive and competitive nature encouraged
- Be First (#1) mentality

## 8. mobility

- a people on the move
- vertical (social / economic) as well as physical mobility

## 9. volunteerism

- belief in helping others (related to equality concept)
- philanthropy admired
- a personal choice not a communal expectation
- involves associations / denominations rather than kin-groups

## 10. action and achievement oriented

- emphasis on getting things done
- priority on planning and setting goals
- tendency to be brief and businesslike
- practical
- measure results
- focus on function and pragmatism

## Appendix 4  Improving Your People Presence

I n these tense times it's worth reflecting on whether you are the kind of person others enjoy swapping ideas with. There's a chance they feel trapped and ambushed in your presence.

Which of the following describe you?

- Do you smile when you meet and talk with people?
- Do you make the conversation easy?
- Are you really interested in what other Americans do and believe?
- Are you friendly with a good sense of humor?
- Do you give the impression that you enjoy life?
- Are you generous with praise?
- Do you look for the good in others?
- Are you patient, helpful, and considerate?
- Do you reflect optimism when facing problems?
- Do you express yourself using positive words and approaches?
- Do you avoid criticizing the unimportant and overlook what you can?

If you couldn't answer an enthusiastic "Yes," take stock and make improvements. We all can.

# Appendix 5

# How Are People Influenced?

## WHICH DO YOU THINK RESEARCHERS HAVE FOUND TO BE TRUE?

1. Attempts to persuade people are more likely to reinforce their existing opinions than to change their opinions.
2. People tend to read and listen to arguments that support their existing views and to ignore arguments that don't.
3. When exposed to information inconsistent with their beliefs, people frequently distort the new information.
4. People tend to remember information that supports their views better than information that doesn't.
5. In many situations people are influenced more by other individuals ("opinion leaders") than they are by mass communication (advertising, reports).
6. If the audience is friendly (agrees, already uses your approach) or is not likely to hear opposing arguments, then a one-sided message that stresses only favorable information is most effective.
7. People who are critical, well educated, likely to hear opposing claims, or hostile (already disagree) are more influenced by two-sided messages that both support one view and refute the other.
8. The credibility of the source strongly affects how much a message influences beliefs.

9. Men who tend to be socially withdrawn or who are overtly hostile toward people they encounter remain relatively uninfluenced by any form of persuasion.

10. Studies typically find women to be more persuasible than men.

11. Because different people have different beliefs, interests, and attitudes, an influence strategy which is believable to some people will not be believable to others.

12. More than one single attempt to influence people is needed, if they are required to change their minds.

13. An influence attempt must get noticed and be relevant to the person's own needs and interests.

14. Arouse someone's needs before presenting information relevant to those needs.

15. When three or more messages are given in a row, the first and last tend to be remembered best.

16. Typically the first information presented is more effective than the last.

17. Some of the most effective messages are those whose purpose is disguised until virtually the last minute, probably because forewarning gives the audience the ability to think of counterarguments.

18. People tend to overestimate their persuasiveness via text-based communication.

19. People tend to believe what is socially reinforced (what their friends, family, and authority figures believe) and what is consistent with their own experience.

20. People believe what they want to believe. (There is a stronger correlation between belief and desire than belief and evidence.)

## ALL OF THE ABOVE ARE TRUE.

# Methods for Dealing with Organizational Resistance

J ohn P. Kotter and Leonard A. Schlesinger described six methods for dealing with resistance to organizational change on a
continuum from slower to faster approaches.[1] In their excellent HBR article you will find common uses plus advantages and
disadvantages of:

1. Education + communication
2. Participation + involvement
3. Facilitation + support
4. Negotiation + agreement
5. Manipulation + co-optation
6. Explicit + implicit coercion

These are strategies worth considering for dealing with resistance
to family, community, or national changes. Each approach works
depending on the situation, and I'll attest to that based on my consulting practice.

The first two methods (education + communication and participation + involvement) can be very time consuming but often elicit
excellent implementation results. When people are informed and
comprehend a change, some resistance disappears.

No other approach works as well as facilitation + support when
people have trouble adjusting.

Negotiating a deal with a workable compromise can sometimes be easy but often results only in a cease-fire, not true buy-in for the long haul. In some situations, it's the only feasible option.

The final two strategies of manipulation and coercion can be speedy and tempting in the short run, but risky long term. Unfortunately, when one party's goal is to force a health care policy, regulatory change, or Supreme Court nominee, the other retaliates. America becomes less rather than more unified. Choose your approach wisely, because the harder you push the stronger the push back.

# Practice Coping through Positive Self-Talk

## COGNITIVE RESTRUCTURING

| Replace Negative Self-Talk | with | Positive Self-Talk |
|---|---|---|
| I can't possibly handle this. | → | I'll find ways to deal with this. |
| I'm not doing as well as I should. | → | I've had some progress. |
| This really makes me angry! | → | Relax. Slow down. Find out more. |
| This is going to be awful. | → | Prepare. |
| This will never work. | → | |
| They must be crazy! | → | |
| What's going to happen next?! | → | |

**Successful athletes tell themselves "ONE MORE" and "BREATHE".**

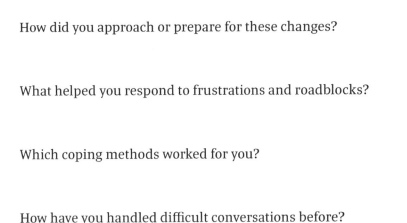

# Appendix 8  Using Appreciative Inquiry

## HOW HAVE YOU HANDLED CHANGE BEFORE?

**List significant events or periods in your life.** (High or low points such as, high school, first job, college, job or career change, move, marriage, divorce, becoming a parent, surgery)

How did you approach or prepare for these changes?

What helped you respond to frustrations and roadblocks?

Which coping methods worked for you?

How have you handled difficult conversations before?

What did you learn that you can build on now?

## Appendix 9

# Cultivate Confidence— What could you say instead?

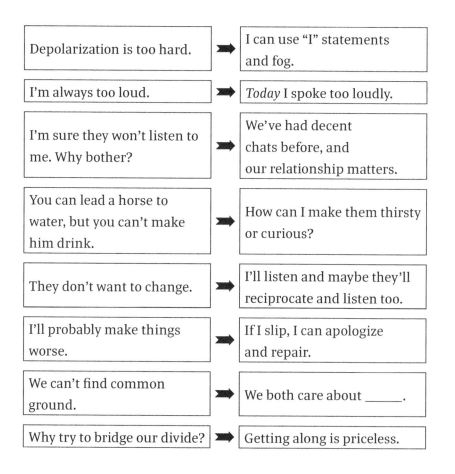

| | | |
|---|---|---|
| Depolarization is too hard. | ➡ | I can use "I" statements and fog. |
| I'm always too loud. | ➡ | *Today* I spoke too loudly. |
| I'm sure they won't listen to me. Why bother? | ➡ | We've had decent chats before, and our relationship matters. |
| You can lead a horse to water, but you can't make him drink. | ➡ | How can I make them thirsty or curious? |
| They don't want to change. | ➡ | I'll listen and maybe they'll reciprocate and listen too. |
| I'll probably make things worse. | ➡ | If I slip, I can apologize and repair. |
| We can't find common ground. | ➡ | We both care about _____. |
| Why try to bridge our divide? | ➡ | Getting along is priceless. |

**PEAK PERFORMERS PERSEVERE BECAUSE
THEY BELIEVE IN THEIR VISION
AND IN THEIR ABILITY TO CARRY IT OUT.**

# Notes

## CHAPTER 1

1. Brooks, A. C. (2019). *Love your enemies: How decent people can save America from the culture of contempt,* HarperCollins.
2. Garfield, C. (1986). *Peak performers: The new heroes of American business,* William Morrow.
3. https://animalhow.com/horse-pull-capacity/
4. http://www.ruralheritage.com/messageboard/frontporch/5517.htm
5. Cole, G. (2004). *Management theory and practice* (6th ed.). Cengage Learning.
6. Fisher, R. & Ury, W. (1983). *Getting to yes: Negotiating agreement without giving in,* Houghton Mifflin.
7. https://www.tandfonline.com/doi/full/10.1080/15534510.2016.1171796
8. https://static1.squarespace.com/static/50faacdee4b0dc8c8e2b878b/t/50fd68e5e4b0dcfb3cb6776b/1358784741782
9. Duckwork, A. (2016). *Grit: The power of passion and perseverance.* Scribner.
10. Markova, D. & McArthur, A. (2015). *Collaborative intelligence: Thinking with people who think differently.* Spiegel & Grau.
11. https://www.strateg-business.com/article06207?gko=f1af3
12. https://www.strategy-business.com/article/06207?gko=f1af3
13. Patterson, K. Grenny, J., Maxfield, D., McMillan, R., & Switzler, A. (2008). *Influencer: The power to change anything.* McGraw-Hill.
14. https://psycnet.apa.org/record/2015-28930-001
15. https://www.huffpost.com/entry/a-freedom-lesson-to-remem_b_8510934
16. Frankl, V. (1997). *Man's Search for Meaning.* Pocket Books.
17. https://libquotes.com/robert-benchley/quote/lbp6t8h

## CHAPTER 2

1. https://www.people-press.org/2016/06/22/6-how-do-the-political-parties-make-you-feel/
2. https://www.forbes.com/sites/andrewsolender/2020/06/07/80-of-voters-think-the-country-is-out-of-control-and-most-see-biden-as-the-one-to-fix-it-poll-finds/#693fa66c644c
3. https://www.people-press.org/2019/06/19/public-highly-critical-of-state-of-political-discourse-in-the-u-s

4. http://fortune.com/2015/08/07/ceo-pay-ratio-sec-income-inequality/

5. https://www.pewresearch.org/fact-tank/2018/09/06/the-american-middle-class-is-stable-in-size-but-losing-ground-financially-to-upper-income-families/

6. https://www.vox.com/policy-and-politics/2017/9/18/16305486/what-really-happened-in-2016

7. Ibid.

8. https://theconversation.com/the-most-unpopular-presidential-election-winner-ever-could-win-again-in-2020-115752

9. https://www.washingtonpost.com/politics/poll-trump-draws-low-marks-for-transition-response-to-russian-hacking/2017/01/17/0926302a-dc25-11e6-ad42-f3375f271c9c_story.html

10. https://www.people-press.org/2016/11/21/voters-evaluations-of-the-campaign/

11. https://www.washingtonpost.com/news/monkey-cage/wp/2016/12/18/a-new-poll-shows-an-astonishing-52-of-republicans-think-trump-won-the-popular-vote/

12. https://time.com/4457110/internet-trolls/

13. https://www.journalism.org/2019/10/02/americans-are-wary-of-the-role-social-media-sites-play-in-delivering-the-news/

14. https://news.gallup.com/poll/267047/americans-trust-mass-media-edges-down.aspx

15. https://www.journalism.org/2018/09/25/democrats-and-republicans-remain-split-on-support-for-news-medias-watchdog-role/

16. https://www.journalism.org/2017/05/10/americans-attitudes-about-the-news-media-deeply-divided-along-partisan-lines/

17. https://www.journalism.org/2019/10/02/americans-are-wary-of-the-role-social-media-sites-play-in-delivering-the-news/

18. https://guides.lib.umich.edu/c.php?g=637508&p=4462444

19. https://www.aeaweb.org/articles?id=10.1257/aer.20160812

20. https://www.vox.com/policy-and-politics/2017/9/8/16263710/fox-news-presidential-vote-study

21. https://www.newsbreak.com/news/0ONxRwiU/the-right-wing-medias-contempt-for-truth-has-never-been-more-dangerous

22. https://www.nytimes.com/2020/04/16/us/politics/michael-savage-trump-coronavirus.html?referringSource=articleShare

23. Frankl, V. (1997). *Man's Search for Meaning*. Pocket Books.

24. https://medium.com/@alexey__kovalev/message-to-american-media-from-russia-6e2e76eeae77

25. Ibid.

26. https://firstdraftnews.org/latest/recent-research-reveals-false-rumours-really-do-travel-faster-and-further-than-the-truth/

27. https://www.cbsnews.com/news/mass-shootings-2019-more-than-days-365/

28. https://www.nytimes.com/interactive/2020/04/01/business/coronavirus-gun-sales.html?action=click&module=Latest&pgtype=Homepage

29. Guinness, O.. (2008). *The case for civility: And why our future depends on it.* HarperCollins.

30. http://www.npr.org/2017/07/03/535044005/americans-say-civility-has-worsened-under-trump-trust-in-institutions-down

31. https://www.splcenter.org/20160413/trump-effect-impact-presidential-campaign-our-nations-schools

32. https://thehill.com/policy/national-security/416418-hate-crimes-up-for-third-year-in-a-row

33. https://www.salon.com/2019/10/14/white-house-press-organization-condemns-pro-trump-video-depicting-violence-against-journalists/

34. www.pewresearch.org/global/2018/10/01/trumps-international-ratings-remain-low-especially-among-key-allies/

35. https://www.politico.com/news/2020/03/13/trump-coronavirus-testing-128971

36. https://www.cbsnews.com/news/andrew-cuomo-new-york-coronavirus-trump-politics-fight/

37. https://www.bcg.com/en-us/publications/2019/fixing-the-flawed-approach-to-diversity.aspx

38. https://www.ted.com/search?cat=talks&q=%22We+Need+to+Talk+About+Injustice%22+-+Bryan+Stevenson

39. https://time.com/longform/south-lynching-history/

40. https://www.civilrightsproject.ucla.edu/research/k-12-education/integration-and-diversity/harming-our-common-future-americas-segregated-schools-65-years-after-brown/Brown-65-050919v4-final.pdf

41. https://www.pewresearch.org/fact-tank/2014/12/12/racial-wealth-gaps-great-recession/

42. https://www.prri.org/research/poll-race-religion-politics-americans-social-networks/

43. https://immigrationtounitedstates.org/491-farm-and-migrant-workers.html

44. https://www.goodreads.com/quotes/1402815-we-all-came-in-on-different-ships-but-we-re-all

45. https://www.politico.com/magazine/story/2019/09/08/shawn-rosenberg-democracy-228045

46. https://www.vox.com/2016/3/1/11127424/trump-authoritarianism

47. Hetherington, M. & Weiler, J. (2009). *Authoritarianism and polarization in American Politics.* Cambridge University Press.

48. https://www.vox.com/2016/3/1/11127424/trump-authoritarianism

49. Stenner, K. (2005). *The authoritarian dynamic,* Cambridge University Press.

50. Ibid.

51. https://verdict.justia.com/2017/07/07/altemeyer-trumps-supporters

52. https://www.salon.com/2018/03/16/more-than-one-in-four-americans-prefer-authoritarian-politics/

53. https://www.pewresearch.org/fact-tank/2020/02/27/how-people-around-the-world-see-democracy-in-8-charts/

54. https://pursuit.unimelb.edu.au/articles/
liberal-democracy-why-we-may-be-losing-it
55. https://www.pewresearch.org/global/2020/02/27/democratic-rights-
popular-globally-but-commitment-to-them-not-always-strong/
56. https://www.nytimes.com/2017/01/20/opinion/the-internal-invasion.html
57. https://www.vox.com/policy-and-politics/2019/9/30/20891096/
impeachment-inquiry-ukraine-whistleblower-arrest-treason-adam-schiff-
donald-trump
58. https://www.apa.org/monitor/2009/11/terrorism
59. https://www.statista.com/statistics/207579/
public-approval-rating-of-the-us-congress/
60. https://www.foxnews.com/us/congress-exempt-from-several-federal-laws
61. https://www.newsweek.com/coronavirus-relief-bill-includes-tax-benefit-
millionaires-that-will-cost-taxpayers-90-billion-1498956
62. https://www.newsweek.com/republicans-think-witnesses-testify-trump-
impeachment-mcconnell-1483264
63. https://www.pbs.org/newshour/politics/
most-americans-support-stricter-gun-laws-new-poll-says
64. https://www.federalregister.gov/presidential-documents/executive-orders
65. https://www.factcheck.org/2016/09/obama-did-not-ban-the-pledge/
66. https://www.jacksonville.com/reason/fact-check/2016-08-30/story/
fact-check-no-obama-has-not-banned-pledge-allegiance
67. http://www.leaderu.com/common/nationsdie.html
68. Acemoglu, D. & Robinson, J. (2012). *Why nations fail: The origins of power,
prosperity, and poverty.* Random House.
69. Friedman, T. and Mandelbaum, M. (2011). *That used to be us: How America fell
behind in the world it invented and how we can come back.* Picador.
70. Sieff, M. (2012). *That should still be us: How Thomas Friedman's flat world myths
are keeping us flat on our backs.* Wiley.
71. https://www.forbes.com/sites/jimpowell/2013/02/05/
how-dictators-come-to-power-in-a-democracy/#2279a607ff70
72. Ibid.

## CHAPTER 3

1. https://www.google.com/imgres?imgurl=https://cdn.theatlantic.com/static/
mt/assets/hua_hsu/height3.png&imgrefurl=https://www.theatlantic.com/
sexes/archive/2013/01/why-its-so-rare-for-a-wife-to-be-taller-than-her-husb
and/272585/&tbnid=w41fBAHMlsIKhM&vet=1&docid=SXa94Oze2ufDrM&w=
615&h=469&itg=1&q=us+heights+for+male+female&hl=en&source=sh/x/im
2. https://spcl.yale.edu/sites/default/files/files/Shelton_
Richeson2005(intergroup).pdf
3. https://spcl.yale.edu/sites/default/files/files/Shelton_
Richeson2005(intergroup).pdf
4. https://time.com/4457110/internet-trolls/

5. https://www.theguardian.com/technology/2016/nov/10/
facebook-fake-news-election-conspiracy-theories
6. https://ed.stanford.edu/news/stanford-researchers-find-students-have-
trouble-judging-credibility-information-online
7. https://news.stanford.edu/2019/11/18/
high-school-students-unequipped-spot-fake-news/
8. https://www.pnas.org/content/116/7/2521
9. https://misinforeview.hks.harvard.edu/article/
emphasizing-publishers-does-not-reduce-misinformation/
10. https://doi.org/10.1016/j.cognition.2018.06.011
11. https://www.researchgate.net/publication/331532481_IdeoLogical_
Reasoning_Ideology_Impairs_Sound_Reasoning
12. https://www.sciencedirect.com/science/article/abs/pii/
S0749597819301633?via%3Dihub
13. https://www.bmj.com/content/369/bmj.m1432
14. Nichols, T. (2017). *The death of expertise: The campaign against established knowledge and why it matters.* Oxford University Press.
15. https://www.nytimes.com/2020/04/08/world/europe/coronavirus-
conspiracy-theories.html?referringSource=articleShare
16. https://www.usatoday.com/story/news/nation/2014/04/06/
anti-vaccine-movement-is-giving-diseases-a-2nd-life/7007955/
17. https://journals.sagepub.com/doi/abs/10.1177/0093650219854600
18. https://www.ncbi.nlm.nih.gov/pubmed/23211778
19. https://pubmed.ncbi.nlm.nih.gov/23211778/
20. https://en.wikipedia.org/wiki/Asch_conformity_experiments#/media/
File:Asch_experiment.svg
21. https://www.tandfonline.com/doi/
abs/10.1080/13669877.2010.511246?journalCode=rjrr20
22. http://www.cjcj.org/uploads/cjcj/documents/jpj_firearm_ownership.pdf
23. https://www.acrwebsite.org/volumes/8213/volumes/v25/NA-25
24. https://psycnet.apa.org/buy/1999-15054-002
25. https://hbr.org/2011/07/lets-abolish-self-appraisal.html
26. Nichols, T. (2017). *The death of expertise.* Oxford University Press.
27. https://www.theatlantic.com/health/archive/2018/03/
you-dont-know-yourself-as-well-as-you-think-you-do/554612/
28. https://www.livescience.com/26914-why-we-are-all-above-average.html
29. https://www.researchgate.net/publication/227619159_Self-esteem_and_
culture_Differences_in_cognitive_self-evaluations_or_affective_self-regard
30. https://www.huduser.gov/portal/AHS-neighborhood-description-study-2017.
html
31. https://www.statista.com/chart/19635/
wealth-distribution-percentiles-in-the-us/
32. https://www.census.gov/library/publications/2010/compendia/statab/130ed/
population.html

33. Woodard, C. (2012). *American nations: A history of the eleven rival regional cultures of North America*. Penguin Books.
34. https://news.gallup.com/poll/188918/democrats-republicans-agree-four-top-issues-campaign.aspx
35. https://www.pewresearch.org/fact-tank/2020/04/21/how-americans-see-climate-change-and-the-environment-in-7-charts/
36. https://www.people-press.org/2019/01/24/publics-2019-priorities-economy-health-care-education-and-security-all-near-top-of-list/
37. https://www.cbsnews.com/news/majority-of-americans-dont-want-roe-v-wade-overturned-cbs-news-poll-finds/
38. https://poll.qu.edu/national/release-detail?ReleaseID=2604
39. https://www.pewresearch.org/fact-tank/2019/11/12/americans-immigration-policy-priorities-divisions-between-and-within-the-two-parties/
40. https://www.pewresearch.org/fact-tank/2019/01/16/how-americans-see-illegal-immigration-the-border-wall-and-political-compromise/1-6/
41. https://news.gallup.com/poll/1714/taxes.aspx
42. https://slate.com/news-and-politics/2019/04/trump-tax-returns-voters-polls-show-americans-want-them.html
43. https://www.reuters.com/article/us-usa-trump-impeachment-poll/let-them-speak-most-americans-want-witnesses-in-trump-impeachment-trial-reuters-ipsos-poll-idUSKBN1ZL33O
44. https://www.people-press.org/2020/04/16/most-americans-say-trump-was-too-slow-in-initial-response-to-coronavirus-threat/?referringSource=article Share
45. https://www.cnn.com/2019/04/07/politics/democratic-positions-majority/index.html
46. https://www.theatlantic.com/national/archive/2012/06/21-charts-that-explain-american-values-today/258990/
47. Ibid.
48. https://www.theatlantic.com/national/archive/2012/06/21-charts-that-explain-american-values-today/258990/
49. https://www.huffpost.com/author/kpasha72-231
50. https://careercenter.lehigh.edu/sites/careercenter.lehigh.edu/files/AmericanValues.pdf
51. Ibid.
52. https://careercenter.lehigh.edu/sites/careercenter.lehigh.edu/files/AmericanValues.pdf
53. https://www.nytimes.com/2017/01/18/opinion/retweeting-donald-trump.html

## CHAPTER 4

1. Hochschild, A. (2016). *Strangers in Their Own Land: Anger and Mourning on the American Right*. New Press.
2. https://www.vox.com/policy-and-politics/2017/5/9/15592634/trump-clinton-racism-economy-prri-survey

3. https://www.theatlantic.com/politics/archive/2017/05/white-working-class-trump-cultural-anxiety/525771/

4. https://www.citylab.com/equity/2017/03/what-is-really-behind-the-populist-surge/519921/

5. https://www.cnn.com/2019/03/19/opinions/what-progressives-should-know-about-trump-voters-hanson/index.html

6. Omer Sanan, retired physician, United Hospital, Iowa City, IA.

7. https://www.usatoday.com/story/opinion/2020/02/12/trump-stock-market-few-gains-millennials-regular-americans-column/4707868002/

8. Ibid.

9. https://www.brookings.edu/blog/fixgov/2016/11/16/economic-marginalization-reality-check/

10. https://www.washingtonpost.com/outlook/2020/03/26/surprisingly-few-voters-think-trump-cares-about-people-like-me/

11. Ibid.

12. https://papers.ssrn.com/sol3/papers.cfm?abstract_id=2822059

13. https://www.pewresearch.org/fact-tank/2016/11/09/behind-trumps-victory-divisions-by-race-gender-education/

14. https://www.census.gov/newsroom/press-releases/2017/cb17-51.html

15. https://www.people-press.org/2018/08/09/an-examination-of-the-2016-electorate-based-on-validated-voters/

16. https://papers.ssrn.com/sol3/papers.cfm?abstract_id=1451343

17. https://faculty.wcas.northwestern.edu/~jnd260/pub/Rothschild,%20Howat,%20Shafranek,%20Busby%202018.pdf

18. http://files.clps.brown.edu/jkrueger/journal_articles/clement-1998-liking.pdf

19. https://www.goodreads.com/quotes/search?q=Dalai+Lama+compassion

20. Haidt, J. (2012). *The righteous mind: Why good people are divided by politics and religion.* Pantheon Books.

21. https://en.wikipedia.org/wiki/Dar_al-Salam

22. https://www.nytimes.com/interactive/2019/10/02/upshot/these-526-voters-represent-america.html

23. https://www.businesswire.com/news/home/20191003005272/en/500-Person-"America-Room"-Deliberative-Polling-Experiment

24. https://www.better-angels.org/evaluation/?link_id=4&can_id=04319c5de0eedf8b1fe4f518c3c0460f&source=email-save-our-republic-in-2020&email_referrer=email_645871&email_subject=save-our-republic-in-2020

25. https://science.sciencemag.org/content/352/6282/220.full

26. https://econpapers.repec.org/article/cupapsrev/v_3a105_3ay_3a2011_3ai_3a01_3ap_3a135-150_5f00.htm

27. https://www.tandfonline.com/doi/abs/10.1080/10584609.2013.828143?scroll=top&needAccess=true&journalCode=upcp20

28. https://www.newsweek.com/former-federal-prosecutors-trump-indicted-wasnt-president-1439716

29. https://www.nytimes.com/2020/04/11/us/politics/coronavirus-trump-response.html?referringSource=articleShare

30. https://www.politico.com/magazine/story/2017/09/05/negative-partisanship-explains-everything-215534

31. Hetherington, M. & Weiler, J. (2018). *Prius or pickup? How the answers to four simple questions explain America's great divide.* Houghton Mifflin Harcourt.

32. Ibid.

33. https://www.researchgate.net/publication/257045805_Obedience_to_traditional_authority_A_heritable_factor_underlying_authoritarianism_conservatism_and_religiousness

34. https://www.pewresearch.org/fact-tank-/2013/12/09/study-on-twins-suggests-our-political-beliefs-may-be-hard-wired/

35. Ibid.

36. https://doi.org/10.1111/ajps.12016

37. https://www.motherjones.com/politics/2013/02/brain-difference-democrats-republicans

38. https://www.ncbi.nlm.nih.gov/pubmed/17032067

39. https://www.washingtonpost.com/news/inspired-life/wp/2017/11/22/at-yale-we-conducted-an-experiment-to-turn-conservatives-into-liberals-the-results-say-a-lot-about-our-political-divisions/

40. Bargh, J. (2017). *Before you know it: The unconscious reasons we do what we do.* Atria Paperback.

41. https://www.npr.org/2018/10/03/654127241/nature-nurture-and-your-politics

42. Hibbing, J., Smith, K., & Alford, J. (2013). *Predisposed: Liberals, conservatives, and the biology of political differences.* Routledge.

43. Ibid.

44. https://doi.org/10.1371/journal.pone.0052970

45. https://www.ncbi.nlm.nih.gov/pmc/articles/PMC3265335/

46. https://www.cell.com/current-biology/fulltext/S0960-9822(11)00289-2?_returnURL=https%3A%2F%2Flinkinghub.elsevier.com%2Fretrieve%2Fpii%2FS0960982211002892%3Fshowall%3Dtrue

47. https://www.ncbi.nlm.nih.gov/pmc/articles/PMC3268356/

48. https://www.theatlantic.com/ideas/archive/2020/04/each-briefing-trump-making-us-worse-people/609859/

49. https://www.tandfonline.com/doi/abs/10.1080/02650487.2014.996199

50. https://www.vox.com/2015/3/20/8260445/underdogs-psychology

51. https://doi.org/10.1177/0146167207307488

52. https://lincolnproject.us

53. Ibid.

54. https://greatergood.berkeley.edu/article/item/do_mirror_neurons_give_empathy

55. https://dx.doi.org/10.1177%2F2374373517699267

56. https://www.tedxmarin.org/speaker/jamil-zaki/

57. https://doi.org/10.1037/a0036738

58. Goleman, D. (2005). *Emotional intelligence: Why it can matter more than IQ.* Bantam Books.
59. https://www.ncbi.nlm.nih.gov/pmc/articles/PMC2944261/
60. https://www.ncbi.nlm.nih.gov/pmc/articles/PMC4112600/
61. https://journals.sagepub.com/doi/10.1177/1088868310361239
62. Lama, D., Tutu, D. & Abrams, D. (2016). *The book of joy: Lasting happiness in a changing world.* Avery.
63. Fredrickson, B. (2009). *Positivity: Top-notch research reveals the 3-to-1 ratio that will change your life.* Three Rivers Press.
64. https://www.people-press.org/2020/04/16/most-americans-say-trump-was-too-slow-in-initial-response-to-coronavirus-threat/
65. Ibid.

## CHAPTER 5

1. https://shop.themyersbriggs.com/Pdfs/CPP_Global_Human_Capital_Report_Workplace_Conflict.pdf
2. Bramson, R. (1981). *Coping with difficult people.* Anchor Press.
3. Gottman, J. & DeClaire, J. (2001). *The relationship cure: A 5 step guide to strengthening your marriage, family, and friendships.* Three Rivers Press.
4. https://kilmanndiagnostics.com/a-brief-history-of-the-thomas-kilmann-conflict-mode-instrument/

## CHAPTER 6

1. Haidt, J. (2012). *The righteous mind: Why good people are divided by politics and religion.* Pantheon Books.
2. https://www.ncbi.nlm.nih.gov/pubmed/30973236
3. Obama, Michelle. (2018). *Becoming.* Crown Publishing.
4. Brown, B. (2019). *Braving the wilderness: The quest for true belonging and the courage to stand alone.* Random House Trade Paperbacks.
5. Molberg, A. (2003). *Making live training lively: 50 tips for engaging your audience.* Crisp Learning.
6. https://www.ncbi.nlm.nih.gov/pmc/articles/PMC3830455/
7. https://hbr.org/2017/04/a-new-more-rigorous-study-confirms-the-more-you-use-facebook-the-worse-you-feel
8. https://academic.oup.com/aje/article/185/3/203/2915143
9. https://hbr.org/2011/02/why-face-to-face-meetings-make
10. Keller, E. & Fay, B. (2012). *The face-to-face book: Why real relationships rule in a digital marketplace.* Free Press.
11. McGinnis, A. (1985). *Bringing out the best in people: How to enjoy helping others excel.* Augsburg Publishing House.
12. Covey, S. (1989). *The 7 habits of highly effective people: Powerful lessons in personal change.* Simon & Schuster.
13. Jourard, S. (1972). *The transparent self.* Van Nostrand Reinhold Inc.

14. https://www.researchgate.net/publication/43476256_Communication_openness_conflict_events_and_reactions_to_conflict_in_culturally_diverse_workgroups
15. https://psycnet.apa.org/doi/10.1037/0022-3514.33.2.184
16. https://onlinelibrary.wiley.com/doi/abs/10.1002/jls.21265
17. Ibid.
18. https://hbr.org/2013/03/the-ideal-praise-to-criticism
19. Ibid.
20. Blanchard, K. (1982). *The one minute manager*. William Morrow.
21. Cialdini, R. (1995). *Influence: Science and practice* (3rd ed.). HarperCollins.
22. https://www.theatlantic.com/education/archive/2014/01/lavishing-kids-with-praise-can-make-them-feel-worse-about-themselves/282772/
23. Chapman, G. (1992). *The five love languages: How to express heartfelt commitment to your mate*. Northfield Publishing.
24. https://www.pnas.org/content/117/19/10218
25. https://www.ajoconnor.com/blog/learning-agility-2020-leadership-competency
26. Gottman, J. & Silver, N. (1999). *The seven principles for making marriage work*. Three Rivers Press.
27. Gottman, J. & DeClaire, J. (2001). *The relationship cure: A 5 step guide to strengthening your marriage, family, and friendships*. Three Rivers Press. p. 25.
28. https://www.annualreviews.org/doi/pdf/10.1146/annurev-orgpsych-032516-113147
29. https://www.pewresearch.org/fact-tank/2019/09/19/americans-perceptions-about-unethical-behavior-shape-how-they-think-about-people-in-powerful-roles/

## CHAPTER 7

1. https://www.nbcnews.com/politics/white-house/trump-new-hampshire-you-have-no-choice-vote-me-n1043001
2. Hetherington, M. & Weiler, J. (2009). *Authoritarianism & polarization in American politics*. Cambridge University Press.
3. https://doi.org/10.1002/jls.21265
4. Ibid.
5. Tannen, D. (1995). *You just don't understand: Women and men in conversation*. Virago.
6. Gray, J. (1995). *Men are from Mars, women are from Venus*. HarperCollins.
7. https://www.quotes.net/quote/374
8. https://opentextbc.ca/socialpsychology/chapter/person-gender-and-cultural-differences-in-conformity/
9. Covey, S. M. R. (2006). *The speed of trust: The one thing that changes everything*. Free Press.
10. https://www.tandfonline.com/doi/full/10.1080/02699931.2017.1422696
11. https://www.researchgate.net/publication/250168730_The_Role_of_Advertising_in_Word_of_Mouth

12. https://files.clps.brown.edu/jkrueger/journal_articles/clement-1998-liking.pdf
13. Ibid.
14. https://www.vox.com/2016/8/18/12423688/donald-trump-speech-style-explained-by-linguists
15. https://www.politifact.com/factchecks/2017/jan/25/sean-spicer/sean-spicer-wrongly-uses-pew-study-bolster-claim-n/
16. https://psycnet.apa.org/record/1971-02324-001
17. Goldstein, N., Martin, S., & Cialdini, R. (2008). *Yes! 50 scientifically proven ways to be persuasive.* Free Press.
18. Ibid.
19. Ibid.

## CHAPTER 8

1. Rock, D. (2006). *Your brain at work.* HarperCollins.
2. https://www.politico.com/news/magazine/2020/04/11/america-two-decade-failure-prepare-coronavirus-179574
3. https://abcnews.go.com/Politics/george-bush-2005-wait-pandemic-late-prepare/story?id=69979013
4. https://www.strategy-business.com/article/06207?gko=f1af3

## CHAPTER 9

1. https://www.monticello.org/site/research-and-collections/i-never-considered-difference-opinion-politicsquotation
2. Goldstein, N., Martin, S., & Cialdini, R. (2008). *Yes! 50 scientifically proven ways to be persuasive.* Free Press.
3. Ibid.
4. Welch, S. (2009). *10-10-10: A life-transforming idea.* Scribner.
5. Faber, A. & Mazlish, E. (1980). *How to talk so kids will listen & listen so kids will talk.* Avon.
6. https://www.ted.com/talks/ron_gutman_the_hidden_power_of_smiling/transcript?language=en
7. https://www.psychologytoday.com/us/blog/slightly-blighty/201509/can-botox-treat-depression-facial-expression-can-cure-you
8. https://online.uwa.edu/news/benefits-of-smiling-and-laughter/
9. https://hbr.org/2017/04/a-face-to-face-request-is-34-times-more-successful-than-an-email
10. Goleman, D. (1995). *Emotional intelligence: Why it can matter more than IQ.* Bantam Books.
11. Fournies, F. (1978). *Coaching for improved work performance.* F Fournies & Associates.
12. https://www.vox.com/2016/8/18/12423688/donald-trump-speech-style-explained-by-linguists
13. https://pdfs.semanticscholar.org/0f34/fb934cbddd03b80550ef7f222e8ae435afd3.pdf

## CHAPTER 10

1. https:www.fs.fed.us/eng/pubs/htmlpubs/htm95512855/page13.htm
2. De Becker, G. (1999). *The gift of fear: Survival signals that protect us from violence*. Dell Publishing.
3. https://www.youtube.com/watch?v=RjJJojXIV3M
4. https://pubmed.ncbi.nlm.nih.gov/17576282/
5. https://doi.org/10.1016/j.tics.2005.03.010
6. https://www.drweil.com/health-wellness/body-mind-spirit/stress-anxiety/breathing-three-exercises/

## CHAPTER 11

1. MSNBC, April 2020
2. https://news.yale.edu/2012/01/09/even-healthy-stress-causes-brain-shrink-yale-study-shows
3. https://news.berkeley.edu/2013/04/16/researchers-find-out-why-some-stress-is-good-for-you/
4. Lazarus, R. & Folkman, S. (1984). *Stress, appraisal, and coping*. Springer Publishing.
5. Driskell, J. & Salas, E. (1996). *Stress and human performance*. Lawrence Erlbaum.
6. https://www.theguardian.com/commentisfree/2017/feb/13/donald-trumps-doctrine-unpredictability-world-edge
7. http://arno.uvt.nl/show.cgi?fid=142697
8. https://www.nytimes.com/2003/02/04/health/behavior-finding-happiness-cajole-your-brain-to-lean-to-the-left.html
9. https://www.psychologytoday.com/us/blog/the-brain-and-emotional-intelligence/201106/retrain-your-stressed-out-brain
10. https://psycnet.apa.org/doi/10.1037/1061-4087.51.2.83
11. https://psycnet.apa.org/record/1980-21134-001
12. https://psycnet.apa.org/fulltext/1993-09706-001.html
13. Frankl, V. (1997). *Man's Search for Meaning*. Pocket Books.
14. Seligman, M. (1991). *Learned optimism: How to change your mind and your life*. Free Press.
15. https://www.ncbi.nlm.nih.gov/pmc/articles/PMC2832856/
16. https://object.cato.org/sites/cato.org/files/pubs/pdf/pa798_1_1.pdf
17. https://doi.org/10.1016/j.tics.2005.03.010
18. Garfield, C. (1986). *Peak performers: The new heroes of American business*. Avon Books, p.160.
19. https://doi.org/10.1080/02640410500128221
20. https://psycnet.apa.org/doi/10.1037/0022-3514.83.5.1178
21. https://www.wsj.com/articles/how-you-make-decisions-says-a-lot-about-how-happy-you-are-1412614997
22. https://www.prnewswire.com/news-releases/americans-check-their-phones-96-times-a-day-300962643.html

3. https://www.nytimes.com/interactive/2016/08/08/us/politics/national-security-letter-trump.html
4. https://www.nytimes.com/2016/08/09/us/politics/national-security-gop-donald-trump.html?referringSource=articleShare
5. https://www.huffpost.com/entry/is-donald-trump-mentally_b_13693174
6. Lee, B. (2018). *The dangerous case of Donald Trump*. Thomas Dunne Books.
7. https://www.theatlantic.com/politics/archive/2020/06/james-mattis-denounces-trump-protests-militarization/612640/
8. https://www.nbcnews.com/think/opinion/trump-s-photo-op-pushed-general-mattis-finally-speak-truth-ncna1226306
9. https://www.psychologytoday.com/us/conditions/narcissistic-personality-disorder
10. https://www.youtube.com/watch?v=Y_JL8Dx4vyw
11. American Psychiatric Association. (2013). *Diagnostic and statistical manual of mental disorders* (5th ed.). American Psychiatric Publishing.
12. https://www.psychologytoday.com/us/blog/evolution-the-self/201711/the-catch-22-dealing-narcissist
13. https://www.tandfonline.com/doi/full/10.1080/01402382.2019.1599570?af=R
14. https://www.cjr.org/analysis/trump-mental-health.php
15. https://www.forbes.com/sites/davidmarkowitz/2020/05/05/trump-is-lying-more-than-ever-just-look-at-the-data/#7866e5691e17
16. https://www.independent.co.uk/news/world/americas/us-elections/harvard-professors-us-president-barack-obama-grave-concern-donald-trump-mental-stability-a7482586.html
17. https://www.foxnews.com/politics/spicer-digs-in-on-trumps-illegal-voting-claim-as-ryan-distances
18. https://www.psychologytoday.com/us/blog/evolution-the-self/201112/narcissism-why-its-so-rampant-in-politics
19. https://www.independent.co.uk/news/world/americas/us-elections/harvard-professors-us-president-barack-obama-grave-concern-donald-trump-mental-stability-a7482586.html
20. https://www.huffpost.com/entry/is-donald-trump-mentally_b_13693174
21. https://www.youtube.com/watch?v=Y_JL8Dx4vyw
22. https://www.psychologytoday.com/us/blog/evolution-the-self/201112/narcissism-why-its-so-rampant-in-politics
23. https://poll.qu.edu/national/release-detail?ReleaseID=3654
24. https://www.reuters.com/article/us-usa-trump-impeachment-poll/let-them-speak-most-americans-want-witnesses-in-trump-impeachment-trial-reuters-ipsos-poll-idUSKBN1ZL33O
25. https://theconversation.com/you-think-this-is-a-witch-hunt-mr-president-thats-an-insult-to-the-women-who-suffered-129775
26. https://www.cbsnews.com/news/trump-inspectors-general-internal-watchdogs-fired-list/
27. https://www.newsweek.com/former-federal-prosecutors-trump-indicted-wasnt-president-1439716

28. https://www.nationalreview.com/news/over-1000-ex-doj-officials-call-on-ag-barr-to-resign-following-roger-stone-sentencing/
29. https://www.nbcnews.com/new/us-news/obama-warned-trump-against-hiring-mike-flynn-say-officials-n756316
30. https://www.nytimes.com/2017/12/01/us/politics/michael-flynn-guilty-russia-investigation.html
31. https://www.nytimes.com/2020/05/07/opinion/michael-flynn-charges-dropped.html
32. https://www.theatlantic.com/ideas/archive/2020/05/michael-flynn-learned-to-play-by-trumps-rules/611332/
33. https://www.nytimes.com/2019/12/16/us/politics/michael-flynn-sentencing.html
34. https://www.psychologytoday.com/us/blog/evolution-the-self/201112/narcissism-why-its-so-rampant-in-politics
35. https://www.psychologytoday.com/us/blog/shame/201508/the-populist-appeal-trumps-narcissism
36. https://www.usnews.com/news/the-report/articles/2017-01-27/does-donald-trumps-personality-make-him-dangerous?src=usn_tw
37. https://www.psychologytoday.com/us/blog/the-time-cure/201702/the-elephant-in-the-room
38. https://www.usnews.com/news/the-report/articles/2017-01-27/does-donald-trumps-personality-make-him-dangerous?src=usn_tw
39. https://www.businessinsider.com/trump-says-gut-tells-him-more-than-anybody-elses-brain-2018-11
40. https://www.deepdyve.com/lp/wiley/narcissism-confidence-and-risk-attitude-sVrmyfGhla
41. Collins, J. (2001). *Good to Great*. HarperCollins.
42. https://hbr.org/2000/03/leadership-that-gets-results
43. Maccoby, M. (2007). *Narcissistic leaders: Who succeeds and who fails.* Harvard Business School Press.
44. https://hbr.org/2016/01/help-your-team-manage-stress-anxiety-and-burnout
45. http://www.awair.eu/wp-content/uploads/2017/03/Kaiser-LeBreton-J.-Hogan-20132.pdf
46. http://citeseerx.ist.psu.edu/viewdoc/download?doi=10.1.1.626.2666&rep=rep1&type=pdf
47. https://pro.psychcentral.com/exhausted-woman/2016/03/how-narcissists-use-the-courts-to-continue-their-abuse/
48. https://doi.org/10.1016/j.paid.2019.109627
49. https://www.npr.org/2019/02/13/694199256/u-s-national-debt-hits-22-trillion-a-new-record-thats-predicted-to-fall
50. https://www.medpagetoday.com/psychiatry/generalpsychiatry/67728
51. https://www.nytimes.com/2020/05/20/us/coronavirus-distancing-deaths.html
52. https://pdfs.semanticscholar.org/dc0e/a72886b73b50a918d2171019e677491e27db.pdf

53. https://dx.doi.org/10.1177%2F2374373517699267

54. Bazelon, E. (2014). *Sticks and stones: Defeating the culture of bullying and rediscovering the power of character and empathy.* Random House Trade Paperbacks.

55. https://www.forbes.com/sites/pragyaagarwaleurope/2018/07/29/workplace-bullying-here-is-why-we-need-to-talk-about-bullying-in-the-work-place/#286766913259

56. https://www.theguardian.com/us-news/2020/may/15/donald-trump-coronavirus-response-world-leaders

57. https://www.irishtimes.com/opinion/fintan-o-toole-donald-trump-has-destroyed-the-country-he-promised-to-make-great-again-1.4235928?mode=sample&auth-failed=1&pw-origin=https%3A%2F%2Fwww.irishtimes.com%2Fopinion%2Ffintan-o-toole-donald-trump-has-destroyed-the-country-he-promised-to-make-great-again-1.4235928

## APPENDIX 2

1. Wilhelm, K. & Hoffman, N. (2020). *How to talk to the "other side": Finding common ground in the time of coronavirus, recession, and climate change.* Kevin Wilhelm.

2. https://townhall.com/columnists/dennisprager/2017/01/17/a-guide-to-basic-differences-between-left-and-right-n2271475

3. https://www.google.com/search?client=safari&rls=en&q=how+many+amendments+does+the+constitution+have&ie=UTF-8&oe=UTF-8

4. Wilhelm, K. & Hoffman, N. (2020). *How to talk to the "other side": Finding common ground in the time of coronavirus, recession, and climate change.* Kevin Wilhelm.

5. https://files.clps.brown.edu/jkrueger/journal_articles/clement-1998-liking.pdf

6. Wilhelm, K. & Hoffman, N. (2020). *How to talk to the "other side": Finding common ground in the time of coronavirus, recession, and climate change.* Kevin Wilhelm.

7. Ibid.

8. https://townhall.com/columnists/dennisprager/2017/01/17/a-guide-to-basic-differences-between-left-and-right-n2271475

## APPENDIX 3

1. https://www.andrews.edu/~tidwell/bsad560/USValues.html

## APPENDIX 6

1. https://hbr.org/1979/03/choosing-strategies-for-change-2

# Recommended Readings

- Berg, J. (2017). *America, we need to talk: A self-help book for the nation.* Seven Stories Press.
- Booher, D. (1994). *Communicate with confidence: How to say it right the first time and every time.* McGraw-Hill.
- Bramson, R. (1981). *Coping with difficult people.* Anchor Press.
- Brooks, A. (2019). *Love your enemies: How decent people can save America from the culture of contempt.* Harper Luxe.
- Carnegie, D. (1981). *How to win friends & influence people* (revised ed.). Pocket Books.
- Cialdini, R. (2006). *Influence: Science and practice* (5th ed.). Allyn and Bacon.
- David, T. (2014). *Magic words: The science and secrets behind 7 words that motivate, engage, and influence.* Prentice Hall.
- Duckworth, A. (2016). *Grit: The power of passion and perseverance.* Scribner.
- Faber, A. & Mazlish, E. (1980). *How to talk so kids will listen & listen so kids will talk.* Avon.
- Fisher, R. & Ury, W. (1981). *Getting to yes: Negotiating agreement without giving in.* Penguin Books.
- Flake, J. (2017). *Conscience of a conservative: A rejection of destructive politics and a return to principle.* Random House.
- Frankl, V. (1997). *Man's Search for Meaning.* Pocket Books.

- Fredrickson, B. (2009). *Positivity: Top-notch research reveals the 3-to-1 ratio that will change your life.* Three Rivers Press.

- Garfield, C. (1986). *Peak performers: The new heroes of American business.* Avon.

- Gartner, J. (2016, January 5). How to pick a president: What we want in a leader and what we need in a leader may be two different things. *Psychologytoday.com.*

- https://www.psychologytoday.com/us/articles/201601/how-pick-president

- Gerzon, M. (2016). *The reunited state of America: How we can bridge the partisan divide.* Berrett-Koehler Publishers.

- Goldstein, N., Martin, S., & Cialdini, R. (2008). *Yes! 50 scientifically proven ways to be persuasive.* Free Press.

- Goleman, D. (1995). *Emotional intelligence: Why it can matter more than IQ.* Bantam Books.

- Goleman, D. (1998*). Working with emotional intelligence.* Bantam Books.

- Gordon, A. (1978). *A touch of wonder: An invitation to fall in love with life.* Jove Books.

- Gottman, J. & DeClaire, J. (2001). *The relationship cure: A 5 step guide to strengthening your marriage, family, and friendships.* Three Rivers Press.

- Greitens, E. (2015). *Resilience: Hard won wisdom for living a better life.* Mariner Books.

- Hosie, R. (2017, January 30). 'Malignant narcissism': Donald Trump displays classic traits of mental illness, claim psychologists. *The Independent.co.uk.*

- https://www.independent.co.uk/life-style/health-and-families/

donald-trump-mental-illness-narcisissm-us-president-psy-chologists-inauguration-crowd-size-paranoia-a7552661.html

- Lakoff, G. (2014). *The all new don't think of an elephant!* Chelsea Green Publishing.

- Lewis, S. (1935). *It can't happen here.* Signet Classics.

- Luntz, F. (2007). *Words that work: It's not what you say, it's what people hear.* Hatchette Books.

- McGinnis, A. (1979). *The friendship factor: How to get closer to the people you care for.* Augsburg Publishing House.

- McGinnis, A. (1985). *Bringing out the best in people: How to enjoy helping others excel.* Augsburg Publishing House.

- Milligan, S. (2017, January 1). Temper tantrum: Some say President Donald Trump's personality isn't just flawed, it's dangerous. *USA Today.*

- https://www.usnews.com/news/the-report/arti-cles/2017-01-27/does-donald-trumps-personali-ty-make-him-dangerous?src=usn_tw

- Nichols, T. (2017). *The death of expertise: The campaign against established knowledge and why it matters.* Oxford University Press.

- Nichols, T. (2020, March 31). Why I watch Trump's daily coronavirus briefings (and no, it's not because I'm a mas-ochist). *USA Today.* https://www.usatoday.com/story/opin-ion/voices/2020/03/31/trump-coronavirus-briefings-watch-ing-to-bear-witness-column/5094794002/

- Patterson, K., Grenny, J., McMillan, R., & Switzler, A. (2002). *Crucial conversations: Tools for talking when stakes are high.* McGraw-Hill.

- Patterson, K., Grenny, J., Maxfield, D., McMillan, R., & Switzler, A. (2008). *Influencer: The power to change anything.* McGraw-Hill.

- Plouffe, D. (2020). *A citizen's guide to beating Donald Trump.* Viking Books.

- Seligman, M. (1990). *Learned optimism: How to change your mind and your life.* Pocket Books.

- *Seligman, M. (2002). Authentic happiness: Using the new positive psychology to realize your potential for lasting fulfillment.* Free Press.

- Siegel, L. (2017, February 22). Avoiding questions about Trump's mental health is a betrayal of public trust. *Columbia Journalism Review.*

- https://www.cjr.org/analysis/trump-mental-health.php

- Snyder, T. (2017). *On tyranny: Twenty lessons from the twentieth century.* Tim Duggan Books.

- Stone, D., Patton, B., & Heen, S. (1999). *Difficult conversations: How to discuss what matters most.* Penguin Books.

- Sword, R. & Zimbardo, P. (2017, February 28). The elephant in the room. *Psychologytoday.com.*

- https://www.psychologytoday.com/us/blog/the-time-cure/201702/the-elephant-in-the-room.

- Tavris, C. (1989). *Anger: The misunderstood emotion* (revised ed.). A Touchstone Book.

# Acknowledgments

I mitating a good corporation, I gathered a wonderful board of dedicated individuals with different skills and perspectives to help me get this book out. It was started three years ago just after Trump's election, shelved, and now finally is in your hands with the help of many.

A corporate executive, blue-necked psychology professor, Republican party leader, book rep, clinical psychologist, church communications director, lawyer, CEO of a non-profit, ICU nursing supervisor, and neighbor with a masters in counseling spent hours reading, suggesting, and editing. All are intelligent, trusted, amazing friends. I can't thank Joline Brown, Tom Brothen, Gerry Blumberg, Mary Kay Ulness, Deirdre Lopez, Nan Ross, Deb Duoos, Paul Lopez, Vic Matin, and Letitia Shields enough. Numerous others also provided ideas, feedback, and insights.

My big sister Beth Molberg, with a background in public policy and journalism, began to pour over every word, sentence, and comma. How lucky I am to just have her in my life as well as initially in the editor role.

Incredibly committed and supportive, paralegal Ann Lange not only read, advised, and encouraged but took over the red pen challenge for which I am forever grateful. She made all the difference.

Creative and patient cover designer Matt Caffelle of RED-FACKTORY transformed ideas into images, and David Wogahn of AuthorImprints designed the interior layout to capture your attention.

Both my daughters went through my angst and anger about our current state of affairs and heard me say, "I have to do something." At times those wise women, a neuroscientist and an organizational psychologist, counseled me to give up, yet they supported my efforts every step of the way. So did my true partner and husband Hank Greenleaf, who not only is a wordsmith but a gift in and of himself.

Many, many thanks!

# About the Author

Doubly trained as both an organizational and counseling psychologist, Dr. Andrea Molberg has spent her career helping people get along and organizations be more effective. As consultant, trainer, and executive coach she has worked with Fortune 500 companies, professional and trade associations, health care organizations, non-profits, start-ups, governmental agencies, and educational institutions for over 35 years. Her executive coaching clients include physicians, police chiefs, executives, and entrepreneurs.

A frequent speaker, Andrea has been a faculty member of the College of Executive Coaching since 2000. From 1974 to 2009, she was an extremely popular, respected part of the University of St. Thomas Center for Business Excellence faculty where she taught thousands how to manage conflict, handle change, influence others, and collaborate.

She holds a PhD from the University of Minnesota. University of St. Thomas students chose her Teacher of the Year in Social Sciences, and her first book *Making Live Training Lively!* is a Crisp/Thomson Learning Fifty-Minute Series Book. A former Midwesterner, Andrea is now headquartered in Tucson.

Learn more about her and her work at **www.andreamolberg.com**.

Made in the USA
Middletown, DE
10 July 2020